The West Highland
White Terrier

POPULAR DOGS' BREED SERIES

The West Highland
White Terrier

D. Mary Dennis
Revised by Catherine Owen

POPULAR DOGS
London Sydney Auckland Johannesburg

*To my husband who all his life has been
a staunch supporter of this lovely breed—
and also to all my dogs who have given me
so much pleasure*

Popular Dogs Publishing Co. Ltd
Brookmount House, 62–65 Chandos Place, Covent Garden,
London WC2N 4NW

An imprint of Century Hutchinson Ltd

Century Hutchinson Australia (Pty) Ltd
20 Alfred Street, Milsons Point, Sydney 2061

Century Hutchinson New Zealand Limited
191 Archers Road, PO Box 40-086, Glenfield, Auckland 10

Century Hutchinson South Africa (Pty) Ltd
PO Box 337, Bergvlei 2012, South Africa

First published 1976
Revised editions 1970, 1973, 1976, 1979, 1982, 1986
Copyright © D.M. Dennis 1967, 1970, 1973, 1976, 1979
Copyright © Chapter 14 and revisions to sixth, seventh and eighth editions
Catherine Owen 1982, 1986, 1989

The Breed Standard copyright © The Kennel Club 1987

Set in 10/11 Times Roman
Printed and bound in Great Britain
by Mackays of Chatham PLC, Kent

British Library Cataloguing in Publication Data

Dennis, D. Mary
  The West Highland White Terrier – 7th ed.
  1. West Highland White Terriers
  I. Title
  636.7′55   SF429.W4

ISBN 0 09 174335 4

Contents

Illustrations

Author's Introduction

My introduction to West Highland White Terriers began when I was but sixteen and first met the boy who was later to become my husband. His father, Nelson F. Dennis, had two or three Westies as early as 1910 and from that time the family were never without one. After the First World War Mr Dennis senior purchased from Mrs Bernard Lucas, Highclere Rose, the winner of three reserve C.C.s, and from this bitch the first West Highland I ever owned was descended. After his father's death in 1921, my husband and his mother kept the dogs in partnership, registering the prefix 'Oughton'. At that time they resided in West Hartlepool, Co. Durham, travelling facilities were not too good, and so their attendance at shows was confined to the north-east of England. In 1923 they moved south into Essex, taking eleven bitches and one dog with them. Shortly afterwards five of the bitches were sold to Miss Errington who, later, was to become better known as Mrs Hewson, the owner of the large and well-known 'Clint' Kennel. Many of the later 'Clints' were descended from the five bitches bought from Mrs Dennis.

In marrying someone who had owned West Highlands from his youth it could have been forecast that I, too, would quickly come to love them as my husband did. I had always been fond of dogs but had never thought seriously of having one as anything other than a pet. Soon after we were married, my mother-in-law told me that the house would never be home without a dog, and as, for her, there was only one breed it would, of course, have to be a West Highland White Terrier. So, when the next litter of puppies arrived, I became the owner of my very first Westie, a bitch we called Judy, whom I remember quite clearly to this day. She was a wonderful character and most intelligent. From her first litter I kept a dog, and it was with him I had my initiation into show business. I do not think he was a very good dog, and I know that I was quite inexperienced in show preparation, but I remember the judge, Mrs D. F. Gardiner, taking the trouble to tell me some of the mistakes I had made in handling my dog and advising me about his good and not so good points. I have never forgotten her kindness to me that day; constructive advice from judges can be so helpful to beginners, and hers had really fired my interest in dog-breeding. I bought a pair of West Highlands from my mother-in-law and from them bred some quite good specimens. By now I was learning fast and well and truly bitten by the show bug. In those days I had little hope of winning anything, except in the most lowly classes. The Wolveys, the Rushmoors, the Clints, the Leals, the Breans, and the Furzefields were in an impregnable position and quite unbeatable. But every dog has his day, and mine was looming on the horizon. In 1939, the war brought everything to a standstill, and my kennel, like so many others, had to be closed down. Deciding how to dispose of about thirty dogs was a heartbreaking task, but I managed to retain ten; eight bitches and two dogs, which had to go to a friend's boarding kennel for the duration. With these ten I had hopes of making a start again in what, at that time, some people thought would be only a year or two. However, by the time it was possible to get a home together again and have what was left of the dogs back—only six of them—they were getting elderly, and only two bitches were fit to breed from. From these two, and Belinda of Branston in particular, the present-day Branstons were revived.

I shall never forget the thrill of breeding my first champion. From that time on other champions followed in fairly quick succession: so many lovely dogs, each wonderful in its own way, but my beloved Ch. Barrister I shall always consider one of the greatest dogs I ever bred. He was a great showman and a wonderful stud dog, siring many champions. But every champion one breeds gives a feeling of satisfaction, and it seems impossible to imagine that a day may come when interest in them will wane.

Dog breeding is hard work. No one can expect to get to the top by an easy way. The only certain way of knowing dogs is to be able, when necessary, to do every task yourself: staying up all night with a bitch whelping, and seeing to her welfare and comfort; knowing the joy of being the first to handle what you hope may be the best Westie ever bred; enduring the small hours, cold and stiff, when nothing much seems to be happening; scrubbing out kennels and washing blankets and sacks; preparing innumerable bowls of milk, and scraping raw meat for the baby puppies, especially in winter when you would much rather be indoors by a fire. And this, seven days a week and at Christmas and on other holidays too. If you can do that and keep a cheerful countenance then you love dogs and deserve some reward.

Breeding and showing dogs has always been one of my greatest pleasures, and my husband's. Without his help none of my success would have been possible; it has always been a combined effort. We have travelled thousands of miles together, year in year out, hardly ever missing a show, and enjoying every bit of it. We often talk of the days when we used to set off in a car that was none too reliable. The journey had to be planned almost as a major operation, and it took about twice as long as it would today. But through these travels we made many good friends and met some of the nicest people one could wish to meet, all with the same interest in life: the furtherance of our lovely breed.

Both my husband and I have been judging for a great many years, and in 1964 I had the pleasure of judging a very nice entry at Crufts. In 1969 my husband, G. B. Dennis, judged a very large entry at this most famous of all shows—a task anyone is very honoured to be invited to undertake. I can ask nothing better for anyone than that they should reap as much pleasure and satisfaction from breeding and showing West Highland White Terriers as I do.

1970

It is very satisfactory to report that in 1972 West Highlands still continued to hold the top placings for all the terrier breeds. It is good to know that more and more people appreciate the many fine qualities of the breed—great sturdy little dogs with fine temperaments that appeal to so many people.

In this third edition of the book, five photographs and two new pedigrees have been introduced to keep readers up-to-date with the history of the breed.

I should like to make a special appeal to all breeders and owners of dogs at this time when there is a great deal of suffering among animals for various reasons. So much is just lack of thought and sensitivity to the dog's feelings. To leave a dog shut up for hours or more can cause intense distress. Because of the whimsical vagaries of railways or airlines, dogs have been known to arrive in a collapsed, or at the least very distressed state at the end of a long journey and I feel sure that the genuine dog lover will take any and every step to see to the welfare of animals subjected to the ordeal of travel.

1972

It was with great pleasure that in 1973 I accepted the invitation to judge Westies at the Californian Terrier Show, where so many exhibits were beautifully presented. Some I found overweight and larger than is customary here, but such an array of champions was overwhelming. Yet I found my top winners from the more junior ranks. I counted it a great privilege to handle and admire them.

In 1974 I had a most pleasant visit to Sweden where I judged the West Highland White Terrier Club Show in Stockholm. The breed has made great progress there in the last few years and I was delighted to find so many good ones. The Swedish are so enthusiastic and their frequent visits to the major shows in this country are manifestly worthwhile as they are almost as conversant with the breeding and performance of the exhibits here as at home. The Swedish people, after those of Great Britain and the USA have, I think, done more than most to increase the popularity of the breed.

As this edition goes to press, I should also like to record one of the greatest moments of my career in dogs. On 1 November 1975 I judged the combined West Highland White Terrier Clubs' Show at Wakefield with a near record entry of 210, with 130 exhibits. The quality of all was so high, and winning dogs and bitches were so excellent, that I feel I can never again hope to see their equal. Ch. Glengordon Hannah is as near perfect as anyone could wish, but still had to give place to Ch. Glenalwyne Sonny Boy who is a real aristocrat. This was a day I shall remember for the rest of my life.

And now I must express my appreciation to those who have written to me from all over the world about this book. I am very glad to know that so many people who, like my husband and myself, love the Westie have found it helpful. In this fourth edition I have made some minor additions to the text, brought the appendices up to date again, and replaced four more photographs.
1976

Since the last edition appeared in 1976 it has been a time of great achievement for the breed. In 1976 Ch. Dianthus Buttons was Best in Show at Crufts. All breeders and exhibitors of Westies were as delighted as if it were their own personal triumph.

Following that we saw the great success of Ch. Glenalwyne Sonny Boy, owned by Miss J. Herbert. Over a period of two-and-a-half years he won thirty-two C.C.s and twenty-two Best of Breed awards and five Best-in-Shows. In all, a record for the breed in this country.

Now I have sadly to record the death of my dear husband on 20 November 1977. In our long years of marriage our chief and all-consuming interest was the welfare, breeding and exhibiting of West Highlands. He served on the W.H.W.T.C. committee continuously for forty years, latterly being chairman and then president of the club. The tributes paid to him from far and wide have been a great comfort to me in my sorrow. The wonderful pictorial history of the breed from 1899—which he originated, compiled and arranged—is to be continued in perpetuity as a lasting and fitting memorial to him.

Once again I have made some small revisions and brought up-to-date the appendices in this fifth edition. Two new pedigrees have also been included, and two photographs have been added.
1979

As I am no longer breeding and exhibiting dogs myself, this seems an appropriate time to seek assistance from someone who is actively involved. Therefore I am most happy that Miss Catherine Owen has accepted my invitation to be responsible for the revisions to this and to any future editions of *The West Highland White Terrier*. Her years of experience in breeding, showing and caring for dogs make her eminently suited to keep this book as interesting and as helpful as possible to owners of our beloved West Highlands.

In addition to amending the text where necessary and to bringing the appendices up to date, Miss Owen has contributed a fresh chapter on the progress of the breed in the last decade. Two of the photographs have been replaced and two new pedigrees have been added.

Clacton-on-Sea   D.M.D
Essex, 1981

It has been an exciting and exacting challenge for me to undertake the updating of this book which has been described as one of the finest informative and technical volumes on the West Highland White Terrier.

There are some changes in the text especially on whelping, puppy rearing and grooming; also some added information on the general care and welfare of older dogs. Since there has been much interest in the pedigree section, I have updated these and added a further line, making them up to five generations.
1986   Catherine Owen

I am delighted that the last edition of *The West Highland White Terrier* has been so well received. In this eighth edition I have corrected a few minor errors in the text, revised the Breed Standard, and the appendices, which include the record of the breed champions, have been brought up to date.

The principle news is that the breed has again hit the dog world headlines with the Best in Show records set in the 1970s by Ch. Dianthus Buttons and Ch. Glenalwyne Sonny Boy now being surpassed by Mr Derek Tattersall's Ch. Olac Moon Pilot. During the last two years Moon Pilot has taken command of the showring and at the time of going to print has amassed 9 Best in Shows, 6 Res. Best in Shows, 16 Groups, 8 Res. Groups, 4 Club Best in Shows, 39 Best of Breeds, 43 Challenge Certificates, 11 R.C.C.s and a Junior Warrant. He was also Top Dog all breeds in 1988 and is in contention for the title this year.

1989   Catherine Owen

1

Origin and Development

THE West Highland White Terrier has attained a degree of popularity that could never have been visualised when the first clubs were formed in Scotland and England in 1905, when, according to many writers on the breed, the little white dogs were beginning to be picked out from the small mixed terriers that had abounded as working dogs in the Scottish Highlands for some three hundred years. It would seem that the breed was first classified at the annual show of The Scottish Kennel Club held at Waverley Market, Edinburgh, 26th to 28th October 1904, the following being a copy of a letter sent by the Secretary of the Scottish Kennel Club to Mr J. A. Urquhart of Rothesay.

'My dear Sir,

I have been requested to provide a short classification for West Highland or Poltalloch Terriers and to ask if you would agree to judge them. The gentleman who makes the request is a specialist in this particular line and does not approve of the Scottish type of these Terriers. He says they should be judged from the working point of view. He says they are the old stock from which the Show Skye has been developed but are not to be judged by the length of the coat, that would be in their way for working. They should have black noses and their weight not over 18 lbs for dogs or 16 lbs for bitches. He says that as to general shape it should make for activity, and the heads and necks for biting and fighting. He also says "the general type would be evident at a glance". I hope you can see your way to judge the variety and I shall be glad to hear from you.

Yours faithfully,
A. P. Simpson.'

The ancestors of the breed were in the past known under various names such as Poltalloch, Roseneath, White Scottish, Cairn and Little

Skye, and in about 1904 all these were merged to become known as West Highland White Terriers. (The Cairn Terrier was given a separate register and Championship status in 1912.)

I am indebted to the Secretary of The Kennel Club for the following article which appeared in *The Dog Owners' Annual*, Canine Literature 1892.

The Poltalloch Terrier

'A white variety of the Scottish Terrier existed at one time (and stray specimens may exist) under the cognomen of Poltalloch Terriers, and Captain Mackie, who went expressly to Poltalloch to see this variety, describes it as follows:

'"The Poltalloch Terrier weighs from sixteen to twenty pounds, has a determined, vermin destroying look about it, it is well knit together, is a sort of linty white in colour. The hair is hard and bristly, and will be from an inch to two-and-a-half inches in length, excepting on the face and head where it is short, hard and wiry.

'"The body is a medium between cobby and long, but is very deep and stands upon short bony legs, the fore ones nearly straight. Head very long; nose broad and often flesh coloured; teeth extremely large for such a small dog; ears small, prick, and covered with a velvety coat. The tail is slightly bent and carried gaily.

'"I have had the breed and hope to have it again. I know exactly what these dogs are fit for, and may add that no water was ever too cold and that no earth was ever too deep for them."

'A dog answering the above description is in the possession of Mr M'Gavin the Laird of Balumbie and comes to Dundee with him regularly. The ears of Mr M'Gavin's dog are tipped with black, the head and body being a light creamy colour.'

'The Dog Owners' Supplement' to the *Bazaar*, dated 27th November 1899, included the following article on Roseneath Terriers. The illustration of the three dogs opposite page 64 is from an old print but will indicate the great similarity with the breed as we know it today.

White Roseneath Terriers

'Under the above name is classed a sub-variety of the Scottish Terrier distinguished chiefly by the coat colour being white instead of that identified with the familiar Die Hard of our shows. These white Scottish Terriers are by no means modern productions, although it is only of recent years that they have come into prominence. To the late Captain Keene belongs the credit of owning in the past an excellent specimen of a White Scottish Terrier in White Heather, and at the last Crystal Palace Show was to be seen a puppy out of White Heather by White Victor in the money. This was bred by Mrs Keene and shown by Lady Forbes. Doubtless if Captain Keene had lived we should have seen a strain established which would have been identified with his name. The perfecting, however, of the White Scottish Terrier has been left chiefly to Dr Flaxman (Mayfield House, Pittenweem, Fife), whose capital team at the last Crystal Palace Show formed the subject of many favourable remarks. Strange to say, alike in the case of Captain Keene's bitch White Heather and Dr Flaxman's finest specimens, they were bred from dark (exceptionally dark in the latter case) parents; and this also was the case, if we mistake not, with a white specimen bred by the well-known Scottish fancier Mr Thomson-Gray. Many difficulties have had to be encountered by those who undertook to revive the old strain, for that a similar strain existed half-a-century ago there is abundant evidence alike on canvas and in print. One difficulty was, we believe, the pink nose, which frequently was found in the progeny of some of the earliest productions. Dr Flaxman's dogs, however, boast noses of the blackest jet.

'There has been some considerable correspondence evoked by the revival of this colour variety of the Scottish Terrier (or is it the working Skye?). The working Skye it must be remembered is a very different dog on the island from the one familiar to us at shows. We have it on the authority of Mr Thomson-Gray that the Skye Terrier as found on the island is a dog something between a Scottish Terrier and a Skye Terrier with sometimes drop and at other times prick ears. These working dogs are much smaller than the modern production, which would be of no use for ousting foxes from the hill cairns, or others from the rocks on the sea shore or from river banks. They moreover have a shorter and harder coat and are not so long in body or so level in back. Her Majesty was at one time the possessor of a brace of working Skyes. One came from the Duke of Argyll's Kennels and the other from that of Dugald Ferguson the Lochgilphead fox-hunter who died a few years ago. The Skye Terrier of the show ring is unknown in the district whence it takes its name.

'Dr Flaxman has very kindly placed at our disposal an excellent illustration of a well-known trio of prize-winning Roseneaths from which the great likeness to the Scottish Terrier as we know him is at once apparent. We sincerely trust that the colour variety will continue

3

to find favour, for such a dog should prove of the greatest service to the sportsman, as the terrier would be readily distinguished even at a very long distance, which is impossible in the case of the dark brindles and the other colours which are common. The dogs depicted in the illustration are Pittenweem Miss Tich, Pittenweem Nipper and Pittenweem Bessie and they have many times carried their owner's name to victory. These dogs are white or creamy white in colour, have a hard outer coat and soft inner one to protect them from the cold, prick ears, dark eyes and dense black noses. These white terriers are every bit as game as their dark-coated relatives and they are, as a rule, several pounds lighter. In the future, Roseneath Terriers should prove very popular as house and companion dogs, whilst those who are on the lookout for a dog which with these will combine sporting and workmanlike qualities could hardly have a better dog, no matter by what name it is known.'

The credit for the development of the modern West Highland White Terrier must be largely attributed to Col. E. D. Malcolm of Poltalloch. At the beginning of the present century in Cassel's *New Book of the Dog*, published about 1911 by Robert Leighton, Col. Malcolm wrote and I quote—

'I have been asked to give an account of these dogs because I ventured to show them some years ago and to bring before the general public the claims of this most ancient race. When I first showed in Edinburgh an old gentleman came up to me and thanked me most warmly for having revived in his breast the joys of fifty years before when he used to hunt otters on the shores of Loch Fyne with Terriers just like mine, colour and all. I can answer personally for their having been at Poltalloch sixty years ago, and so they were first known as Poltalloch Terriers.

'When public attention had been called to them, as I cared for the breed only and had no ambition to be known as a doggy man, I joined with a few of those interested in the breed to form a Club for the promotion of the interests of the West Highland White Terrier.

'It is still to be found all along the West Coast of Scotland. I myself have seen good specimens belonging to Ross-shire, to Skye, and at Ballachulish on Loch Leven, so that it is a breed with a long pedigree and not an invented breed of the present day, so I thought it right to disassociate it from the name of Poltalloch.

'The West Highland Terrier of the old sort—I do not of course speak of bench dogs—earned their living following fox, badger and otter wherever they went underground, between, over, or under rocks that no man could get at to move and some of such size that a hundred men could not move them (and Oh! the beauty of their note when they came

4

across the right scent). I want my readers to understand this and not to think of a highland fox cairn as if it was an English fox earth dug in sand; nor of badger work as if it was a question of locating the badger and digging him out. No, the badger makes his home among rocks, the smaller ones weighing perhaps two or three tons and probably he has his "hinner end" against one of three or four hundred tons—no digging him out—and moreover the passages between the rocks must be taken as they are; no scratching them a little wider. So if your dog's ribs are a trifle too big he may crush (squeeze) one or two through the narrow slit and then stick. He will never be able to pull himself back—at least not until starvation has so reduced him that he will probably, if set free, be unable to win (as we say in Scotland) his way back to the open.

'I remember a tale of one of my father's keeper's terriers who got so lost the keepers went daily to the cairn hoping against hope. At last one day a pair of bright eyes were seen at the bottom of a hole. They did not disappear when the dog's name was called; a brilliant idea seized one of the keepers, the dog evidently could not get up, so a rabbit-skin was folded into a small parcel round a stone and let down on a string. The dog at once seized the situation and the skin, held on and was drawn up, and fainted on reaching the mouth of the hole. He was carried home, nursed and recovered.'

This illustrates the intelligence of the West Highland of bygone days. It is still evident today although few of them get the opportunity of displaying their working qualities. The writer was recently informed that one of the famous Hunts still uses a West Highland Terrier in preference to any other breed for bolting foxes. In the West Country they are regularly used as working dogs and are sent on their own without human assistance to fetch up the herd of milking cows from the pastures.

Mr Holland Buckley senior, a very early authority on West Highland White Terriers, recorded in his book on the breed in 1911, that he had seen papers at Versailles and pictures, bearing the imprint of the time of Louis The Great, that were identical with the modern West Highland except that some were prick-eared and others drop-eared or semi-erect.

There are, of course, the two famous paintings by Sir Edward Landseer, R.A., of about 1839, 'Sporting Dogs' and 'Dignity and Impudence', both of which include a West Highland White Terrier.

Many romantic stories are told of their early days, among which is the famous request of James the First of England, in the early seventeenth century, to send to Argyllshire for six little white 'earth dogs' to be forwarded as a present to the King of France. It is certain that he must have placed much value on them because he gave specific instructions that they should be sent in two ships lest one should be lost on route. A letter from India was recently received by the Author stating that the ships of the Spanish Armada carried small white dogs of West Highland type to catch the rats on the ships. History has recorded that after a disastrous naval battle in the late sixteenth century, several of the galleons were driven northwards, where most of them were wrecked on the coasts of the Western Isles of Scotland. If this is true it may account for the little white dogs of Scotland being found in Spanish ships. In fact, Mr Holland Buckley states in his book that, 'Col. Malcolm of Poltalloch claimed by an attenuated chain of reasoning (which although picturesque and vivid, scarcely carried conviction to the student) that the Scottish Terrier owed its existing type to the influence of outside blood and that the original terrier was actually of the type of the West Highlander.' If Col. Malcolm was right, perhaps the outside blood came from Spain. That the original West Highland Terrier was bred for its working and sporting qualities has been firmly established. Their intelligence is very much above average and they are really clever schemers when it comes to worrying vermin out of their holes, and their tenacity of purpose invariably means there is only one end to their work.

Mrs Lionel Portman, in 1910, wrote an article in *The Field* about the happy days spent hunting badger with a team of West Highland Terriers, and the same dogs were exhibited with considerable success. Mrs Portman prefaces her article with: 'Badger digging is, undoubtedly, the supreme test of a working terrier. Rabbiting improves his nose and condition. Ratting combines business with pleasure. But to find a badger deep in the labyrinths of a large earth, and to stick to him, possibly for hours together, baying and sniffing at him so that he has no time to dig—a thing he can do much faster than two men—is a task requiring perseverance, grit and stamina of the highest order. As we feel these qualities are worth at least as much encouragement as show points, we invariably enter all our terriers to badger soon after they have received their preliminary training.'

The foregoing will give the reader some idea of the hard work put in by the old stalwarts on the several regional types to develop them into a single breed, and the controversy that must have existed over the selection of a name to suit all regions. It is quite possible, although there is no evidence to prove it, that the present name was a compromise to include all the white dogs of the West Highlands, hence the name, the West Highland White Terrier.

Show Development

The earlier part of this chapter has given a brief outline of the early West

Highland White Terrier under its various aliases as a working terrier, and I now propose to chronicle its evolution into a show dog.

At a show held in Birmingham, in 1860, classes for 'Scotch Terriers' were included. It appears to have been the first time any terriers were classified, and a 'White Skye' was among the winners. The first show held in Scotland was at Glasgow in 1871, and here again 'Scottish Terriers' were classified, but I can find no record of the winners, and the term probably covered all the short-legged terriers of Scotland.

A White Scottish Terrier puppy by White Victor out of White Heather (it does not appear to have had a name) was shown by Lady A. Forbes at the 1899 Crystal Palace Show, and was among the winners. At the same show, also, Dr Flaxman showed a team of Roseneath Terriers. The first show where West Highland White Terriers were separately classified was at the Annual Show of the Scottish Kennel Club held at Waverley Market, Edinburgh, 26th to 28th October 1904.

At the next Scottish Kennel Club Show, held in October 1905, Morven won the Championship Certificate at the age of seven-and-a-half months, and in 1907 became the first Champion in the breed. Morven was born 28th March 1905, by Brogach out of Callaig, and was owned by Mr Colin Young of Fort William. Brogach has been described in some books as being a biggish terrier with great bone and substance generally, yet weighing only 17 lb. I can find no record of the weight of Morven, who was stated to be smaller than his sire. It is also recorded that Athol, reputed to have been Morven's best son, weighed 16 lb, and Ch. Glenmohr Model, the son of Athol, also weighed 16 lb.

Also in 1907, Ch. Cromar Snowflake, by Morven out of Snowdrift, and Ch. Oronsay, by Conas out of Jean, both gained their titles and were owned by the Countess of Aberdeen.

The first three Champions were therefore produced in 1907, and these together with their contemporaries laid the foundation of the breed. In this same year, also, 141 dogs and bitches were registered.

Between 1907 and 1916 the total registrations of West Highland dogs and bitches amounted to 3,947 and 27 Champions were made up. The names of their owners, among others Miss Viccars (Childwick), Mrs M. A. Logan, Mr Holland Buckley and his daughter Miss W. Buckley, and their 'Scotia', Mrs Lionel Portman, Mr C. Clare, Mrs B. Lucas of Highclere fame, and Mr John Lee, have now become legendary.

Among other breeders and exhibitors during this period were Mr E. Mullard who was known to many of the present-day exhibitors as a judge in the 1950s, and, of course, the famous Mrs C. Pacey who, in the fifty-odd years until her death in 1963, did more for the breed than anyone else and possibly more than anyone will ever do. She became one of the best, if not the best, all round judge in the world and officiated on every continent and in practically every country where dog shows were held, and was very much in demand. In her book, Mrs Pacey says that she made a start and won a lot of awards with a dog called Wolvey MacNab, born 28th June 1911, by Athol out of Weddington Sanna, and bred by Mrs H. Shawe. The first of the many (58) Wolvey Champions was seen in 1916 in Ch. Wolvey Piper, born 24th July 1914 by Ensay out of Culloch and bred by Mrs S. McLeod on the Isle of Skye, followed in the same year by Ch. Wolvey Rhoda.

After 1916, all shows were stopped by the war. Breeding was prohibited in 1917 and 1918 and no dogs born during this period, except under licence, were allowed to be registered. Due to very stringent food rationing many dogs had to be destroyed, some kennels never started again, and those that were able to keep one or two dogs alive on any food they could get, were in a good position to make a slow start once the restrictions were lifted.

Breeding started once again in 1919, and during that year 126 dogs were registered. The following year shows restarted, registrations increased to 244, and five Champions were made: Mr C. Viccars's Charming of Childwick, Mrs B. Lucas's Highclere Rhalet and Highclere Romp, Mr J. H. Railton's White Sylph, and Mrs C. Pacey's Wolvey Skylark. Registrations increased to 758 in 1925, the highest pre-Second World War total, and remained fairly static until 1928, then declining to around the 600 mark during the economic crisis of the early 1930s, increasing in 1936 to 757. In 1941 they reached their lowest since 1919. Except for the years 1951 to 1954 there have been annual increases, culminating with a record total in 1965 of 3,113.

The years 1920–39 saw 125 Champions being made up and of these 32 were Wolveys, approximately 25 per cent, quite a record.

A complete list of all Champions will be found in Appendix II. It is possible to take note of only a few of these Champions. (The date the dog obtained its title is shown in brackets after the name.)

Mrs Pacey's Ch. Wolvey Patrician who won many Best in Shows and would appear in an extended pedigree of most of today's dogs, was the sire of International Ch. Ray of Rushmoor, Ch. Rodrick of Rushmoor, both owned by Miss V. M. Smith-Wood, Miss P. Pacey's Ch. Wings, Mrs Hewson's Clint Crofter who, although never becoming a Champion was the sire of many outstanding dogs, including Ch. Clint Cocktail (1931), probably the best of the Clints.

Mrs Innes's Ch. Brean Glunyieman (1934) was an outstanding dog, considered by many to be the best of all the Breans.

Mrs Pacey's Ch. Wolvey Pintail (1936) was to my mind the best Wolvey I ever saw, a perfect model and the ideal West Highland Terrier. The way she showed, always to perfection, must have gladdened the hearts of all who saw her. The impression she made on me at that time has remained with me all the years of seeing and showing wonderful dogs. She won Best in Show at the Great Joint Terrier Show in 1936 and, on the following day, at the L.K.A. Show was best bitch.

Miss A. A. Wright's Ch. Calluna Ruairidh (1937), sired by Ch. Ray of Rushmoor, was sire of Miss Turnbull's Ch. Leal Flurry (1938), who was the sire of Mr Hewson's Ch. Melbourne Mathias (1939). Miss Turnbull's Ch. Leal Sterling (1938) was the outstanding dog of that year.

We have a direct line from the bitch Ch. White Sylph (1920) to Ch. Wolvey Guy (1924): Ch. Wolvey Patrician—Int. Ch. Ray of Rushmoor—Ch. Calluna Ruairidh—Ch. Leal Flurry to Ch. Melbourne Mathias and, missing one generation, to his grandson Furzefield Piper, who became a prominent sire when breeding and showing restarted in 1946.

With the advent of the Second World War in 1939 all showing ceased, but this time breeding was not banned, and food was available although difficult to get. Nevertheless, it allowed a few kennels to keep going in a small way, and during the period 1940–42 the yearly registrations averaged approximately 150, increasing to 277 in 1943 and to nearly 500 in 1944, rising steadily, except for a drop of 200 in 1953 (crisis again), until in 1964 they reached the total of 2,884, nearly 100 per cent above the 1958 figure.

At the outbreak of the War—I then kept Cairns as well—all the Cairns and some of the West Highlands were given away and eight bitches were put into boarding kennels and remained there until 1943. I kept the two male dogs with me but, later, one of the dogs joined the bitches in the kennels.

In 1943 circumstances made it possible for me to get the bitches back. I intended to restart breeding in a small way, and nature made certain that it was in a very small way as only two of the bitches ever had any puppies again. One had one litter and the other three litters, but this was a new start. It was from this latter bitch, Belinda of Branston, born 27th December 1937 by Ch. Clint Constable (1936) out of Clint Coacla, that the present-day Branstons were developed. Belinda's first two litters were by Bobby of Branston and Ch. Clint Cyrus (1937) out of Blossom of Chemstone, and the last by Mrs Beel's Freshney Andy by Ch. Melbourne Mathias out of Freshney Crysta, which produced Ch. Binnie of Branston (1949).

Championship shows were permitted again in 1946, but only as Breed Specialist Shows, and after a lapse of six dreary war-ridden years what a tonic it was to have them again. The West Highland White

Terrier Club of England held its first show at Peterborough on 11th July of that year, and was greeted with a record entry of 225. To Mrs Winnie Barber fell the honour of awarding the first post-war certificates in the breed. This show was to be memorable for some of the exhibitors: The Hon. Torfrida Rollo won her first certificate with Timochenko of the Roe by Irish Ch. Tam O' Shanter of the Roe, out of Whisper of the Roe. Timochenko gained his full title in 1947. The bitch certificate went to Mr Charles Drake's Macairns Jemima by Ch. Leal Sterling out of Macairns Jeanne, and this was Mr Drake's first Championship Show, his bitch gaining her full title in 1948.

The West Highland White Terrier Club held its first show in Edinburgh on the following August the 11th, with Miss M. Turnbull as judge, and awarded the dog certificate to Mrs Beel's Freshney Andy by Ch. Melbourne Mathias out of Freshney Crysta who, except for his tragic death a month later, would have been a certain champion and also a very dominant sire, for during his short time at stud he sired six champions, including Ch. Cruben Crystal (1948), Ch. Athos of Whitehills (1949) and Ch. Binnie of Branston (1949).

The 'of England' Club held its second show on 28th November 1946, with Mrs Thornton as judge. The dog certificate was awarded to Mrs Pacey's Wolvey Prospect by Ch. Wolvey Prefect (1936) out of Wolvey Poise, and the bitch certificate to Miss E. E. Wade's Freshney Fiametta, by Ch. Melbourne Mathias out of Freshney Felicia, which in 1947 became the first post-war Champion in the breed, going Best in Show at the all breeds Championship Show held at Cambridge 10th July 1947, and the winner of six challenge certificates and six best of breeds. Fiametta was a glorious bitch—althouth some people considered her too big for a bitch—well balanced, with charm and character which were brought out to perfection by her handler, Arthur Wade, who was one of the greatest professional handlers in Great Britain. Although handling many terriers his great loves were West Highlands and Sealyhams, and his knowledge of both breeds was almost unsurpassed. He had a genuine love for all dogs, and many new exhibitors owed much to his readiness to pass on the vast knowledge he had gained during his lifetime of work with them. In his younger days he managed the famous Childwick Kennels of Miss Viccars.

The beginning of general all-breed Championship Shows was 1947, the first being held at Peterborough by the East of England Ladies Kennel Society on 29th–30th May. Here the dog certificate went to another new breeder, Mrs Finch. Shiningcliff Simon by Ch. Leal Flurry out of Walney Thistle gained his title at Leicester the same year, but the greatest achievement for Simon and his owner was still to come, for at Crufts in 1950 he was Best Terrier in Show, and in the following month at the Scottish Kennel Club Show at Glasgow he was awarded Best in Show all Breeds. He was the sire of several champions. It was a great loss to the breed when Mrs Finch gave up breeding in about 1955.

It is not proposed to detail all the championship shows since 1947, the few mentioned above being intended to give the reader some insight into the efforts that were made to re-start breeding after the Second World War and to prove to the new exhibitor that if they have the right dog it can win.

During the early period of the post-war years the quality of the dogs - was very high, which may have arisen because during the war years, although so many of the cream of the fancy were sent to America and other places abroad, a few of the most devoted followers of the breed overcame almost insurmountable difficulties to keep two or three good brood bitches as a future foundation. The breed was also fortunate in having the services of the last pre-war champion, Melbourne Mathias, now owned by Mrs McKinney. He was the grand sire of Furzefield Piper from whom so many of today's dogs are descended, as family tree 'B' so clearly illustrates. This 'tree' does not include all the champions sired by the several dogs, but only some of the main branches, but it should be noted that earlier in this chapter I showed how Ch. Melbourne Mathias was directly descended through champions from Ch. White Sylph in 1920.

There is no doubt that Furzefield Piper was the leading stud dog at this time—Piper was a grand dog although a somewhat fiery showman—and would have become a champion except for being penalised for having lost some teeth in a kennel fight. He was the sire of nine champions of whom the most notable was Ch. Hookwood Mentor owned by Miss E. E. Wade who, in turn, sired eleven champions. His greatest son is generally recognised as being my Ch. Barrister of Branston, who also sired eleven champions, and several with two certificates.

Since the resumption of championship shows in 1946, 168 champions have been made up to the end of 1964, and it is obviously not possible to review the merits of all the glorious dogs who have won their titles (a complete list is in Appendix II). I have, however, selected a few who have left their mark on the breed in one way or other.

My Ch. Baffle of Branston, by Feshney Frinton out of Baroness of Branston, is mentioned here as she was the first of the many Branston champions and is still remembered by some who saw her in the ring, a grand-daughter of Ch. Melbourne Mathias.

Mr A. H. Salsbury's Ch. Macconachie Tiena Joy, by Ch. Shiningcliff Simon out of Macconachie Pearlie, well-named, was a very beautiful bitch and the winner of twelve challenge certificates—still a record.

My Ch. Barrister of Branston, by Ch. Hookwood Mentor out of Bloom of Branston, through his eleven champion sons and daughters and several near champions has undoubtedly left his mark on the breed.

Dr and Mrs Russell's Int. Ch. Cruben Dextor, by Ch. Hookwood Mentor out of Am. Ch. Cruben Melphis Chloe, quickly gained his title and went to America where he continued his winning ways with many Best in Shows. He has sired more champions in America than any other dog.

Mrs Allom's Ch. Furzefield Pilgrim, by Furzefield Piper out of Furzefield Purpose, is the sire of several champions, including Ch. Wolvey Pied Piper.

Mrs Beel's Ch. Calluna the Poacher, by Calluna Bingo out of Calluna Vermintrude, born 1952, died 1965, was winner of ten challenge certificates and ten best in breeds in just under a year, a record that will take a lot of surpassing. He sired five English champions and several in America, including a complete litter of four.

The Hon. Torfrida Rollo's and, later, Mrs K. Sanson's Ch. Eoghan of Kendrum, by Ch. Barrister of Branston out of Ch. Isla of Kendrum, was sire of several champions, including Ch. Quakertown Questionaire.

Miss Cook's Int. Ch. Famecheck Viking, by Ch. Calluna the Poacher out of Famecheck Fluster, a daughter of Ch. Barrister of Branston exported to America and reputed to have won more Groups and Best of Shows than any other West Highland, was still being shown when ten years old.

Mrs E. A. Green's Ch. Nice Fella of Wynsolot, by Fan Mail of Wynsolot out of Shiningcliff Star Turn, gained fame when winning Reserve Best Terrier at Crufts in 1956. He was a very useful stud, and sired Ch. Banessa of Branston and Ch. Sollershot Sun-up.

My Ch. Banker of Branston, by Ch. Barrister of Branston out of Binty of Branston, sired six champions, the most famous being Ch. Bandsman of Branston and Am. Ch. Rainsborowe Redvers, now owned by Mrs Barbara Sayers, and the winner of many Best in Shows.

Mrs Kenny Taylor's Ch. Sollershot Sun-up, by Ch. Nice Fella of Wynsolot out of Cotsmoor Crack O'Dawn, sired five champions, including Eng. and Aust. Ch. Busybody of Branston, out of Ch. Brindie of Branston, and Mrs Estcourt's Ch. Citrus Lochinvar of Estcoss. Mrs Pacey's Ch. Wolvey Pied Piper, by Ch. Furzefield Pilgrim out of Wolvey Padella, was the sire of four champions.

My Ch. Bavena of Branston, by Ch. Banker of Branston out of Famecheck Teresa, was winner of the Terrier Group at Birmingham National and Hove Shows. Exported to Mrs R. K. Mellon, she soon gained her American title.

Miss Cook's Ch. Famecheck Gay Buccaneer, by Ch. Famecheck

Gay Crusader out of Ch. Famecheck Lucky Mascot, is probably the most outstanding of all the Famecheck champions.

My Ch. Bandsman of Branston, by Ch. Banker of Branston out of Ch. Banessa of Branston, winner of seven consecutive challenge certificates and Best of Breeds in three months, was reserve Best Terrier at Windsor Championship Show in 1960. He was sire of three champions and several other certificate winners.

Mr and Mrs Granville Ellis's Ch. Slitrig Shining Star of Lynwood, by Ch. Famecheck Gay Buccaneer out of Slitrig Sweet Suzette, was one of a long line of Lynwood champions and a magnificent bitch.

Mrs Kenney Taylor's Ch. Sollershot Soloist, by Ch. Bandsman of Branston out of Citrus Silhouette, was winner of twelve challenge certificates. It was a very great loss to the breed when, in 1965, Mrs Kenney Taylor, owing to domestic reasons had to give up breeding and exhibiting, and her Kennel was disbanded.

Mrs K. Sanson's Ch. Quakertown Quistador, by Ch. Alpin of Kendrum out of Quakertown Querida, was an outstanding dog and an exceptional showman, winner of twelve certificates, Terrier Groups and Best in Shows. He should be a very great influence on the breed.

Among the many other experienced breeders and exhibitors are: Mrs P. Welch from Worcestershire (Glengyle) who although only keeping a fairly small kennel always manages to show something good, and so far has made four champions; Mrs J. Sinclair (Miss Herbert) from Galashiels (Glenalwynne), President of the West Highland Terrier Club (Scotland), who is a very dedicated breeder and exhibitor but unfortunately prevented from showing during the summer months because of business commitments; Mr and Mrs Billy Thompson, from Lancashire (Waideshouse), who have made three champions in their comparatively short time in the breed; Mrs B. Graham, in partnership with her mother Mrs G. Hazel, is a great supporter of the breed; her first champion was Lasara Lee in 1963, and she has also exported several dogs to Scandinavia where they have very quickly gained their local titles; Mrs Sylvia Kearsey, from Warwickshire (Pillerton), one of our younger enthusiasts who in a very short space of time has bred an excellent type. Her first champion was Ch. Pillerton Pippa who was Best of Breed at Crufts 1965. In the West country Mrs J. Beer (Whitebriar) produces stock of high quality, some of the best having made their mark in Canada and the U.S.A. The Citrus kennel, owned by Mr and Mrs G. Lemon, has produced two champions.

The popularity of the West Highland White Terrier has, during the past few years, increased by leaps and bounds, and new names are constantly before us—such as Miss Sheila Cleland (Birkfell) who by her devotion to the female of the species has bred three bitch champions.

Mr and Mrs Bertram have made three lovely champions in a short space of time and no doubt more will be heard of the Highstile prefix in the future. Miss Fisher (Lindenhall) has an excellent type and has bred two champions, one of which is owned by Mrs Millen who really had the traditional beginner's luck by making her first Westie a champion. The Alpinegay prefix first became well known when Mrs Wheeler made Impressario a champion and later exported him to Mrs Church in America where he had instant success. A year later, in 1968, his younger brother, Alpinegay Sonata, gained his title in the capable hands of Miss C. Owen. There are many others, like Mrs Murial Coy (Cedarfells) with two champions, and Mrs Pratten whose Rainsborowe prefix occurs in many of the pedigrees of recent winners, while from Scotland come such well known names as Mr C. Berry (Incheril), Mr W. Stevenson (Parkendot), and Mr and Mrs Gellan (Backmuir).

In 1965 it was on record that West Highlands had maintained their position of second in the Terrier group but this has now been surpassed and they head the group with a record registration of 4,160 in 1968. It must be hoped for the good of the breed that, as the numbers increase, standards are not allowed to fall.

The demand for top class show stock from this country is incredible and very complimentary as it proves that the large majority of exports are well up to standard.

In 1974 the number of registrations was 4,630. This number has only twice before been surpassed with 4,837 in 1969 and 4,933 in 1970. It would seem that the economic problems are not sufficient to deter either newcomers or veterans when their minds are fixed on making their first or fiftieth champion.

In 1975 so many British exports are making the headlines. In Sweden the expected entry in classes is often more than treble what it would have been ten years ago. Stock from Birkfell, Lasara, Quakertown and other kennels is doing well. In New Zealand Lasara Landlubber gained ten C.C.s in eight months including two reserve Best-in-Shows. In the U.S.A. Ch. Ardenrun 'Andsome of Purston, bred by Mr C. Oakley and exported by Mr M. Collings, excelled himself by winning the Terrier Group at the Westminster. In Spain Int. Ch. Kirkgordon Mariniello, bred and exported by Mrs M. Dickinson, has competed in Portugal, France and Spain with outstanding success.

Since this book was first published, many of the well-known and often famous names have faded from the scene, but fortunately there are always new names and prefixes to add to the honours of the breed. In 1978 names that are regularly in the news are, to name a few, Mrs J. Abbey (Kristajen), Mr and Mrs Armstrong (Justrite), Mrs K. Gallagher

(Gleneyre), Mrs Greening (Tollcross), Mr and Mrs Thomson (Ash-gate), Mrs A. Millen (Sarmac), Mrs T. Lees (Carillyon), Mrs M. Torbet (Newtonglen), Mr and Mrs Tattersall (Olac), Miss E. Wilson (Treth-more), Mrs B. Strivens (Angligate), Mrs B. Hands (Crinan), Mr and Mrs B. Pogson (Meryt), Mr and Mrs R. Wilshaw (Domaroy), Mrs M. Webster (Kilbranon), and Mrs H. Wysocki (Sursumcorda).

With such keen competition it is virtually certain that the breed will continue to prosper.

2

The Breed Standard

IN Great Britain there are four Specialist Clubs, the senior one being The West Highland White Terrier Club, based in Scotland and known to one and all as The Scottish Club, founded in 1905. Shortly afterwards, in the same year, the West Highland White Terrier Club of England was formed. It was not until 1959 that a breed club started in Northern Ireland and in 1980 the Southern West Highland White Terrier Club was formed.

The standard we know today has altered very little from the time it was first set out and recognised by the Kennel Club, in about 1908. The interpretation in some instances is perhaps a little different, as for instance colour, which was always described as white, but rarely, as far as can be gathered, meant the same as we mean by white today. In all the old records I have come across it was freely admitted that a sandy or yellowish streak down the back was usually present and permitted. Now the description means what it says, and a poor-coloured coat is penalised.

The most significant change was made in 1948, at a joint meeting of the committees of the Scottish and English Clubs held in Edinburgh, when it was agreed that the height should be about eleven inches at the shoulder as against the previous eight to twelve inches which had been the accepted height from the days of the original standard. Also, the weight standard of 14 lb to 18 lb for dogs and 12 lb to 16 lb for bitches was abandoned and no weights, therefore, are shown in the present standard. In my opinion this was a grave error because now, except for height, there is no guide to body size and bone formation. A dog can be the correct height as laid down by the standard but be very light and shelly, and conversely, it could be very coarse, due to having an over-heavy body. On the other hand, there must be enough body and bone to give the breed strength to fulfil its original purpose, which the dogs in the early days obviously had since they were regularly used for badger hunting. Of recent years there has been a tendency with some breeders to produce a West Highland White that looks, in body, like a Scottish Terrier. This is quite incorrect and should be guarded against.

The following is the Kennel Club Standard, reproduced by permission.

General Appearance Strongly built; deep in chest and back ribs; level back and powerful quarters on muscular legs and exhibiting in a marked degree a great combination of strength and activity.

Characteristics Small, active, game, hardy, possessed of no small amount of self-esteem with a varminty appearance.

Temperament Alert, gay, courageous, self-reliant but friendly.

Head and Skull Skull slightly domed; when handled across forehead presents a smooth contour. Tapering very slightly from skull at level of ears to eyes. Distance from occiput to eyes slightly greater than length of foreface. Head thickly coated with hair, and carried at right angle or less, to axis of neck. Head not to be carried in extended position. Foreface gradually tapering from eye to muzzle. Distinct stop formed by heavy, bony ridges immediately above and slightly overhanging eye, and slight indentation between eyes. Foreface not dished nor falling away quickly below eyes, where it is well made up. Jaws strong and level. Nose black and fairly large, forming smooth contour with rest of muzzle. Nose not projecting forward.

Eyes Set wide apart, medium in size, not full, as dark as possible. Slightly sunk in head, sharp and intelligent, which, looking from under heavy eyebrows, impart a piercing look. Light coloured eyes highly undesirable.

Ears Small, erect and carried firmly, terminating in sharp point, set neither too wide nor too close. Hair short and smooth (velvety), should not be cut. Free from any fringe at top. Round-pointed, broad, large or thick ears or too heavily coated with hair most undesirable.

Mouth As broad between canine teeth as is consistent with varminty expression required. Teeth large for size of dog, with regular scissor bite, i.e. upper teeth closely overlapping the lower teeth and set square to the jaws.

Neck Sufficiently long to allow proper set on of head required, muscular and gradually thickening towards base allowing neck to merge into nicely sloping shoulders.

Forequarters Shoulders sloping backwards. Shoulder blades broad and lying close to chest wall. Shoulder joint placed forward, elbows well in, allowing foreleg to move freely, parallel to axis of body. Forelegs short and muscular, straight and thickly covered with short, hard hair.

Body Compact. Back level, loins broad and strong. Chest deep and ribs well arched in upper half presenting a flattish side appearance. Back ribs of considerable depth and distance from last rib to quarters as short as compatible with free movement of body.

Hindquarters Strong, muscular and wide across top. Legs short, muscular and sinewy. Thighs very muscular and not too wide apart. Hocks bent and well set in under body so as to be fairly close to each other when standing or moving. Straight or weak hocks most undesirable.

Feet Forefeet larger than hind, round, proportionate in size, strong, thickly padded and covered with short harsh hair. Hindfeet are smaller and thickly padded. Under surface of pads and all nails preferably black.

Tail 13–15 cm (5 to 6 ins) long, covered with harsh hair, no feathering, as straight as possible, carried jauntily, not gay or carried over back. A long tail undesirable, and on no account should tails be docked.

Gait Movement Free, straight and easy all round. In front legs freely extended forward from shoulder. Hind movement free, strong and close. Stifle and hocks well flexed and hocks drawn under body giving drive. Stiff, stilted movement behind and cow hocks highly undesirable.

Coat Double coated. Outer coat consists of harsh hair, about 5 cms (2 ins) long, free from any curl. Undercoat, which resembles fur, short, soft and close. Open coats most undesirable.

Colour White.

Size Height at withers approximately 28 cms (11 ins)

Faults Any departure from the foregoing points should be considered a fault and the seriousness with which the fault should be regarded should be in exact proportion to its degree.

Note Male animals should have two apparently normal testicles fully descended into the scrotum.

With a standard so briefly but clearly written it should be easy to form a mental picture, even to one who is not very familiar with the breed. Truly to appreciate the many sterling qualities and wonderful temperament of this fascinating terrier one must really own one or, if possible, two or more. One thing the standard fails to lay enough emphasis on is the character and adaptability and all-round purpose of this versatile dog, the best-tempered of all terrier breeds, who is a worker, game and energetic and yet able to adapt with ease to the artificial life of the city dweller. So distinctive is his white coat and black nose and piercing expression that he will always stand out in a crowd, and rarely passes along a street without drawing looks of admiration.

For anyone intending to breed West Highlands, whether for the occasional litter for pleasure or for more serious breeding, with sights set on the summit of success, which means at least one champion or more, then the standard must be studied until it is known by heart; not just casually but until it is known so well that any particular point leaps to mind. It may be difficult to breed the perfect Westie, but one should know instinctively what one is trying to achieve. To have some vague idea of what the standard is all about is not enough. It costs no more to rear a prospective champion than some ill-begotten pup with every imaginable fault, and there is a great deal more pleasure in looking at the result. First, let it be remembered that the West Highland is a working terrier. Not 'was' but 'is', and a true one is as tough as the rocks of its native land. It is a distinctive name—West Highland White Terrier—so descriptive that its name indicates what to expect from the breed: a dog that is hardy, tough and game, intelligent, cheerful and independent, and ready to do a good day's work. It must always be remembered that from their very earliest days they were highly thought of, chiefly for their ability to kill rats, hunt and kill badgers, and to dig and squeeze their way into almost inaccessible places. It is important, therefore, to know what sort of ribs they should have and why so small a dog has such muscle and strength and all else that makes up a really typical specimen of the breed. Unfortunately, today many never get the opportunity to show their skill as vermin killers, but to be true to the breed their structure must be right so that if occasion ever arises they may be a credit to their ancestors.

One of the most descriptive phrases appeared under the heading General Appearance in the old standard—'A small, game, hardy terrier, possessed of no small amount of self esteem', a description that is exactly right and describes the whole dog in a nutshell. Add to this the piercing look in their eyes, the pricked attentive ears, the proud way the head is held, the look of quiet assurance and self confidence, the free gay movement that makes one think of a bonny Scotsman with his kilt swinging to the sound of the pipes, the gay devil-may-care look, the smart appearance with a straight white coat and black points, and a substantial though not too heavy body, and the whole portrait is of a dog with great vitality and strength in a neat compact frame.

Although no mention of weight is made in the standard of today, it is generally accepted that the ideal for a dog is about 16 to 18lb, though some almost certainly weigh considerably more. It should be carefully watched to see that they do not become too big or coarse, nor, on the other hand, should they be too small. A bitch should be proportionately smaller, with a weight of about 14 to 16 lb.

In his book. *The West Highland White Terrier*, written in 1911, Holland Buckley wrote that Brogach, the sire of Morven, was 17lb weight, Atholl, Morven's best son, 16 lb, Model, the best great-grandson of Brogath, 16 lb.

They should have neither the appearance of the Scottish Terrier with its lower-slung heavy body nor the lightness of bone and body of the Cairn Terrier. For weight and size the West Highland is fairly and squarely between its two Scottish cousins. It will be a great pity if the lovely head we associate with the breed is ever allowed to be spoilt.

It must be remembered that the standard says, 'the distance from the occiput to the eyes should be slightly greater than the length of the foreface'. If this description is kept firmly in mind the long foreface, which occasionally creeps in, will rapidly disappear.

It is important, too, that the muzzle is not thin and nipped in. It is a strong foreface because it needs to have room in the jaw bone to contain those good strong teeth which have the power to kill, at one snap, a good-sized rat.

The possession of a decided 'stop' is vital if the head is to look right. The stop is formed by the heavy bone ridge or eyebrow, with a slight indentation between the eyes. Without a good stop the head is almost always long and lean in appearance, the eyes narrow-set, and the typical expression quite lost.

A good dark well-shapen eye of medium size is important. The socket is, near enough, almond-shaped, and together with the black eye rims and the very dark eye the expression gives a piercing look. Nothing spoils the expression more than a light eye, which is quite out of keeping and should never be condoned because it spoils the characteristic charm of the true West Highland.

Ears, too, are another feature to correct expression, and in some ways they do more for the head than the eyes. The real terrier look and character can be seen when the dog is on the alert and the ears are pricked forward inquisitively, asking, listening, and all-aquiver for any exciting bit of sport that may be coming up next. Neat, well-pricked ears are most desirable, placed so that they look neither too wide nor too narrow. They must not be too wide at the base, too thick, or even a bit soft. Carried alertly they are a great asset. Carried too wide gives the expression a mulish and unhappy look not at all characteristic of the breed.

The nose, which must be black, should protrude beyond the end of the muzzle only very slightly and should blend into the foreface. A large nose is unsightly. Occasionally the colour of a nose will fade a little and

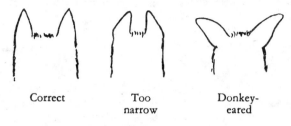

| Correct | Too narrow | Donkey-eared |

Figure 1 Ears

become a pale brown, but this, if it happens, is generally only in the winter months or, sometimes, if a dog is not in top condition. It is usually only a passing phase of a few weeks' duration. Years ago I had a dog with the blackest of toe nails, but at the beginning of winter they turned a very pale brown and stayed so until the spring, when they again reverted to black. Oddly enough, his nose was black all the time.

The description of the mouth, in the standard, seems a little inadequate since it makes no mention of the number of teeth in the mouth as a whole, and refers only to the six incisors in top and bottom jaws between the canines, and of the scissor fashion bite of the top incisors over the lower incisors. Molars and pre-molars are not considered so important in the United Kingdom as they are in some other countries, and they are not mentioned in the standard, which is a pity because in some circumstances they can be important. In at least one continental country dogs are not eligible for show, and in others heavily penalised by some judges, if their teeth do not conform to set standards, but more of this in another chapter. In a fully grown dog a full complement of teeth is forty-two, six incisors and two canines in each jaw. The molars and pre-molars can be remarkably difficult to count up correctly, but a perfect mouth should have a full set of teeth, although points are not lost here if a few pre-molars are missing. They, the pre-molars, are often quite late in coming through the gums and sometimes do not appear before the dog is eight or nine months old, or even more.

The standard says the teeth should be large for the size of the dog. It certainly gives great pleasure to find a good strong set of teeth but I have yet to find a Westie that, even with smaller than normal teeth or an elderly dog with some missing, could not kill a rat with the greatest of ease. The strength must, to a large degree, lie in the jaw, as I have personally known a four-months-old puppy catch and kill a rat, and the way they can gnaw through a marrow or shin bone is quite extraordinary.

The final item of charm to a lovely head is, of course, the hair, which is usually referred to as 'furnishing'. It grows naturally and needs no great amount of trimming. The hair on the head is a little softer than elsewhere on the body and usually needs only the ends tidied up to keep it from covering the eyes completely and hiding the expression.

The neck and forequarters are almost indivisible, in that one part depends so much on the other. The neck must be of good proportions, strong and muscular and fairly long, but not too long. A neck that is too long can make a dog look unbalanced and is almost as bad, though not quite, as one with too little neck. The neck must merge smoothly into the shoulders, which it will do if the shoulders have the correct lay-back. This is of the utmost importance.

The apex of the shoulder blades should be very close together, almost, but not quite, touching. The scapula makes almost a right angle with the humerus. If the shoulders have the correct lay-back the back will be shorter and the neck longer. If the shoulders are straight the whole conformation is spoilt and the shoulders become like those of a cart-horse instead of a thoroughbred.

Together with good shoulder placement there will be the long free stride which really covers the ground and so delights the eye of the beholder. Hand in hand with straight shoulders will go a stilted gait, when the feet seem to be very busy getting nowhere.

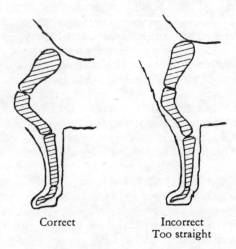

Correct   Incorrect
          Too straight

Figure 2 Shoulder Placement

When a well-made dog is moving away from you in a straight line it should be impossible to see past the hindquarters to the shoulders. If the dog is heavy and thick on the shoulders at the point where the scapula and humerus join, then the dog will have 'loaded' shoulders, which give an appearance of coarseness and heaviness.

The best description I ever heard of shoulders was made by Dr Russell of 'Cruben' fame. He said that good shoulders resembled more nearly the neck of a champagne bottle than that of a beer bottle.

The shoulders and front quarters should be refined in comparison to the hindquarters which have the muscular strength and roundness that can supply the power that gives the great drive for the strong thrusting movement so typical of a West Highland.

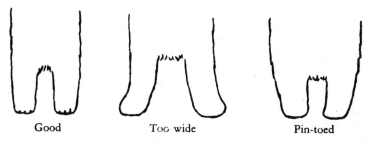

Good   Too wide   Pin-toed

Figure 3 Fronts

The West Highland White should be fairly wide across the loin with a feeling of firmness and strength under an outspanned hand. The stifles must be well bent but not exaggeratedly so. The hind legs must have really good muscle, for here lies all the driving power. Straight stifles and lean shanks go together with cow hocks and weak stilted movement, about the worst faults a West Highland can possess.

A good tail is a great asset. It must be short, thick at the root, gradually tapering to a point. Although the standard says the tail should be about six inches long, most people prefer it to be shorter, between four or five inches. A better guide is that the tail should be in proportion to the size of the dog. When a dog is standing alert, with head and tail well held up, the tip of the tail should be about level with the top of the head between the ears. It is most important that the tail has a good set, high rather than low, which quite detracts from the appearance. A well-shaped tail, inclining just the slightest bit, but no more, towards the ears, looks most natural and also gives the impression of a short back. Thin, long or gay tails are undesirable.

23

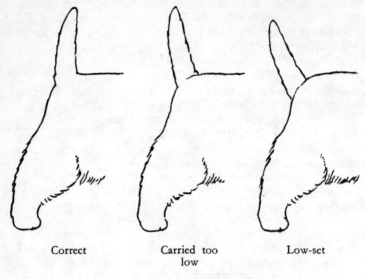

| Correct | Carried too low | Low-set |

Figure 4 Tails

Good tight feet, well padded, are another essential. Thin feet, down on the pasterns with toes splayed out, do not fit in with the picture of a game hardy terrier that can do a hard day's work on rough ground. Last, but not least, is their weather-resistant jacket, a coat that is rain- and wind-proof, to give protection to its wearer as he fights his way through a bramble hedge after a rabbit. The soft undercoat provides the warmth, and the top coat repels most of the rain. The genuine white adds the final touch of smartness; any other breed looks drab and ordinary standing beside a well-kept Westie.

It is small wonder that with so many good things wrapped up in so small a parcel, discerning owners who want a really distinctive dog around come back time and again for another West Highland to replace old faithfuls who have passed on to their happy hunting grounds.

3

Planning a Kennel

THE majority of kennels come into being as a result of a dog being bought as a family pet with no other purpose than to enjoy its companionship and love. Quite by chance, someone suggests it is worth showing, particulars are obtained of the next local show and, believe it or not, before the owner knows anything more she is coming home with a red card and the assurance from a friendly judge that 'you have a champion there'. Whether this proverbial beginner's luck lasts or not, more often than not freedom has been signed away, the disease of dog breeding and showing has been caught, and the dog owner must resign himself to a lifetime of ecstasy and despair. The real dog lover rarely gives up. If he has had a bad day, there is always next time. Before long the original pet is supplemented with one or two bitches, which is all right in a small house with a small breed like the Westie, but when they have puppies even the most strong-minded find excuses for keeping a puppy from this or that litter. That is when the trouble starts, for unless outside kennels are erected there is not much room left in the house for the owner.

Kennels today are designed for every size and shape of dog; most are good but many are too small and dark and uncomfortable, especially for the long, dark, dreary days of winter.

First consideration, of course, is a suitable site and space for the chosen kennel and run. The ground must be well drained and the kennel should, if possible, face south with room to have pens or runs on either side.

Profiting from my early experience with the first kennel I ever bought, I advise against anything that cannot be walked into and stood upright in while working. There is no joy on a wet winter's day in feeding puppies with one's head in the kennel and the rear end out in the wet and cold.

Plan to build the kennel or kennels as near as possible to the house,

25

for our breed likes human companionship and does not thrive when shut away. They are inquisitive little creatures and like to know what is going on. A largish building will cost more but will be worth the extra expense in the comfort acquired, when spending hours giving its inmates the attention they need.

As there are many restrictions in these days, it is best to find out from the local council if planning permission is necessary and it will be if the house is in a residential area. Also, if you have close neighbours, find out their attitude to your project, otherwise they may not be co-operative and will complain about barking, and so on. Time and money will be wasted if, after erecting smart new kennels, near neighbours complain to the council that the dogs disturb them.

Usually, the intention is to limit the numbers kept to at the most three or four bitches but when, having bred two or more litters, the temptation to keep the best puppy from each litter has proved irresistible, numbers soon outstrip the original plan. While about it, therefore, it is better to allow for expansion. Before beginning to build, try to get some good, workable ideas from other established kennels. They have probably thought of things that could be improved in their own buildings and will freely advise against the mistakes they feel they made when they were drawing up plans for their kennels originally.

A good deal of thought needs to be given to eventual requirements before any building is erected. If the plan is to limit the number of dogs kept at any one time to six, with probably one or two of them living in the house at times, a building of about 20 to 24 ft long by 10 to 12 ft wide should be sufficient. This could easily be divided into three compartments, with reasonable space for dogs and their attendant to move around. Always guard against overcrowding or cramped quarters. There are many good designs of sectional building, and I have even seen a sectional garage erected and then divided up to suit individual requirements, but it was then necessary to put in additional windows.

With wooden kennels it is essential to insulate all external walls with hardboard, packing the space between the outer wall and the hardboard with wood wool or, better, lining it with polystrynol. It is inadvisable to use glass fibre as an in-filler as this could prove dangerous should a dog decide to try to chew through the wall. Although unlikely, it could happen.

When dividing up the kennel it is as well to plan for a corridor of adequate width the whole length of the building, to give easy access to each compartment. If possible, a small section should be left as a working area for grooming etc., with cupboard and shelves for storage of tools, toilet requisites and first-aid kit.

The divisions between each compartment should be at least 4 ft 6 inches high and constructed of chain-link fencing, of heavy gauge, on timber framing. Should it be required to segregate a compartment completely, solid portable wooden panels could be fitted within the timber frame of the chainlink partitions.

Lighting and heating must also be available in the kennel, and the safest and most satisfactory way is to use electricity, the installation of which should be carried out by a qualified electrician. No electrical fitting should be within reach of a dog.

Should it be thought desirable to heat the kennel during the winter months two infrared 750-watt strip-heaters, thermostatically controlled, should be adequate. Most kennels need some form of heat, and dogs are more contented when the air is slightly warm. If it is proposed to use the kennel for whelping or puppy rearing, points should be provided for 250-watt infrared dull emitters to hang directly over the whelping box. I have found the Elstein agricultural infrared radiators most effective, resulting in contented mothers and babies. For puppies to thrive they must be comfortably warm. Some heat, therefore, is almost always required for the first week or two, and through the winter it will be required for an indefinite period. The height of the lamp above the box should be carefully adjusted and the instructions supplied with each heater strictly adhered to. These heaters can be obtained from most dog equipment specialists at Championship Shows or from P. & R. Electrical (London) Ltd, Pearl House, Acton, London, W.3.

Sleeping boxes should always be raised off the floor to avoid draughts. Dogs always seem to prefer to have a box to go into rather than an open bench on which to sleep. The most commonly used is probably the ordinary tea chest, adapted so easily for a small dog, and quite draught-proof. To lift the box off the floor it is quite simple to fix a length of 1 in by $1\frac{1}{2}$ in timber on each side of the bottom of the chest. A piece of timber about 6 inches high fixed along the bottom front will keep the bedding in place. More elaborate arrangements for sleeping can be made if required, and ready-made cages may be bought with half-barred fronts and doors so that the dogs may be kept enclosed at night. This arrangement is quite good as long as the dogs are not shut in for too long, nor confining the dogs during the day time. I do not approve of dogs having to spend a large part of each and every day in a cage. No doubt it is possible to keep a far larger number at one time under those conditions, but no self-respecting West Highland should have to endure it.

Let the kennels be as near to the house as convenient because they need the companionship of humans as much as possible. If the dogs can have a good view of comings and goings they are going to be very much happier. They really do like to know what is going on.

The outside runs or pens should be formed with 4 ft-high chain-link fencing on concrete posts, if possible, but good timber or steel will suffice. The bottom line wire should be fixed as close to the ground as possible and secured to the stakes driven into the ground at intervals. This is important as West Highlands are expert excavators and will leave no stone unturned and no sod 'un-dug' if given half a chance.

The pens should be divided as required and a gate of adequate size should be provided to give access to each pen. The pens should be as long as possible to give plenty of scope for the dogs to chase about and amuse themselves. Long pens are better than square ones as they can extend themselves more when racing other dogs in adjacent pens. In reason this type of exercise is very beneficial for warming up and for developing good, well-muscled quarters, so important in this breed. Grass pens are pleasant in summer but of little use in winter when they soon become like ploughed fields. The best way to have both surfaces is to grass the centre of each pen and to provide a wide strip of concrete or paving stones all the way along the sides. All pens should be provided with raised benches on which the dogs can rest off the damp ground.

If the pen is large enough, a suitable shrub planted in the middle adds greatly to their enjoyment. Puppies especially get much pleasure and can have great fun and games dashing underneath the outspread branches and romping round and about it. Straight concrete pens look oh so neat and tidy but are too terribly dreary for lively little characters like West Highlands.

If, after a time, it is decided to expand, and more kennelling is needed, it will have to be decided whether to build a separate puppy house or a very secure kennel for bitches on heat. Everyone has their own ideas about first priorities, which vary according to the type of business it is intended to conduct. Always study the comfort and well-being of the dogs first, and never keep more than can be properly cared for.

If there are good outbuildings that can be converted into kennels, so much the better. Brick-built stables and barns, when lined and made draught-proof, give so much more room than sectionalised timber kennels and there is almost unlimited space for exercise under cover in inclement weather. It can be a slow job adapting these buildings to suit one's particular needs, but when eventually accomplished they can be a real joy to the dogs, owner and attendants. A large barn can be converted to house a great number of dogs in comfort. In the worst of winters, with weeks of snow and outside exercise impossible, the dogs can be kept busy and interested. Once the building has been satisfactorily lined throughout and divided up as required the living conditions are ideal for all times of the year, cool in summer and warm in winter.

If using this type of building be sure to let in plenty of extra windows wherever possible. Dark dreary kennels should never be tolerated.

If a fairly large number of dogs are to be kept it will soon be found most desirable to have a kennel kitchen for preparing the dog's food and where the feeding dishes can be washed, stacked and put ready for the next mealtime. If hot and cold water is available dirty dishes are quickly disposed of after every meal. An electric mincer does away with the tedious job of mincing pounds of meat by hand. The more efficiently everyday chores are planned the greater amount of time there is to spend with the dogs. A separate place for isolating a sick or injured dog is a great asset; it should be heated and quiet.

No matter how good the kennels are every dog enjoys being taken up to the house for a change and treated as a house pet. Two or three can often be brought into the house to sleep and then returned to the kennels in the morning, while others can come to the house during the day and return to sleep in the kennel. This sort of custom is much more important than is often realised. To some it may seem an unnecessary bit of extra work but it is the sort of thing that pays high dividends in building an equable-tempered dog, who is not nervous and who responds to all with whom it comes in contact, quietly confident that the world is a very nice place for little dogs. These are the dogs that make the most of themselves in the show ring. They are so interested in all that is going on around them that they enjoy life and show it by their happy alertness.

4

Breeding

To make a success of breeding the first essential is to start with a good bitch, for the old saying that, 'The strength of a kennel lies in its bitches' is as true now as it always was. It is not disputed that the stud dog plays a very important part but in founding a kennel the first priority must go to quality bitches.

A great deal of thought is needed, first in choosing the bitch, and then in finding the most suitable mate with blood lines in common. The more that is known of the bitch and her ancestors the better. To know that her sire and dam consistently produce a certain desirable type is reassuring and will prove a help in deciding what pattern to follow in breeding plans. Assess the bitch carefully both as to good and weak points, not forgetting the importance of temperament.

Should you wish, and who does not, to establish a strain easily recognisable as particularly your own, you may be sure that it is going to take many years of dedicated work and attention to detail. Endeavour to stick always to the type that is your ideal.

If you are a beginner don't think that anything will do to start with. Choose a bitch from a line that is renowned for its ability to produce with almost monotonous regularity a succession of good ones of both sexes.

Price too often being the governing factor a newcomer will often decide to make do with something a little inferior at less cost, hoping that the use of a good champion dog will be sufficient to counterbalance any faults and failings the bitch may have. Just occasionally such a mating may by a lucky fluke produce a good one, even perhaps a champion, but it is rather unlikely. Years of disappointment and frustration can follow this type of 'flash in the pan' success simply because there is no real quality background. The beginner will wonder why it seems impossible to repeat the original success, and put it down to bad luck. Luck? Of course there is an element of luck sometimes, and one should be duly grateful for it, but more often it is good judgement and common sense, and the fact that the right foundation stock was used in the beginning, having first made an extensive study of blood lines and followed out a well-considered breeding schedule.

There are many good kennels who, over the years, have worked out for themselves a sound breeding policy. If a bitch has been obtained from one of these successful kennels with an established line of breeding, then you will be wise to ask and be ready to accept the sound advice that will be readily given if asked for. You may be treated to a learned discourse on the theory of Mendel, if your mentor is blessed with scientific and biological knowledge, but it is more likely that you will be dealing with a breeder who is concerned more with the practical knowledge gained through years of hard and sometimes bitter experience. The experienced breeder will have strong feelings about line breeding, inbreeding and blood lines and can usually produce a good collection of pedigrees going back several generations to prove a point.

With a quality bitch that satisfies you in all the essentials, breeding back to her grand-sire or to a half-brother is considered a good plan. However, if neither of these is available, look around for some other with suitable blood lines as near as possible to the desired type and possessing a pedigree that contains at least three or more of the most dominant dogs recurring in your bitch's pedigree. The experienced breeder when studying a pedigree is able to conjure up a picture of the dog concerned, seeing not only a collection of names but conformation, character and temperament.

Do not let the bogy of the word 'inbreeding', about which so much nonsense is talked, frighten you. The term inbreeding is applied when mother and son or father and daughter or brother and sister are bred together. Inbreeding is not common in West Highlands but at times it has been used with satisfactory results. It is one way of stamping the type, but it is vital that both should be absolutely sound and as near perfection as any dog can be. The temperament must be quite reliable, with no sign of nervousness. It would be folly indeed to inbreed with something unsound either mentally or physically, for faults as well as virtues are intensified by inbreeding. Only the best should be kept, and if any dog or bitch shows the slightest weakness or fault he or she should not be kept, or bred from. The beginner should seek advice from a reliable source before embarking on any plan to inbreed. At the right time it can be good, and helps to fix a desired type, but you must know what you are about and it should not be lightly undertaken.

Line breeding, which is generally considered to be good, is to mate grandfather to grand-daughter or half-brothers and sisters. Unless, of course, both dog and bitch are good specimens of the breed, line

31

breeding is unlikely to achieve anything of quality.

To outcross is to breed to another line that is completely unrelated. This is generally resorted to only after several generations of line-breeding and its object is to bring in fresh blood; for example, in the hope of regaining size if it is considered that the progeny are getting too small.

It should be possible to learn quite a lot from the first one or two litters you breed. Get someone, either the owner of the stud dog or the breeder of the bitch, to look at the puppies and advise you which, if any, to keep. If you do sell them all and are able to keep in touch with them in their new homes, so much the better. By the time you are ready to breed from the bitch a second time you will be able to decide to repeat the mating or try another dog. If the first litter produces nothing of outstanding quality then see if another sire can do better. Much has been written, by a famous breeder of another breed, against repeat matings, suggesting that each succeeding litter is less satisfactory than the last. I cannot accept this as from my own experience I have proved it to be quite contrary to the facts. If it is found that a certain dog suits a bitch and can produce champions in successive litters there is surely nothing to be gained by trying elsewhere. Whenever I was ill-advised enough to try another dog the results were always very disappointing. Bloom of Branston bred to Ch. Hookwood Mentor three times and produced a champion in each litter. Binty of Branston mated to Ch. Barrister of Branston also was responsible for another three champions. Binty also had one other champion when mated to Barrister's full brother Ch. Brisk of Branston. Bono of Branston likewise produced three champions when mated to Ch. Banker of Branston on three consecutive occasions. Ch. Brindie of Branston also bred a champion on each of the three occasions that she was mated to Ch. Sollershott Sunup, but with Brindie, alas, wanting very much to bring in another line, I sent her on a visit to another very good dog twice, but with disappointing results.

There must be many other kennels with similar successful repeat matings. One that particularly comes to mind are Miss F. Cook's 'Famechecks'. In four litters Ch. Famecheck Lucky Mascot when mated to her nephew Ch. Famecheck Gay Crusader produced five champions. Surely that is successful breeding by any standard. Again, out of Ch. Famecheck Lucky Charm, bred to her cousin Ch. Happy Knight, came three champions out of two litters. Unfortunately Happy Knight died very young or there would probably have been even more champions.

The Stud Dog

A stud dog should look masculine. He should have all the traits one associates with the male. A good strong head carried proudly and with a determined, assertive look. That does not mean that he is a born fighter but rather that he will stand his ground and dare anyone to touch what is his. He must always be kept in the prime of condition. Well fed on good meat, both raw and cooked. An egg each day if he enjoys them, also milk. Biscuit should be only a secondary item of his diet as he should not be allowed to become unduly fat. With mainly meat he will be hard and active. A good stud dog is worth his keep and should not be kept short of anything to keep him in the peak of condition.

If a bitch is to be mated during the day he should have his early morning exercise and then be kept quiet until the mating is accomplished. Always insist that any bitch that is visiting him arrives well before feeding time. Never allow a dog to be used directly he has had a meal.

It is wise to limit the number of bitches that may visit him especially while he is still young. The age a dog should first be at stud varies according to the way he has matured. A West Highland is usually ready to serve a bitch at ten or eleven months but after that he should not be used more than once a month until he is considerably older. Later, a strong healthy dog will manage one or more in a week. Mrs Pacey, who was such a great authority on everything pertaining to dogs, told me that she had found that if a dog was used too frequently when he was young he would go off stud work for a time.

With a young dog giving his first service it is better if the bitch has been bred from previously. If he is started with a maiden bitch, who may be a little difficult or refuse completely to be mated, it can be most unfortunate and sap his confidence.

If much stud work is to be undertaken it is best to have a small room or kennel kept solely for the purpose. All that is necessary is that it should be clean and uncluttered. When scrubbed out it is better to use strong soda-water rather than a strong-smelling disinfectant which can sometimes put a dog off, the scent from the bitch being camouflaged. The only 'furniture' required is a cage or travelling box, in which the bitch can be placed after mating or any other time, a table, a bowl of cold water, cotton-wool, a towel and a jar of Vaseline.

Be sure that the door of the room you are using is securely closed. Nothing could be worse than to allow a bitch in season to escape. If the bitch is good-tempered and ready for mating she will like to flirt and play for a few minutes and it is quite delightful to watch this preliminary lovemaking. As soon as the bitch seems ready to stand and turns her tail

33

invitingly sideways, hold her steadily so that the dog may position himself comfortably. A little Vaseline smeared on the finger and then inserted into the vaginal passage will usually facilitate an easier mating. Some people prefer the mating to take place on a table, and it certainly saves backache, but not all dogs like this procedure. If, however, you do use a table, be sure it is firm and substantial and covered with thick material such as sacking so that the animals can get a firm foothold. Never allow your attention to be distracted while they are on the table, particularly during the actual mating or when they are 'tied'; a slip off the end of the table might cause serious injury to one or both. Once the mating has been successfully accomplished put the bitch in the box to rest for half an hour or so. If the bitch objects to the dog very strongly directly she sets eyes on him, however, more likely than not she is either not ready or her season is over. Owners are not always too sure of the day their bitches come into season, and in any case the length of time each individual bitch is actually on heat varies quite a lot. Some are quite ready at ten days or earlier, others at fourteen to sixteen days, or even longer, *but the eleventh day is about normal.* An experienced stud dog will, however, rarely show much interest unless the bitch is quite ready.

If it is possible to have an assistant to hold the bitch, so much the better, for it allows the other person to give the necessary attention to the dog. The dog can be helped quite considerably by placing one hand under the bitch and slightly raising the vulva. If there is no stricture or obstruction and the bitch stands quietly the dog should penetrate without trouble. If, on the other hand, after repeated attempts he is unable to mate the bitch, it is better to make a further examination of her before the dog exhausts himself. Dip the finger into Vaseline, gently insert the finger into the vagina, and if there is a stricture it will be quickly found. If slight, it can be easily broken with the finger and there should be no more difficulty. If the bitch is malformed or has some more serious obstruction, however, it will be necessary for a veterinary surgeon to examine her more thoroughly.

Directly the dog's penis penetrates and the dog is obviously working, hold him firmly in position until such time as the tie is complete. When the dog and bitch are satisfactorily tied the dog is usually ready to turn and will lift one hind leg over the bitch's back so that they will be standing tail to tail. Most people consider it more satisfactory if there is a tie, but some dogs never attain it, and yet beget good litters. Always talk quietly to them both while they are in this position, and see that the bitch remains steady. If she is allowed to fidget the dog may be injured. It is best to hold one of the dog's and one of the bitch's hind legs together so that it is impossible for them to move before the penis is withdrawn. As mentioned above, directly the mating is completed place the bitch in a cage or box so that she may rest quietly for half an hour or so. Make sure that the dog is fully retracted before returning him to his normal kennel or living quarters.

If the mating has been satisfactory there seems little value in repeating the performance, but sometimes the owner of the bitch will request that two matings be given. Most owners of a stud will accede to the request if feasible, but if the dog is in great demand it may not always be possible to do so. If a second mating is given, it may be either the next day or the next but one. If a maiden bitch has been reluctant to be mated then it is desirable that she has a second service, when she will probably be more co-operative.

It is the usual practice to give a free service on the next heat if the bitch proves not to be in whelp after the first, but it should be made quite clear that if there are no puppies the owner of the stud dog should be informed without delay.

Stud fees should always be paid at the time of service and, in return, the pedigree of the dog used should be given to the owner of the bitch.

5

Whelping

When the bitch has finished her season let her return to her normal routine without any fuss. There is little or no sign of pregnancy in the first month though a very lively bitch may be quieter or her demeanour may change. If she acts more lovingly towards her owner it may indicate that she has 'taken'. A veterinary surgeon can diagnose pregnancy by palpitation as early as 18 to 21 days. It's a technique that requires a good deal of practice. However, in an obese bitch you can't be certain and damage can be done if you are clumsy. Personally, if all is well I am not in favour of visiting the surgery as most of the 'patients' in the waiting room will be sick animals. Try to curb your natural impatience. Even the most experienced breeders can be wrong in their estimation of the number of puppies the bitch will produce; some have been kept guessing till the last day. It is usually about five or six weeks before it is possible to say with any certainty that puppies are on the way. Around this time the abdominal enlargement will be progressive, with a barrelling effect of the ribs, the teats will protrude and take on a bright pink colour and there may be a slight, odourless, colourless, sticky discharge around the vulva. At this stage it is advisable to kennel the bitch alone, the reason being that expectant 'mums' give off a scent that arouses aggressive instincts in kennel-mates with whom they are normally the best of friends.

One sometimes finds that a bitch becomes finicky over her food during early pregnancy, and even has occasional bouts of sickness. Generally this phase only lasts for a short time and no concern need be felt if she seems otherwise in good health.

Strong, healthy puppies are unlikely to be produced by a bitch unless she is fed well and kept in good health and excellent condition during her pregnancy. A good, balanced diet should continue to be fed throughout, but during the last three weeks the amount should be increased so that she is given a third to half more than usual, chiefly in the form of extra protein i.e. meat and fish products. The bitch will probably appreciate this extra quantity fed as a separate meal as it will be difficult for her to eat a full meal at one sitting. Apart from seaweed powder, which is rich in iodine and other minerals and is beneficial to dogs of all ages, additional supplements are usually unnecessary if you are feeding a sensible and varied diet high in protein e.g. meat, fish, tripe, mixed with pre-soaked wholemeal puppy biscuit, plus raw vegetables etc. Today so many foods are already fortified with added vitamins it is superflous to give more. If the bitch enjoys a bowl of warm milk with a raw egg broken into it during the last weeks of pregnancy, so much the better. It is the quality of the food rather than just the quantity that counts at this stage. Guard against the temptation to overfeed, and so make her too fat, as the extra weight can make the delivery more difficult. There is an increasing tendency to think that pregnant bitches and infant puppies benefit from Vitamin C, and Raspberry Leaf given from the time of mating until two days after whelping helps to cleanse and strengthen the reproductive organs which may help the whelping.

Keeping the bitch fit and active is another important part of her pre-natal care. She should continue to receive daily exercise in the fresh air throughout her pregnancy. Several short walks a day instead of one long one are desirable though they should not be too vigorous. This has the beneficial effect of maintaining muscle tone so that when the time of whelping arrives the bitch has plenty of strength to expel her puppies. Sluggish bitches, not necessarily very fat ones, are rather common subjects for inertia. She should be encouraged to take some exercise right up to the last minute even if it is only a leisurely stroll. Obviously, however, the bitch should not be permitted to overexert herself and certainly never to become overtired.

Take great care when lifting or carrying the bitch not to put pressure on her abdomen. Lift with one arm around her chest and elbows and the other at the back of her hindquarters supporting her firmly. She should also be discouraged from running up and down stairs or jumping on and off objects of any height. Unnecessary car journeys are best avoided whenever possible.

Unless you have a specific infection to deal with which must be treated, do not give any medication and radiography definitely should be avoided throughout pregnancy. The bitch should have been in good condition when mated and cleared of worms. However it is advisable to give a routine treatment for roundworms at least a month before she is due to give birth, helping to reduce contamination of the puppies' environment later, though this is a matter to discuss with your vet. To increase the amount of maternal antibodies which will be passed on to the puppies, the bitch's vaccinations should be up-to-date. If this has not been done prior to mating, a *killed* vaccine should be used thereby avoiding foetal damage. It is recommended to give this in the *last* two or three weeks of pregnancy.

With the increase in size of the abdomen, pressure will build up against the bladder so naturally the bitch will pass water more frequently. There may be some accidents especially during the night. Also, she usually consumes more drinking water and so to summarize the rules for a healthy bitch and her litter: good diet and regular exercise to keep her in hard muscular condition, but do not cosset her.

Whelping Quarters

The period of gestation is sixty-three days so there is plenty of time to make the necessary preparations for the expected litter. Once you are certain your bitch is pregnant, start giving thought to the whelping box. Everyone has his or her own ideas on which type of box is best; my preference is for one strongly constructed of plywood which is still light enough to move around and, ideally, raised from the floor to avoid draughts. It should be long enough for the bitch to lie full length in

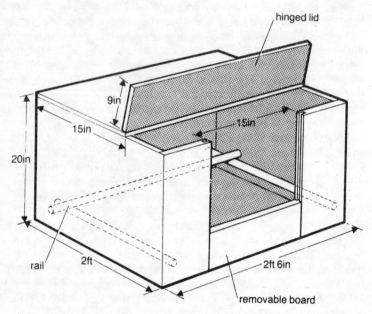

Figure 5 Whelping box

comfort. The most suitable size I have found is 2 feet 6 inches × 2 feet wide and 20 inches high. It has a half-hinged lid so it can be closed down for warmth or snugness but can be folded back to allow an infrared lamp to warm a corner of the box. The front has grooves into which a removable board can be fitted to prevent the puppies falling out of the bed. A rail should be fitted into the box for the first week or two to afford small puppies some protection from being squashed against the side of the box by their mother. It can be removed later when they are stronger, to give more room.

During the whelping the room temperature should be kept around 70° (21°C). An infrared lamp hung over the whelping box at a suitable height will keep the bed warm and dry. It is best to have the lamp hung by a chain so that the height can be adjusted to give more or less heat. Even during warm weather newly born puppies get chilled, and the more quickly they are dried and warm the less risks there are of losses.

Arrangements for the whelping room should be made in good time and whether the room or kennel chosen requires additional heating depends largely on the time of the year. Whenever possible it is far more convenient to have the bitch close at hand in a quiet room in the house, especially if the confinement is an all-night affair. The important thing is for all to be ready and waiting so that the bitch can be accustomed to her new living quarters at least a week before the litter is due.

Make sure the whelping area is scrupulously clean and clear of anything that is not absolutely essential. Assemble the necessary items for the whelping to cover all eventualities. These include piles of clean newspapers for the box and floor, hand towels for drying pups, thermometer, K-Y lubricating jelly, vet's phone number, clock, hot-water bottle, cardboard box and blanket (which may be required to accommodate the pups temporarily), Snugrug (veterinary approved fur fabric bedding), notebook and pen to record data of whelping activities as they occur (also for future reference), scales for registering the puppies' birth weight, Welpi or similar supplement equivalent to bitch's milk plus baby feeding bottle. A table at a convenient height should be available in good light, and an ample supply of hot clean water, soap, nailbrush and towels which are essential accessories for the attendant.

Whelping

You will not necessarily have to call your vet at all for the whelping, nevertheless it is a good idea to notify the surgery beforehand of the expected date. The routine then is to telephone during the first stage of labour, allowing the vet to make arrangements should his services be required. Normal whelpings may vary as much as seven days either way from the standard sixty-three days. In the majority of cases the litter will arrive a little early rather than late, although I have known bitches to go six days past their time with no problems arising. Obviously it is more worrying when the litter is delayed, for the babies are growing all the time, but providing the bitch is well in herself, active and there are no disturbing symptoms such as a rise in temperature, sickness, or a black or green vaginal discharge and the bitch has not shown anything like a first stage and then stopped, when some qualified advice should be sought without delay, it is better not to interfere unnecessarily and to be patient for a while.

Temperature checking can be a valuable aid to the recognition of the imminence of whelping. For several days it may hover around 100°F (38°) but in the twelve to twenty-four hours immediately preceding the first stage of labour there is a sharp drop to perhaps 97°F (36°C) but it does come up again before whelping so keep a twice daily chart for several days.

The milk glands steadily develop throughout pregnancy. About ten days before the bitch is due to whelp the vulva and all the surrounding tissue swell up. This is important as only tissue which has become swollen can stretch easily at the time of whelping. For some days before delivery, the bitch passes a few blobs of slimy, *slightly* green or brown-tinged but basically clear discharge. This is the heavy jelly plug at the neck of the womb slowly breaking up.

The first stage of labour, the dilating of the cervix, is not detectable by the observer, but appears to cause the bitch some discomfort. However it is apparent from her behaviour when labour has actually begun; she becomes progressively more restless, shivers and pants. Her eyes glaze over and she looks to be in a trance. Some may vomit at this stage and nearly all will refuse food. If it is a first whelping, the bitch is often apprehensive as she does not quite understand what is happening to her. She paces back and forth usually with her tail tucked underneath her body, glancing nervously at her rear, and probably passes water frequently. During this time the bitch will scratch at and tear up the paper in her box. Some have shredded newspaper so vigorously that it becomes stuck between their teeth and forms a papiermaché wad inside the mouth locking the jaws together.

Any or all of these signs may be present and the preliminary stages may last only an hour or so but can take up to twenty-four hours. The second stage is recognized outwardly by the onset of straining and later by the appearance of the waterbag. Never burst waterbags—leave them to break naturally as they help lubrication and cushion the pups. Once it is evident that labour has genuinely started it is best to be close at hand all the time. Most bitches seem to derive quite a lot of comfort from the presence of their owner. Full knowledge of how things are progressing and in many cases quick action may be the means of saving a puppy. The length of time taken for a bitch to produce her first puppy varies a good deal. Some will deliver a puppy only half an hour or so after the onset of straining, while others may start with mild and irregular contractions and take perhaps two hours or more, having frequent rest periods in between.

However if she continues straining and does not produce a puppy within two hours it is advisable to consult your veterinary surgeon, who would rather make an unnecessary visit than be called out to a case that is past help. Some whelp so easily that one is hardly aware that a puppy has arrived, but others make much ado about it and will cry out in pain continuously. If when the puppy is partly born it seems to get stuck and the bitch is unable to expel it completely, then is the time to give assistance. Using a sterile towel, as the bitch strains grasp the part of the puppy that has appeared and pull down slowly but firmly until it is safely delivered.

Puppies are normally born head first but occasionally they arrive hindleg first. This is known as a breech birth, and more often than not, is the cause of a difficult birth. It is useless to be squeamish at such a time, or give way to agitation. If the bitch is given assistance every time she strains, in a minute or so it will be over. If she has had a struggle with the first puppy she will be only too glad to let someone assist with the cleaning up process. Normally the bitch will rupture the sac in which the puppy is born herself, but if she does not react instantly, break it quickly with your fingers to release the head and clear any mucus from the mouth and nostrils to allow a free passage to the lungs.

The placenta (afterbirth) may still be attached to the puppy's umbilical cord, which should be severed by tearing it with your nails. It is better to leave the cord too long rather than too short, about an inch and a half is safe enough. This quickly dries up and in a couple of days will fall away. Next the bitch should start to devour the afterbirth. This is a normal function and provides her, as nature intended, with some nourishment. However there is still divided opinion on whether or not this should be permitted. Meanwhile the bitch's vigorous licking serves to dry, warm and stimulate the puppy's breathing. By this time it should have given its first cry. When this happens one knows all is well and in a few minutes the puppy will crawl towards the teat and start guzzling. A few gasps by the puppy at birth show it is breathing; otherwise make sure the head is free from fluid and then shake it upside down to clear the back of the throat. Hold the puppy firmly in your hand supporting the head and neck, raise it to shoulder-height and then, with a swinging motion, bring it down to the level of your knee, removing the expelled mucus each time you do this. Vigorously massage over the heart and lung area, and blow into the pup's mouth. Fluid left in the lungs will cause pneumonia.

If all goes well, after a short rest the bitch will start to strain again and repeat the whole performance. Usually once the first puppy is born the rest follow without too much trouble. Suckling by the puppy stimulates the production of hormones which help milk production and start the uterine muscles squeezing again for the next delivery. Sometimes after one or two puppies she will take a longer rest, but there is no hard and fast rule, and one can only wait patiently.

With luck, an easy whelping may well be over in three or four hours, but if the bitch experiences trouble or it is a long drawn out affair, she may be offered warm drinks of milk and glucose from time to time and a short outing to relieve herself may make her feel more comfortable.

Some people prefer to place the puppies in a cardboard box on a well wrapped hot-water bottle as they are born, but many bitches become agitated if they are removed, so it really is a matter of discretion. In a normal whelping your role is to reassure and encourage the bitch, which is all the assistance she requires. The amount of interference should be minimal.

It is advisable to count the afterbirths as they are expelled. Should one become detached from the puppy and not arrive when the puppy is born, as sometimes happens, it is necessary to keep a sharp eye on the bitch in case of a serious rise in temperature, for if an afterbirth is left behind it will almost certainly cause trouble unless prompt steps are taken to avoid complications. New-born puppies cannot regulate their body temperature effectively, and until they are a week old they are unable to shiver. Therefore they are very dependent on external sources of heat, including warmth from the mother. An infrared lamp sited across a corner of the box or a hot-water bottle are the best methods as they allow the bitch a cool area to sleep. Heat for at least three days after whelping, 75°–80°F at floor level.

Care of the Nursing Bitch

If the whelping has been straightforward and the services of the veterinary surgeon have not been required, it is the general practice of many to let him examine the mother next day and, if he considers it necessary, to give calcium, and an antibiotic injection to counteract possible infection. It is not always easy to ascertain that all the puppies have arrived so a check-up saves a lot of worry and, more important by far, saves your bitch a lot of unnecessary suffering. If by some misfortune the whelping does not go according to plan, do not hesitate to call a veterinary surgeon in good time so that he can take whatever steps seem necessary, even a caesarean operation if required. Unfortunately, there are a number of complications which may occur. A malpresentation or oversize puppy, inertia or an exhausted bitch are some of the problems. If it should be decided that a caesarean is necessary, it is better undertaken before the bitch becomes overtired and weakened with fruitless straining. Today this has become a safe and simple matter and now it is the exception rather than the rule to lose any puppies if the operation is done in good time. In a very short time, three or four hours, the bitch will be back home and in her bed with a healthy litter of puppies contentedly feeding away. If it is a first litter it can be a shock for the bitch to wake up and find herself surrounded by a number of squeaking puppies. It is not surprising if at first she does not comprehend how they got there. However with encouragement most accept them quickly. After that, apart from a little stiffness she will soon be back to normal.

Before automatically resorting to a caesarian for a last puppy, some veterinary surgeons use the technique known as episiotomy. Used rather frequently in human deliveries, episiotomy is the cutting of the perineum or area of tissue between the rear opening of the vagina back almost to the opening of the anus. After delivery it is stitched together and barring complications heals easily, presenting no problems in future births.

Once all the puppies have arrived and she has rested awhile, steps should be taken to give her a complete change of bedding. Remove all the soiled paper and bedding, wipe around the box, then replace with clean paper and the Snugrug. Examine each puppy from head to tail to make sure there are no abnormalities and re-check for its sex. Before leaving her to rest give her a bowl of warm milk and glucose. It will be necessary to hold this in the box so that she can drink it comfortably without disturbing herself too much. Make sure she has fresh water to drink and all the puppies are suckling. Check that she has milk in her teats, as sometimes it does not appear until a few hours after whelping. If this happens, still try to make the puppies suckle, as this will stimulate production. It is important that puppies nurse as soon after birth as possible as the 'first milk' or colostrum, which contains antibodies against various diseases, protects them with a passive immunity for several weeks after birth. There are, of course, only antibodies against those diseases to which the mother is herself immune. Once you are satisfied all is well and the new family contented you can safely take a well-earned rest for a couple of hours.

The bitch's food should initially consist of a light diet, semi-solids such as fish, egg and milk, Complan and milk, with the addition of calcium and the aforesaid glucose or honey. After the first twenty-four hours, if her temperature is nearly normal, she will be ready for a small helping of finely chopped meat. From that time onwards, all being well, she will quickly get back to a regular routine of two milk meals and two meat meals alternating, ending the day with meat. If she refuses her food or eats and then vomits it up, take her temperature. The normal is 101.5°F (38.5°C) but it often rises a day after whelping to 102°F (39°C) or half a degree more, without there being anything really wrong. However, if you are unhappy about the bitch do not delay in sending for your veterinary surgeon, who will almost certainly give her an antibiotic injection.

The more quickly any upsets, however small, are attended to the better. If the bitch is making a good recovery she should be encouraged to go outside three or four times a day for a little exercise and to attend to the needs of nature. To begin with she may have to be lifted out of her box and carried outside as she will be reluctant to leave the puppies. At least once a day, for the first few days, it is usually necessary to get a bowl of warm water and wash her tail and rear end, as there will be a little discharge that soon becomes unpleasant if neglected. See that she is well dried before returning her to her puppies. The normal vaginal discharge which at first is dark green, and later becomes red, may continue for two weeks or longer. Her motions for the first day or so after whelping will be loose and almost black, but they should become normal within a few days.

The removal of dew claws is only a minor job and should be done at three to five days. An experienced breeder will attend to this herself but if you are not too sure about how to go about it get your veterinary surgeon to do it for you. It only takes a few minutes to attend to an ordinary sized litter but it should not be done within sight or sound of the dam.

We have in the bitch a ready-made machine for warming, cleaning and feeding puppies; nevertheless it is necessary to check over the litter daily. Pick each puppy up in your hand to see that it has a full tummy and feels warm and firm. Contented puppies will lie peacefully with their dam, but do not be perturbed if you see them twitching in their sleep, for this is the normal thing for a healthy puppy. If the puppies cry a lot, are always restlessly crawling around, or nurse only for a few minutes at the 'milk bar' and then fall off, it is probable that the bitch's milk does not satisfy their needs. In this case it may be necessary to supplement feed. A regular watch to see the mother is keeping tails nicely washed is also important. If you do have to remove any dried excreta from their little behinds it is best to use warm olive oil to soften it, using a piece of cotton-wool.

Newly born West Highlands have pink noses and pads but these gradually turn black within the first few days.

Some breeders avidly weigh their puppies daily, though it is generally apparent that they are thriving as they grow rapidly in the early stages. Weight gains differ considerably but, as a guide line, an average puppy will weigh around 6 ozs (170 grams) at birth and gain 1 oz (28 grams) a day.

The eyes usually begin to open from ten to fourteen days after birth. The lids first part at the inner corner and gradually open to the outside. Occasionally at this stage an infection creates a pus formation which builds up under the eyelid causing the lids to bulge. In this case bathe the eye in a warm saline solution several times a day. The pus will drain from the inner corner and should be wiped gently away with cotton wool swabs. A little chloramphenical ophthalmic ointment is most effective. Once the eye opens up completely the problem goes away. However a veterinary surgeon should be consulted if it is not clear in forty-eight hours. The ears are also sealed at birth and will start to open after about fifteen days. It is preferable to have one specific person to care for the bitch and her litter, who will be responsible for monitoring their progress. Even the most amenable, calm bitch can be upset by strangers, both dogs and people, and it is not worth risking infection being carried into the nursery on 'foreign' shoes so do restrict visitors to the absolute minimum.

The first week is the most critical stage. Once through this period, with care and attention, regular feed times for the mother and the puppies, and a bed-change every day, there should be nothing to worry about. To have happy, healthy litters to watch over is a most pleasant pastime.

Post-whelping Complications

Post-whelping complications are uncommon; nevertheless it is better to be aware of things that can go wrong and acquaint yourself with the possible symptoms rather then wait for a crisis. The following are some of the problems that can occur with a nursing bitch or her puppies.

Abnormalities—Once in a while puppies are born with a deformity, so as soon as they are established each newborn should be thoroughly examined for any congenital faults. Starting with the head, open the mouth to make certain that there is no cleft palate. This is a defect of the roof of the mouth in which the two sides of the structure forming the palate are not properly united. Unless put to sleep most puppies will die of starvation anyway, as the milk, instead of being swallowed, is usually returned through the nasal passages. This condition is thought by many to be a hereditary fault in certain lines and caused by improper development of the foetus during the period when the mouth is being formed. A virus infection during the early part of pregnancy is considered another source of the problem. Riboflavine or Folic Acid tablets (both products members of the Vitamin B group) administered from the day of mating until a week before whelping to bitches with a tendency to produce this problem, have been found helpful. A hare lip is also often associated with a cleft palate.

Another problem that may occur is a malformation of the stomach in which the belly has not completely closed up and some of the intestines are on the outside. (An over-zealous bitch may sever the cord too closely, tearing the navel, but this should not be confused with the deformity). If immediate veterinary attention is available and the opening stitched up in time, puppies have been known to survive. Generally, however, an umbilical hernia will develop and an operation will be necessary later on.

Examine the legs, both fore and hind for obvious malformation of joints or limbs. Check that there are the correct number of toes. Lastly, look at the rear. Tail faults can vary considerably from a slight thickening which is not noticeable unless handled, to kinks of various degrees of severity. It is often possible to achieve considerable improvement, as in the early weeks the tail is like gristle. Although a kinky tail detracts from the dog's appearance, it is not detrimental to its health. A more serious condition is the bob-tail, which is often seen with an imperforate anus where the terminal canal of the alimentary tract has no opening to the outside.

Many of these conditions are detectable at birth and it is not advisable, in the serious cases, to waste time, but accept your disappointment and have the puppy put to sleep. Naturally it is important that any surviving deformed puppy should later be prevented from breeding and thus perpetuating the condition.

Colic—The crying of a puppy from pain is one of the most heartrending sounds in the world. The 'colic cry' is different from the normal 'hunger whimper': it is harsher, an almost continuous wailing. Examine the puppy and look for the telltale distended stomach, hard as a rock. Colic produces a build-up of gas. Just as in human babies, a few drops of gripe water may help eliminate some of the gas. A teaspoon of milk of magnesia given to the bitch will help in the case of her milk being acid.

Eclampsia—This is a disease of the lactating bitch where there is a drop in the calcium level in her blood due to the demands of lactation. The symptoms are shivering, rapid panting, staggering around and some-times collapsing completely. Occasionally the bitch may become hysterical and bark and in these cases the temperature may go as high as 106°F (41°C). Prompt treatment must be by a veterinary surgeon, who will give the bitch calcium by intravenous injection.

Fading Puppies—is the term applied to puppies which appear to be normal and vigorous when born, but become less and less so and die before they are fourteen days old. Fading puppies will seem to suck less ardently in the few days after birth. They become limp, chilled and flabby, their heads often swaying from side to side. The pups are likely to appear smaller than at birth as they become progressively more dehydrated. Bacteria or a virus may be to blame for the problem. Sick puppies lose ground rapidly, but in cases when symptoms have been diagnosed in the early stages and prompt medical therapy administered, there are instances when they have recovered. In some conditions a 'mixed grill', a concoction of Mansi serum (concentrated bacterial and viral mixed canine antiserum), antibiotic and vitamin B12, has been found effective.

Management is still the most critical factor in getting puppies through the first two weeks of life, and chilling accounts for a high proportion of deaths. The temperature at floor level must be maintained at 75–80°F. Puppies may starve if the bitch's nipples are too large, or conversely too small for them to suck effectively.

Hand Rearing—It is extremely rare to lose a bitch during whelping but she may become ill, her supply of milk may fail in quantity or quality, or her maternal instincts may be lacking. Under these circumstances, or in the event of her family being abnormally large, it may be necessary to share the nursing duties. Whatever the reason, rapid action is essential if the puppies are to be saved. Canine foster-mothers are not always available so the alternative is to bring the puppies up by hand-feeding. It is a very demanding and exhausting job but extremely rewarding to rear puppies that would otherwise be lost.

It is vitally important to keep the feeding as close to the routine of the natural mother as possible, and a small feeding bottle fitted with a teat is recommended. Ensure all equipment is kept clean and sterile. Prepare the Welpi or similar proprietary formula according to the makers' directions and cool to blood heat. Maintain the milk at the correct temperature for each puppy. The food should be freshly prepared for each meal. Hold the newborn puppy in your lap in an almost upright position, with the bottle at an angle to allow the entire nipple area to be full. Do not let the puppy nurse too quickly or take in too much air. The amount each one requires often differs and it is difficult to be precise but as a rough guide, half a teaspoon (2½ mls) per newborn puppy should be offered for each meal. Generally they know themselves how much they want, and you can cease feeding when they lose interest. Never try and force more down if the puppy has taken a reasonable amount and then desists. The quantity should increase rapidly as the puppies grow. The timetable generally recommended is feeding every two hours day *and* night, though if the puppies are contented, 'feed on demand' or every three to four hours.

Besides correct feeding, there are two other essentials to the successful hand-rearing of puppies: warmth and excretion. Heat must be supplied either with an infra-red lamp or with constantly refilled hotwater bottles, carefully wrapped to avoid burning the babies, to compensate for the mother's body warmth. The bitch normally briskly licks the puppies at, or after, a feed and the friction and warmth of the tongue induce urination and defaecation. If puppies are hand-reared this process must be imitated by gently massaging the abdomen and under the tail in order to stimulate them to pass waste matter. Use a small pad of warm, damp cotton wool or paper tissue.

Mastitis—an inflamation of the mammary glands, which may occur any time between parturition and weaning. The inflamed teat becomes purple, swollen, hot and very tender, and the bitch's temperature will be high. Immediate veterinary attention is advisable because an abscess may develop in the glands. Warm fomentations of epsom salts in water will induce the abscess to burst. The puppies may need to be hand-fed but should be kept with their mother if possible, as the bitch usually responds to treatment fairly quickly.

Metritis—This usually occurs within a few days of whelping and is often caused by the retention of one or more afterbirth, which causes inflammation of the uterus. The signs are vomiting, restlessness and reluctance to take food. A purulent (reddish or creamy coloured) discharge will be apparent and the temperature will rise quickly. Professional advice should be called for; modern antibiotics correctly and promptly administered usually effect a speedy recovery.

Prolapse of the Anus—This is not a common problem and is caused by the puppy straining to pass faeces. Its appearance is that of an enlarged, very red fleshy mass protruding outside. Persistent licking by the mother should be discouraged. Emergency first aid is to gently press the prolapse back again with wet cotton wool and lubricate the area with liquid paraffin. If the prolapse recurs veterinarian advice should be sought.

Umbilical Hernia—the protrusion of a fat-laden membrane through the abdominal wall where the umbilical ring has not closed properly. When small the hernia has little effect on the puppy, but a large one should be corrected surgically.

6

Puppy Rearing

The importance of the way in which puppies are reared cannot be over-emphasised. Good conditions of housing and feeding are absolutely vital, and no detail unimportant or too much trouble; indeed, the true dog-lover will spare no effort to see that puppies have as near perfect attention as possible. It is not good sense to neglect any aspect, at any age, when rearing puppies if one wishes to produce the best. This means not only puppies that are structurally sound with good pedigrees but also strong in bone and body and with good temperaments. The first essentials are a warm, dry, clean bed without draughts and sufficient food in small quantities at frequent intervals. Contented puppies are thriving puppies and, if their mother has amply supplied them with her own milk, at three weeks they should be nicely round and firm with their eyes and ears open and beginning to walk somewhat unsteadily around their bed. Remember to keep their toe nails cut very short, as they become long and needle sharp, and nothing tends to make their mother more irritable than little sharp claws working on her tummy while they take their nourishment.

Weaning generally starts when the puppies are around three weeks of age and is a somewhat messy process. It is far easier to start with a semi-solid mixture, i.e. tinned baby food—creamed rice pudding and egg custard with rice seem to be the most acceptable, or Welpi thickened with baby rice may be used. Warm the food to body temperature: nothing puts puppies off more than being offered cold food. Using a saucer or shallow dish for the mixture, guide the puppy's nose down to the food. Sometimes the pups have already had a taste from their mother's bowl of milk and will immediately start lapping, whilst others will splutter, are more reluctant and resist. At this first attempt, the puppy is usually so amazed at finding all this food that its feet, chest etc. land in the dish as well. Obviously the puppy will need washing after this messy encounter and often litter-mates are seen licking it clean. Once having tasted this food, they usually lap quite eagerly next time. It is better not to rush the initial introduction to solids, and one meal for the first day is sufficient, increasing gradually to four meals a day. Once the pups are proficient at lapping, offer them half a teaspoon of finely scraped raw meat (use meat fit for human consumption—not pet mince). The preparation of this meat is rather a tedious job but is well worth the effort. The best way to do this is to cut a thick slice of good lean beef and then with a spoon scrape away the meat from the sinew until sufficient puree has been obtained. (A food processor can be used making the meat a mushy consistency, and this can be frozen in individual portions in the freezer all ready for use.) Some puppies prefer meat to their milk meals but both are essential to their growth. By four weeks they will have arrived at four meals a day, two milk and two meat mixtures, and at this stage a little crumbled brown bread may be mixed with the meat juices and scrambled egg may be added to the diet. The rule for weaning puppies is the same as weaning babies: make all changes of food gradually, thus ensuring no digestive problems which quickly lead to diarrhoea. It will be appreciated that these feeds are supplementary, to begin with, to those given by the dam, but, as the meals are gradually increased, the demand made by the puppies on their mother decreases. Over the next week or two the amount of her food should be reduced, and little by little her milk glands will slowly dry up. The following diet from seven weeks onwards is usually satisfactory. A substantial meal given last thing helps to compensate for the longer gap without food overnight.

Diet Sheet

8.30 a.m.	One of the following:
	Warm milk (pre-boiled if cow's milk) sweetened with honey or glucose and fortified with beaten egg and baby cereal
	or
	Complan
	or
	Weetabix or cornflakes in milk
	or
	lightly boiled or scrambled egg with grated cheese
	or
	boned white fish in milk.
1.00 p.m.	Minced or very finely chopped beef (fit for human consumption), either raw or lightly cooked or *Forthlade Tripe Mince* or *Denes Healthmeal*.
5.30 p.m.	Alternative of breakfast

> *or*
> milk pudding, sponge cake or baby rusk soaked in milk,
> *or*
> Bengers
> *or*
> Slippery Elm Food
> *or*
> cottage cheese
> *or*
> plain yoghurt.

10.00 p.m.   Minced warm cooked meat (beef, chicken, rabbit, lambs' hearts or tongues) mixed with brown bread, cooked rice or wholemeal puppy meal scalded with broth. A little grated raw carrot or green vegetable may be added.

Even to an adult dog it is advisable to feed a puppy meal presoaked to a crumbly consistency. Never feed meal *dry* as this product swells in contact with fluid and will cause acute abdominal discomfort. I am aware that this feeding menu is not a particularly economical one, but a nutritious diet helps to build up the puppies' resistance to disease and it is important that each animal should be plump and well-covered but not flabbily fat. At five weeks it is time to let the bitch spend increasingly longer periods away from her puppies during the day. When their little sharp teeth start to come through their gums the dam soon becomes very weary of their perpetual demands. For at least another week the bitch should be left with them at night, but it is a good plan to devise somewhere where she can rest out of their reach if she desires. The dam's instincts are the best guide. If she starts to growl at them the time has come for her to be removed entirely. Otherwise, they should be independent, and she may be released from further responsibilities, when the litter is six to seven weeks old.

Some bitches regurgitate food for their babies. This is quite natural; it contains some of her gastric juices, but it can be highly dangerous if she has been fed on large pieces of meat or paunch. The puppies will eagerly devour it if given the opportunity, with unfortunate results. Therefore if the bitch returns to see her puppies, it is better that she does so before her meal.

As most people with any experience of puppies are aware, round-worms are an ever-present problem. Roundworm infections in puppies can lead to many symptoms ranging from unthriftiness, intermittent diarrhoea and sickness, to pneumonia and death in severe cases. Puppies become infected within the uterus of the dam. Although older dogs rarely have worms in their intestines they invariably have larvae of the roundworms in their muscles and elsewhere in their bodies. In a pregnant bitch these larvae become active and travel to the uterus, cross the placenta and infect the puppies. Thus the pups are born already infected, although it takes about three weeks before the worms mature and begin producing eggs. As puppies may start passing eggs in their faeces as early as three weeks after birth it is important to worm them before this time. Worming at ten days of age, with a suitable roundworm drug (Piperazine Citrate—obtainable from your veterinary surgeon) followed by further worming doses at weekly intervals up to six weeks of age is recommended. A further dose at two-and-a-half months is advisable. The bitch should be dosed each time the puppies are wormed as she may pick up larvae passed out by them.

Regarding training them to clean habits, the first lesson will start when they are about three weeks old and beginning to move around their bed. At this age a puppy instinctively tries to leave its bed to attend to the demands of nature, so now is the time to remove the board in the front of the box so that they can easily walk out to attend to their needs and get back again. When they first start to leave their nest they should have only a fairly small area to move round in, for if they are at liberty to get too far from the box in their first venturings they may get lost, stay at the far end of the kennel, and get chilled; nor should they be able to squeeze behind the box. If the space outside the box is limited to an area of about a metre square, say, for a week they will soon get their bearings and then the space can be increased. The arrangement should also include an area for the mother to take her meals in peace.

The best floor covering is several thicknesses of newspaper, for which purpose every newspaper that comes into the house should be saved, also any that can be obtained from friends or neighbours. Whenever one goes to the puppy pen it is easy to pick up soiled papers and replace them with clean ones. It is surprising how quickly puppies choose one particular corner for toilet routine, leaving the rest quite unsoiled.

At the stage when the dam has just left the puppies, it is very necessary to keep a watchful eye on their posteriors to see that they are managing to keep themselves clean. It is advisable to keep the hair round the anus very short, but in any case it should be examined every day, which also serves the purpose of getting puppies used to being handled by humans.

Always hold the puppy firmly when picking it up so that it feels secure, and be sure that your hands are on the outside and never underneath the pup's elbows, as nothing is more likely to ruin what would normally be a good straight front than wrong handling. Picking up puppies the wrong way and allowing them to go up and down steps at an early age are both equally disastrous. Puppies should be played with and handled from an early age as attention in the early weeks proves priceless in developing their characters and prevents them from being hand shy. It is important that the puppy is fearless of the everyday noises of life, and a radio in the nursery helps to accustom them to a number of sounds from quite an early age. Puppies love to have toys, hard rubber rings or jingle bells and something to push around, so give them a tightly sealed tin containing a few pebbles, which makes a most intriguing noise and gives endless enjoyment.

Absolute cleanliness is another most important factor, not only feeding and drinking dishes but also the bedding. Whether you are using Snugrug or wood wool it should be changed daily. It is a good practice to have a spare box and puppy pen so the litter may be interchanged. This allows a far better chance for thorough cleaning, scrubbing, drying and airing before being re-used.

At about six weeks, if the puppies are fortunate enough to be born in the spring or early summer, it is very good for them to be allowed out for short periods of play, preferably on a lawn or in a sheltered place, as soon as the weather is warm enough. They need to stretch their legs and expand their lungs, and will eat and sleep all the better for so doing. The best time for them to romp and play is before each meal, and after meals they should be allowed to sleep undisturbed. Directly they show signs of tiring—probably in about half an hour on their first outing—they should be returned to their kennel. In an uncertain climate great care must be taken to see that they are not put in a cool wind or allowed to get chilled. They will soon be protesting loudly when they are returned to their kennel earlier than they think necessary.

Winter puppies are, of course, a more difficult problem. They still need a change of scene, and it is often easiest to take them into the kitchen to play around, first having taken the safety precaution of protecting electric fires, telephone wires etc, removing all mats, shoes or brushes and anything too valuable for chewing. The more puppies are accustomed to strange noises, the friendlier they will be. Puppies left too long in a kennel soon become shy and bored; consequently they will become destructive. This extra attention takes up a lot of time but is well worth all the trouble in the long run.

It seems no time at all before they are eight weeks old, when serious thought must be given to which puppies are to be kept and which parted with. Eight to ten weeks is a good age to sell the first ones, but no puppy should be sold under this age. It should be possible to give the buyer a guarantee that the puppy has been wormed, and that it is satisfactorily eating good solid food. Always give a written diet sheet to the new owner so that any sudden change of food which might upset the stomach is avoided. During the period of adjustment the puppy may be overawed by the new surroundings and although otherwise very well and happy could be struck with transient diarrhoea. Stress and tension will be present even if the puppy seems to be having fun. Therefore it is suggested that the youngster be fed on a bland, fat-free diet for the first 3–4 days. A little dry arrowroot powder or All-bran mixed with the food will help rectify the trouble should it arise. During the initial settling-in a puppy may be fussy with its food or may not eat as much as the breeder predicted. This may be due to the fact that it is distracted by new things or because there is no longer the competitive presence of its brothers and sisters. Do not panic! With a little patience the appetite will soon be regained. Leave the puppy in a quiet place with its food for about ten minutes and then remove the dish until the next meal. Dishes of food left lying around soon sicken the puppy and destroy its appetite.

Impress very strongly on the buyer the virtues of having the puppy fully inoculated as soon as it is three months old. Fortunately these precautions seem, nowadays, to be generally accepted, though there are still a few people who are prepared to risk a puppy's life rather than go to any extra trouble or expense. Such people should not be allowed to own a puppy. Anyone who has ever seen the misery of a dog with hardpad or distemper would have to have a heart of stone to withhold the protection afforded these days by simple inoculation against these horrible diseases. The puppy should not come into contact with other dogs or be allowed in public places or streets until two weeks after the last inoculation.

Undoubtedly you will have interviewed the prospective owners and be satisfied that they are responsible people and the puppy will not be a surprise gift or a plaything for the children. As far as possible ensure that they have made adequate provisions for the puppy at home, fenced the garden securely and provided a warm dry place to sleep. Ideally the new owners should collect their puppy in the morning in order that they may spend the day together getting acquainted.

The car journey home will be the first major ordeal for the puppy, and hopefully a passenger will hold it securely and give it the necessary reassurance. A towel and some tissues are useful in case the puppy drools or is sick. The pedigree certificate, correctly made out and signed, should be ready for the purchase, though the registration and transfer documents (or the form to register the pup yourself) most probably will not be back from the Kennel Club and will be sent on at a later date. Many breeders operate an insurance scheme, which is well worth considering.

As the puppy gets older it often seems to get bored with various foods and will refuse the occasional meal. One has to think up ways of getting it to take a balanced diet. Plain cow's milk or diluted evaporated milk may be more acceptable, then being thickened with baby cereal, or try some brown bread soaked in egg and fried until crisp—these make a tasty change. Sometimes a little grated cheese, crumbled digestive biscuit or a minute amount of liver sprinkled on top of the meal will start the puppy eating. Generally this phase coincides with the teething period and although it is worth some trouble to offer tempting meals to the puppy, it should not be pampered or you may well end up with a finicky feeder on your hands.

At around four months the number of meals may be reduced, first by stopping the mid-afternoon milk feed. The two meat meals, however, should be increased in quantity weekly and by six months pups will consume 6–8 ozs (175–225 grams) of meat a day. They develop rapidly, and should be plump, with thick, rubbery skins and solid bone.

It is important that puppies have regular and frequent access to clean fresh drinking water, especially in hot weather; however if you have a youngster who paddles in the water or tips over the bowl and chases it around the floor, it is not feasible to leave a bowl constantly down.

At three months pups will enjoy a hard biscuit to chew, and a large non-splintering marrow bone to gnaw is beneficial in many respects. It will keep them occupied for hours, and even puppies will make a hole in a bone to get at the marrow which they adore and which is very good for them. When they get to about four months old and are about to start losing their baby teeth, the bone will play an important part in loosening the milk teeth and helping the adult ones through the gums. At this time the mouth should be examined every day to see that all is well. Sometimes the canines, which are the tusks at the side, prove rather stubborn, and some assistance may be required to get them out before the second set of canines is through. This is very important, otherwise the second teeth may be misplaced and a bad mouth result. Firmly pressing the thumb against each tooth several times a day will help loosen them without upsetting the puppy. Nothing can be more heartbreaking to a breeder of show dogs than to have a superb puppy with an imperfect mouth, i.e. one whose jaw is either undershot or overshot or with very tiny misplaced incisors. Almost every breeder has, in her time, had to make the decision to sell as a pet a puppy that, up to about four months, seemed to be all that could be desired, but whose teeth have developed wrongly. A kennel run for show purposes must be absolutely ruthless in parting with any animal whose mouth is not up to the required standard. Some minor faults may be forgiven but a dog with an imperfect jaw or poor teeth will never be passed by a good judge, and to be tempted to breed from it is to risk perpetuating the fault for generations to come.

Around twelve to fourteen weeks of age the puppies should be introduced to a collar and lead, and once again all the patience that can be mustered is required. It should be possible to train a puppy to the lead without any show of force whatever. Using a very soft narrow collar it is enough at first to let the puppy get used to the feel of it around its neck and then to trail the attached lead for five or ten minutes at a time, being careful to ensure it does not get caught up in anything and hurt the puppy. The handler should then pick up the lead and coax the puppy to follow a tit-bit or toy; cajole and build the pup's confidence and never force the issue. Once a youngster starts to struggle against the lead it is worse than useless to pull it about; the puppy only becomes frightened.

Some pups will go easily at once whilst others may take days or even longer before capitulating. These first training sessions should always be brief and the puppy must never be overtired. Ideally, a lawn is better than a hard surface at the introductory stage. Once the animal has learned its first lesson of going in the same direction as the handler, all that is required for several weeks more is a few minutes each day, making sure it walks just at your side; so many owners settle for being pulled along, which becomes a tiresome tug when the dog is older. It is still too young to be taken on the road for anything resembling a walk. In any event before the puppy makes its debut on the public highway it should have had its full inoculations. When these are completed it is time to introduce the puppy to the car, and the sooner the better. (His only rides so far will have been home from the breeder and to the vet for vaccinations.) A puppy that is accustomed to short rides from its early days is less likely to be a bad traveller. It is very tiresome when travelling long distances to shows to have to take a dog that is habitually sick.

Another little lesson the puppy should learn in the first few months is to rest quietly in a travelling box. For purposes of house training it is far easier if the puppy is shut in a travelling box at night. A pup will rarely soil its own bed if it has been taken outside last thing at night before the owner retires, and is carried outside immediately on rising in the morning. During the day there are three obvious times a puppy will want to relieve itself—directly it wakes from sleep, immediately after playing and just after it has eaten. These are 'musts' and, if you delay, the puppy's mistakes are your fault. By taking it outside at frequent intervals 'incidents' in the house will be avoided. Each time you see it preparing to squat in the house, pick it up and rush it outside before it has a chance to do anything. Always stay out with it until your object is achieved, then give plenty of praise and allow the puppy to return indoors. Do not scold for any accidents unless you catch it in the act. The transgression is your fault for not anticipating the trouble. Have patience, do not give up, and equally important—praise. As soon as the puppy has become habitually clean at night it is no longer necessary to close the door of the box.

If you have bought a puppy from a breeder, he or she will have shown you how to groom it. Grooming should commence the first week. Apart from keeping the coat healthy and free from tangle it cleans it of dead hair, scurf and dirt, stimulates circulation of the skin and blood, and helps prevent skin troubles. Grooming sessions should be endured with patience as they accustom the puppy to being handled, and regular examinations of ears and eyes can spot any trouble commencing. Nails also require attention: clip them back periodically and trim the excessive hair on the pads of the feet. Many puppies mature with faulty fronts and feet due solely to the neglect of this procedure.

Bad habits need to be firmly curbed early in life and the puppy depends on you for guidance, so start as you intend to go on and be firm. Plan to spend as much time as possible with the new puppy and it will quickly gain a sense of security; frequent rest periods are also essential. A well-trained puppy is a credit to its owner and ready to be accepted into society.

It is advisable to register the new puppy as a patient (and the owner as a client) with a veterinary surgeon and not wait for an emergency.

7

Growing Up

A West Highland puppy grows quite fast during the early months, and in this period it is judicious to ensure every opportunity of fulfilling his mental and physical potential. Good rearing is extremely important, and the feeding aspect of this is dealt with in the Puppy Rearing chapter.

It is important to realize that puppies do not all develop and grow alike, and some grow much faster than others and therefore need more food. As far as quantities are concerned you should remember that each puppy is an individual and will have its own requirements. These are best assessed by watching results. As a general rule it is a good idea to leave each meal down for about ten minutes only and then remove what is not eaten. The puppy menu need not be altered, except of course that all items are gradually increased, until you notice the occasional meal being refused. This varies with age and puppy but frequently coincides with teething. When this happens (at about four months of age) the mid-afternoon 'tea' can be dropped, but increase the other meals in proportion. As the period of rapid growth diminishes (usually from about six to seven months), a thriving puppy can go on to two meals a day. By the time your dog is a year old he will probably have stopped growing and the meals can eventually be combined.

However there are other factors to be considered in this development stage. An early assessment of the puppy's temperament will be valuable in determining how it will mature, and what course to follow in training and upbringing. The over-excitable puppy will test your patience, but perseverance on your part will pay off in the end. When he is pleased to see you it is very hard to calm him down, and he will need help to channel his energy in the right direction. Your reward will come when you finally succeed in teaching him to control himself. A bold puppy, frightened of nothing and who loves everyone, is a joy to own. However, he too requires to be trained in a firm, consistent manner, otherwise he will grow strong-willed and try to boss you. Taught from an early age what is expected of him, the puppy will grow into a nice, steady, predictable dog, showing a typical West Highland spirit. The reserved, quiet puppy has to be encouraged to accept his place in the world by a slow, gentle handling technique, using soft but firm voice commands, building his confidence and reassuring the puppy that all is well.

Puppies, like children, are naturally curious creatures and enjoy having playthings to keep them entertained and active, so you are permanently thinking of their safety. It is imperative that you keep them away from plants or lawns that may have been fertilized or sprayed with insecticides, lawn dressings and garden poisons; also that all household soaps, bleaches, detergents and other cleaning supplies are kept out of reach. Puppies tend to chew a lot especially during the teething process which encourages good strong dental development and jaw growth, so provide suitable items such as clean cardboard cartons (glued sections removed), an old sock knotted to make it firm, a hard rubber ball, ring or bone. Natural marrow bones should be carefully selected so that they do not splinter and create hazards to the mouth and stomach. If such items are not provided, the puppy will choose something for himself and tend to attack your slippers, or that electric cord, or your cushions or some valuable piece of furniture. To relieve the boredom a puppy can and will get into mischief if left on its own for long periods.

Puppies thrive best when they are given human attention—the more the better—and time spent with them is usually well repaid. This critical period of socialization will help the puppy to manage the various experiences that come its way. Subject the young fellow to a variety of everyday noises—a simple and effective method is to keep a radio switched on near him—and accustom him to the sound of the vacuum-cleaner and other general household clatter.

Car travel should continue at every opportunity, so that it becomes second nature to the dog, and many owners like to carry the puppy around in busy places at quite an early age, so that he may see and hear all the bustle of life, while feeling secure and unthreatened in the owner's arms.

Young children should be taught the rights and wrongs of bringing up a dog. They must be kind and gentle and particularly respect the puppy's rest periods when it should not be disturbed. Never allow children to carry the little animal about without supervision, for a wriggly puppy may so easily be dropped and injured. It is wiser for them to fondle or play with it at ground level. And remember particularly where there are children in your household, to worm the growing dog.

Although the initial worming regime has been completed, puppies require regular dosing. They should be treated for roundworms about every two months until perhaps eight months of age and thereafter biannually or as needed.

As your puppy grows older he may lose that attractive appearance that first endeared him to you. He will possibly become rather gawky, with big ears that may drop, and generally look all legs and arms. This means that he has become gangly, rather loose and un-coordinated, and often the body does not seem to fit the legs and head. Do not let this discourage you. As the weeks pass, and the 'teenage' period of uneven growth ceases, you will see the puppy tighten up and become an adult, and hopefully a creature of beauty. The stage of transition from puppyhood to adult is a natural process. As a young male reaches puberty, when the customary leg-raising posture is adopted to facilitate territory marking, he may experience an upsurge of hormones, making him indulge in excessive sexual behaviour. Amorous tendencies may be exhibited by constant sniffing and licking, or by mounting people and inanimate objects. These actions should be discouraged right from the start and the problem will often prove only transient.

The general purpose and plan in pedigree dog-breeding is to produce animals that conform to a standard set down by experts over many years. Only the best should be used to reproduce. They should be sound and healthy, of good type and conformation, and free from structural, organic or hereditary defects. In addition they should be of good sound temperament. It is unfair to keep a male dog which is *not* to be used at stud with bitches that are undergoing regular oestrus cycles, and it is very unwise to use a pet male for breeding even to satisfy someone who makes a casual request.

Anyone who is interested in improving the breed will only use a dog that has a record in the show ring or proven ability to sire quality puppies.

Pet Males

It is unkind and unrealistic to take a pet male who is happy and satisfied as he is and introduce him once or twice to breeding, and then expect him to go back to being the clean, stay-at-home pet he was originally. It is a mistake to assume that every dog should be mated in any case, and if a dog is used only once or twice during his life he tends to become awakened but not satisfied. Naturally once a dog has been stimulated in this direction he will be looking for bitches to breed all the time and will be a much less satisfactory companion. He may well become frustrated and not content to stay at home. An encounter with a bitch can be upsetting to the pet male and inevitably leads to escape plans and wanderlust. Even if he cannot reach his desires he may set up a passionate and annoying howling from the nearest vantage point. The worried owner of an over-sexed dog may feel that if only he were mated it would calm him, but it will not generally solve the problem; in fact the condition will probably be aggravated.

If these sexual tendencies become excessive and the dog becomes an embarrassment, the question of castration should be considered as a last resort. In extreme cases it may be the best solution. Although the operation is carried out under general anaesthesia, neutering in the male does not require abdominal surgery.

Pet Bitches

From the standpoint of health it is not necessary for you to breed from your pet bitch. There is no evidence of any benefits, and the single, so-called 'therapeutic' litter may well unsettle her, arousing maternal and breeding instincts which are then subsequently thwarted if she is not allowed further puppies. A West Highland brought up as a companion will cherish her role as a family member and suffer no ill-effects from not being bred at all. Certainly many maiden bitches have lived healthy lives into ripe old age.

Breeding from your bitch should not be looked upon as a fun, moneymaking or child-educating proposition, and unless there is a definite desire to breed, a certainty of placing the resulting puppies satisfactorily, and ability to provide necessary care and attention, it is not advisable to mate her. There is a good deal of expense involved in stud fees, veterinary fees (which can be substantial) and in providing proper care, food, and facilities for the puppies. Just feeding and keeping a growing litter clean and satisfied is a time-consuming job and not to be undertaken lightly. Remember each little puppy produces innumerable puddles and cleaning up is a messy and continuous business. Nevertheless, with the proper attitude, there is a great deal of experience and satisfaction to be derived from letting your bitch have a litter.

You definitely do not want to try to breed her, however, to a West Highland just because it lives down the road. Not only will you be in danger of producing poor-quality, unattractive puppies that no one wants, but you are likely to end up with a male and female that are frightened, frustrated and even injured. If you just turn two Westies loose together for mating, there is a real danger of one of them being bitten or hurt.

Bitches normally reach puberty and come into season for the first time at about seven or eight months of age. Thereafter they have an oestrus at six-monthly intervals. It is possible for some variation in these times, to as early as four months or as late as fifteen months, and this is not necessarily an indication of any abnormality. The cycle may vary too, and occasionally a bitch will go twelve months between seasons, while in another bitch it may occur again after only a four-month interval. However, if a bitch has three seasons in a year, one of these will not be fertile.

Dogs will often sniff around a bitch and show interest before the season actually starts, and this is frequently a sign that it is imminent. The first stage of the cycle, pre-oestrus, begins with the appearance of a bloody discharge and swollen vulva. Many bitches keep themselves very clean, and if yours is one of these, she should periodically be tested with a swab of cotton wool for the first sign of colour. This stage lasts an average of nine days, and during this time the bitch will attract males, but will not allow them to mate her.

The next stage, 'oestrus' itself, is said to begin on the first day that the bitch will stand for a dog. The vulva has usually reached maximum size and has begun to soften. The colour of the discharge generally fades and there is just a pinkish tinge or straw-colour in contrast to bright red. At this stage the bitch is anxious to escape to meet the male, and must be kept indoors until the end of this period whether mated or not. If she is to conceive, it is important that the bitch is mated at the right time and although many have laid down the maxim that the tenth to the twelfth day after showing colour is the right time, anywhere from the seventh to the twenty-third day is not exceptional. The bitch is receptive if she raises her tail and moves it to one side when she is stroked or scratched just above the base.

West Highlands are usually easily controlled when in season, but if your premises are not completely secure from invasion by trespassing dogs, some form of contraception is preferable to mis-mating and a subsequent unwanted litter. Sprays, lotions and chlorophyll tablets which claim to disguise the odour of a bitch in season are ineffective and a waste of money. For the non-breeding bitch, and where the owner cannot cope, the majority of veterinary surgeons advocate surgical neutering, although the bitch should not be subjected to major surgical interference solely for the convenience of the owner. The other methods of control are injectable or oral preparations to postpone the onset of season or to stop it soon after it has started. Each has advantages and disadvantages and the matter should be discussed with your veterinary surgeon.

A word of warning: if you intend to have your bitch spayed, wait until she has had a season first. If the bitch is operated on when still a puppy there are several major disadvantages due to the lack of maturity. Halfway between the first and second seasons is the best time as the bitch has reached the period when the sex organs and secondary sexual characteristics have fully developed.

The major reasons *not* to spay before the first season are:

1. Personality. She will be juvenile in outlook and will not understand the scents present on a walk. She may become dull and lazy.
2. A greater tendency to run to fat. Usually the immature spayed bitch gains weight very quickly within six months of the operation, and consolidates it in the next two to three years.
3. *Atrestia vulva.* A bitch tends to have a very small vulva before the first season, and if she then runs to fat a large roll develops round the vulva causing sweatiness followed by persistent eczema, which is extremely resistant to treatment. The external genitalia will remain immature, giving rise to urine scalding and dermatitis around the vulva. Also the short hair may grow into the vulva causing an unpleasant dark discharge.
4. West Highlands spayed too early never seem to grow a thick coat; it is always fine and thin in texture.

Mis-Mating

If you are unlucky and your bitch gets out and a mismating occurs, consult your veterinarian regarding the possibility of terminating the pregnancy immediately, as an injection to avert should be given within twenty-four hours of the mating. The drug most commonly used to correct misalliances is stilboestrol. The effect of this will be to reverse the dominant hormones of the bitch's oestrous cycle, so that she will begin her season all over again. Vigilant control will be needed, as the bitch may be even more willing to be mated on a second occasion. Quite frequently the whole cycle seems to be adversely affected and her following season may prove unproductive. Another side-effect may be a loss of coat, and in some cases all the furnishings on the head and legs are dropped and may take months to grow in fully again.

8

General Care

If you are thinking of adopting a dog as a member of the household you should, before embarking on the responsibility, first ask yourself if you are in a position to ensure sufficient attention to its general welfare, e.g. daily exercise and suitable feeding, and if you can withstand the financial burden of vaccinations, medical care, insurance premiums, grooming, boarding kennels, etc. throughout the dog's lifetime of a decade or more. Unless an affirmative answer can be given, you should refrain from becoming an owner. Furthermore, consideration must be given to your own lifestyle. A family with a busy social life or erratic routine is not the ideal household for a dog. The excessively house-proud will not appreciate the home being sullied, as even the most thoroughly groomed dog will shed the odd hair, not to mention dirty footprints from muddy feet and 'sniff marks' on the patio doors from an inquisitive nose. The garden, too, may never again be so immaculate or the lawn so green. Yet the companionship and unstinting devotion given by a faithful friend greatly compensates for what you may lose. Many an owner's health has benefited by the enforced ritual of a daily walk, while others consider a dog an investment as a guard and burglar alarm. Their sensitive prick ears pick up the slightest strange noise and let you know in no uncertain terms that something needs your attention. Whatever the case, ownership should be a total commitment—a pledge.

The decision to buy a puppy is an important one, and as they are not produced to order you must be prepared to wait for the right one and not buy on impulse. There are three sources you can contact so 'shop' with care.

Firstly there is the breeder—and technically anybody who owns a bitch at the time of the litter is the 'breeder', although generally the term is used to mean a specialist in the breed. Next, there is the private individual who has had a litter from a pet bitch (hopefully by a reputable stud dog) but who may not know much about rearing puppies. Finally there is the unorthodox pet shop or puppy farm where the dealer or middle man is without allegiance. He ignores the quality of the puppies in relation to breed standard and in all likelihood short cuts will have been taken regarding rearing the puppy and it will not be in good physical health. A puppy raised in a 'mass production' atmosphere, at a minimal expense, will of necessity have little, if any, human contact so will have got off to a bad start, as both hereditary and environmental factors influence temperament. Considering these points, together with infectious disease and stress-induced illnesses from long journeys, it is not surprising that so many puppies bought at pet shops or from puppy farms by unsuspecting purchasers turn out to be sickly, shy or vicious. The surprise is that *all* of them don't. Another trick employed is to advertise puppies as vaccinated, making it seem a better bargain. However, puppies already vaccinated by eight weeks of age have almost certainly only received serum which gives temporary protection for a few weeks. Then the full course will still be required.

Without hesitation the recognized breeding kennels are to be recommended whose ultimate aim is to produce sound healthy West Highlands and which spare no expense in trying to breed the best they can. Yet contacting one in your locality may be difficult. The Kennel Club will give details of clubs and societies listed with them, and in theory the secretaries should in turn furnish you with various names and addresses. Otherwise you might inquire at veterinary surgeries. Vets, although professional etiquette prevents actual recommendations, might give names of establishments of reliable breeders. Check the listings in the classified advertisements in the weekly dog magazines or attend a dog show. Even if you only want the puppy as a family pet, being familiar with what the better specimens look like is helpful and you learn a lot by observing the dogs in action in the showring where personalities come to the fore.

One you have located a breeder do contact him or her in advance to set up an appointment to view the puppies and don't arrive unexpectedly. The kennel premises should be clean, with no overpowering smell; the puppies healthy, alert and of sound temperament. If a puppy is to be reserved for you, expect to pay a deposit and do not be offended if the breeder questions you to ascertain your suitability as a dog owner.

Buying a puppy may be likened to preparing for the arrival of your first child, as there are a number of items required to coincide with the event—bed, blanket, brush, comb, dishes, collar, lead, and toys etc—which make it an expensive venture. It is best to be advised by the breeder on the correct equipment to obtain.

Unless you are sincerely interested in showing or in breeding there is no reason for you to purchase a 'show prospect.' Any purebred registered West Highland that does not have a disqualifying fault (*see* breed standard) may be shown. This does not make it a show dog. Litters, even well bred ones, contain few real show prospects and many litters contain none at all. A pick of the litter is not necessarily a show prospect because it may not be the best of litters! A 'show prospect' is a puppy that the experienced breeder feels will conform closely enough to the breed standard's ideal to (one day) acquire the coveted title of Champion. These puppies are selected on the basis of their head and body structure, size and coat texture and other subtle qualities obvious only to the trained eye. The puppy that may be most attractive to you may be the least promising show prospect! Some kennels do advertise show quality puppies for sale; however, extremely promising puppies of two or three months of age do not necessarily develop into real show dogs capable of winning in the ring. Conversely the 'ugly duckling' can turn into the 'beautiful swan', so that any so-called guarantee is meaningless.

The breeder from whom you purchase your puppy should provide you with a diet sheet, together with instructions on general care, and usually he or she operates an after-sales service to answer all your queries. It is advisable to obey the rules as to diet, as a sudden change in food can easily cause a digestive upset. The following suggestions will hopefully ease those anxious but happy days when the new puppy initially joins your household. In the beginning it is best to restrict the puppy to one room, and although not absolutely essential it is usually a good plan to devise a small, warm, draught-proof enclosure, a place the puppy regards as its own retreat when it needs to rest, and where it can be confident that it will not be disturbed. An old-fashioned playpen, or panels intended for enclosing compost heaps, make an ideal sanctuary, and are a boon to new puppy and owner alike, keeping the youngster out of mischief and preventing it from getting underfoot when you are busy. A cardboard box with a cut-out entrance makes an adequate bed to start with, as it is easily replaced when it gets chewed or soiled. You will also need some bedding—something warm and cosy such as 'Snugrug'.

When you first bring the puppy into your home he will be feeling lost and probably homesick, missing the familiar company of his littermates who have kept him warm and given vital comfort, so you may well expect an interrupted night. Once the puppy has eaten supper and had a playtime, you will want to settle him down for the night. He may whine, howl or cry as he calls for his mother to rescue him, but if you have done all you can to make him comfortable and there is no way in which he can harm himself, on no account go to him. If you go to give

Roseneath or White Scottish Terriers, 1899

Colonel Malcolm with his Poltalloch Terriers, *c.* 1905

Thomas Fall

Ch. Calluna Ruairidh, 1937

Thomas Fall

Mrs C. Pacey with Ch. Wolvey Pintail, Ch. Wolvey Wings,
Ch. Wolvey Prefect, Ch. Wolvey Poacher and
Ch. Wolvey Peacock, 1935

Thomas Fall

Ch. Freshney Fiametta in 1947, the first post-war breed champion

The Poltalloch Eleven

Ch. Banner of Branston, 1962

Ch. Bardel of Branston, 1965

him a cuddle you will create a problem for yourself and you can be sure he will expect the same treatment the next night. A hot-water bottle, securely and well wrapped to protect the pup and prevent the bottle from being chewed, or a stuffed toy with the eyes removed, may help to substitute for the rest of the litter. It is also advisable to darken the room as much as possible, otherwise the puppy may be awake at daybreak. Naturally there is a certain amount of excitement with a new 'baby' in the family and the puppy, although delighted to be the centre of attention, is bound to be undergoing stress at the complete upheaval and change of environment. For this reason, plus the risk of infection, visitors should be restricted to the minimum while the puppy adjusts to the immediate family.

Further hints on training the puppy to be clean and guidelines on lead training are covered in the Puppy Rearing chapter.

Basic Training

It is generally agreed that half the puppy's disposition is inborn while the characteristics of the owner, together with the environment in which the young dog lives, develop the other half. Puppies should be played with and handled from an early age, as attention in the early weeks prevents them from becoming shy. An intimate rapport is liable to mould the puppy into a well-mannered, manageable, and obedient dog and loveable pet. It is natural to love one's dog, but it is unnatural for it to be spoiled and there are certain things that the puppy must be trained to do and to permit. A small puppy is very trusting and teachable, as long as his confidence in you remains unshaken. So make a few simple rules and stick to them. Teach the puppy to play with its own toys and not to be destructive in the home. Accustom the puppy to being left alone in a room for short periods during the daytime without barking or howling. You should be able to take an object—a toy or food—away when necessary without any growling or snapping. This also instils a respect for your superiority! From puppyhood medication or first aid must be administered without resistance, and above all the young Westie should allow the veterinary surgeon to examine him without a battle. There are other annoying things to curb, like jumping up at people in welcome. This habit might be quite cute with a young and clean puppy but it is exasperating when its feet are muddy, and simply bad manners. Indiscriminate barking should be discouraged so that genuine warnings are recognizable. Incessant barking is infuriating to the neighbours, who are rarely tolerant and those subjected to it are entitled to complain! Growling and biting in the early days are often encouraged in a cheeky puppy, but as it grows big and strong and the teeth and jaws become powerful, the games of puppyhood are no longer funny, and may cause alarm and annoyance to strangers and trades-men. Take care to check any traits that are likely to cause trouble later, such as puppy temper, jealousy, or over-possessiveness. Biting of feet and nipping of fingers must be eradicated immediately, and any puppy making a nuisance of itself at the meal table certainly should not be rewarded with tit-bits. Screaming with rage when the door bell or telephone ring are also anti-social habits that need curbing quickly. Be sure from the start that your puppy amiably tolerates grooming and handling and, if possible, that he becomes acquainted with children if you have none about of your own. The puppy depends on you for guidance. It must be disciplined for its own happiness and safety, and it is up to you to see it has both of these, plus your love. With sensible and consistent handling it will soon become a well-behaved companion who will adjust to all situations and will be a pleasure to own.

Training should be fun at all times and the best instrument to help you is your voice, which should be used to praise and encourage your puppy at all times. The more you speak to it, the more responsive the puppy will become. Punishment by rebuke is usually adequate; physical violence will lose you the pup's respect, and disciplining with a rolled-up newspaper will only make the paperboy an enemy for life. When you are teaching your puppy anything, above all, be consistent. Always use the same words; tell him, don't *ask* him what you want him to do. Remember you are the boss; do not let him think he is. Teaching the puppy to come on command is vitally important since in the future it may prevent an accident. It is futile getting irritated and impatient if he does not co-operate on your first command, and never reward him with a telling-off when he eventually does come. If you do, 'coming' will be regarded as a crime and the punishment avoided. If he is running circles around you without coming within reach he may just be a naughty, mischievous puppy. In this case you will be excused for using tit-bits as bait, and eventually he will learn to come. Until the puppy shows he is reliable in the garden, keep him on the lead when out for a walk in the park (he should always be on the lead in the street). Just like a baby, in the early stages the puppy's routine consists of eating and sleeping with spells of activity in between, but exercise and play should never be overdone, and frequent rest periods are essential, as puppies have a lot of growing to do in a short time. Puppies that run around all day tend to develop long in back, while those that are allowed up and down steps are inclined to be out at the elbow, which naturally disfigures the shape of the adult dog.

Grooming

Puppies must be taught to accept any necessary attention, such as
trimming or grooming, from an early age. Practise standing the puppy
on a sturdy table and encourage him to lie on his side during the daily
grooming sessions. Stroke and praise him to build up his confidence. He
will then become accustomed to being handled in this manner. Later
when his first professional trim is due he will accept it quite readily. Be
careful when lifting the puppy that he does not wriggle out of your arms
on to the floor, and that once you have him on the table he does not
attempt to leap off. The puppy must be restrained all the time as he will
seem to have no sense of danger.

Regular grooming is essential (*see* the chapter on Trimming). In fact
attention to coat, ears, teeth and nails to ensure everything is in good
order is the duty of any responsible owner. A superficial top brushing
serves no practical purpose; indeed it often succeeds in making matters
worse. Allowing a dog to become matted and tangled is neglectful and
could be construed as cruel, resulting in long and painful disentangling
sessions.

Health and environment undoubtedly play a large part in the dog's
coat condition. A good balanced diet together with frequent brushing,
which helps to stimulate the secretion of natural oils, is advantageous.
This is particularly important in the winter when dogs spend more time
indoors, and the dry air of modern central heating systems affects the
skin and dulls the coat. Bitches quite often drop their undercoat after
whelping, and this was probably nature's way of making the nest warm.
Likewise they moult during a false pregnancy. An operation or
anaesthetic will also affect coat condition.

All dogs need some sort of maintenance to keep them in peak
condition and during the grooming process all parts of the anatomy
should be carefully examined. White dogs are prone to sensitive skins.
Pollen, fertilizers and insecticides are all irritants, as are self-inflicted
injuries caused by nibbling, licking and scratching. The dog may collect
chemical irritants on the bottoms of his paws while out walking, and
then only has to scratch his sides for red sore patches to form. Dogs with
skin trouble are rather like children – the spot itches so they scratch it,
not realizing this makes matters worse. With treatment at the onset, the
irritation can be relieved; the soreness will soon die down and new hair
will grow. A clean, well-kept skin is less susceptible to bacterial
infections and other skin disorders so it is imperative to keep it in good
condition.

Older dogs tend to accumulate tartar around the necks of their teeth,
which can turn them a dirty brown colour, causing bad breath.

Occasionally, foreign bodies such as twigs, particles of food, paper or bone get jammed in between the teeth and cause decay. Signs of pain in the mouth are—the dog rubbing its face along the ground, pawing the mouth, holding the head on one side or salivating. If the teeth are very bad or loose, or if the gums are inflamed, the dog should be treated by a veterinary surgeon. Large marrow bones or hard biscuits will help remove tartar.

Ears are a very sore subject in more ways than one and some dogs' ears are frequently inflamed. Each condition requires separate treatment, as the wrong one may do more harm than good by aggravating an already sensitive area. A slight, clear discharge from the eyes is not uncommon and should be carefully removed with damp cotton wool daily or as often as necessary. If left, unsightly brown marks will appear under the eyes. Persistent discharge may indicate conjunctivitis and requires prompt veterinary help. Eyes are too important to risk delay or incorrect treatment.

If the dog is found to be licking its paws, this is often a sign of inflammation caused by interdigital cysts or grass seeds caught between the toes, which can be very painful if not dealt with quickly. Having a clod of mud or matt of hair in the pad will cause the dog great discomfort and may be likened to a human walking with a stone in his shoe. Paw licking can be habit-forming and should be treated by the same method as human nail-biting—some nasty tasting substance, in this case applied to the feet. Constant licking will frequently turn the hair on a dog's feet brown, which is caused by acidity in the saliva. Many dogs have brown mouths from the same cause.

The care of toenails is often neglected and can spoil an otherwise well-kept dog. Long nails are solely the result of bad management and lack of exercise and require gradual and frequent trimming. Be extremely careful: the quick or vein reaches nearly to the end of the nail and it is easy to cut into it, causing the nail to bleed. This is very painful to the dog. If it does occur, a coagulant should be applied. Be guided by looking before you clip. Whereas on black nails the quick cannot be seen, it shows up pink on white nails. Cut the points off the nails, including the dew claws if they have not been removed, and then use a steel file to take off the rough edges. If the quicks should be cut, it will subsequently become a battle royal every time the dog's feet are touched. The frequency of cutting depends on the type of exercise the dog receives, whether on grass or concrete, as well as on the way in which the nails grow. Some dogs may need trimming weekly while others may need no clipping at all. If the nail grows straight out no amount of exercise will wear it down.

Always check through the coat for external parasites such as fleas, lice, ticks, and harvest mites etc. All these points can so easily be spotted during regular grooming sessions and can save the dog a lot of inconvenience and unnecessary suffering.

It must be remembered that dogs, like children, have temper tantrums and it is imperative that you are always in control of the dog and show him who is boss! If the puppy is excessively energetic and excitable a short sharp shake is more effective then any number of smacks. Always be gentle but firm and never hurt the puppy and he will really love the fuss and attention during his grooming sessions. Eventually when the time arrives for your dog to visit his canine beautician, fear of the unknown may cause him to tremble and shake, but providing he is groomed and trained and the coat is ready, the thought will be more painful than the deed.

Feeding the Adult Dog

It is impossible to stipulate the amount of food which should form the daily ration of a healthy adult dog (for puppies, see the Puppy Rearing chapter). Ideally it is just sufficient to maintain the dog in hard, muscular condition, showing neither signs of obesity nor emaciation. A balanced diet is built up by choosing foods which together cover all needs and provide all essential nutrients in the correct quantities. The sensible method of feeding the adult is to find a diet which is liked and on which it thrives.

Dogs are naturally carnivorous, but with domestication they have become adapted to a mixed diet and changes of food can be made from time to time to add interest and variety to the menu. Fresh meat may consist of beef, ox cheek, chicken, rabbit, lambs' tongues and tripe (paunch). Meat offals such as lights, melts, heart and kidney should be used sparingly but may be given as a change. Liver, although rich in vitamins, should be limited to very small quantities owing to its laxative properties. Although there are some foods which can be fed raw, cooking is advisable for the majority of meats as it kills most bacteria. Meat may be cooked with added vegetables such as carrot, onions, leeks, lettuce, spinach, celery, etc. or sometimes noodles, pearl barley or rice can be included to ring the changes. The flavour may be enhanced by adding a little Marmite. Stock cubes should not be used as they are too salty and may cause the dog to drink excessively. The home-made diet should include a good quality wholemeal puppy meal, which should be pre-soaked using the stock, and then the meat and vegetables added, making a wholesome and palatable meal. Both white fish and fatty fish like herrings, cooked and carefully boned, provide valuable protein, and are usually readily eaten by most dogs. Fish is particularly useful during convalescence. Dairy products, whole (cooked) eggs and cheese are highly nutritious and together with tit-bits such as bacon rinds, Yorkshire pudding or similar leftovers, may be included in the menu providing they are put in the bowl and not fed from the table. Amounts to serve are always difficult to assess. As an approximate guide, a Westie needs about six to eight ounces of meat a day, but this may vary with age, exercise and health.

To prepare this kind of diet is often a time-consuming business and the pet food industry have a bewildering choice of prepared foods on the market. The most modern form of feeding is the 'complete diet' which is becoming increasingly popular. Doubtless such meals have been accurately formulated and provide all the important aspects of a balanced diet. They have the advantage of being clean to handle and store, are convenient and time-saving to feed, but they do seem rather monotonous. A dry food diet will also create an excessive thirst. Please read the instructions carefully, whatever package you choose. Other dry products are intended as a 'mixer', to add to meat products and are not sufficient in themselves.

In addition to this type of food there are the semi-moist and deep-frozen products, plus the tinned varieties. Tinned food comes in two categories—those which consist of protein-rich ingredients canned in jelly and those in which the jelly is replaced by cooked cereal. Dogs fed on tinned food seldom appear satisfied for any length of time, and it seems to pass through the intestine rather quickly and so may cause a looseness of the bowels. Again, do read the labels carefully to ensure you are using canned products correctly.

Abrupt changes of diet inevitably cause problems, so any new regimen should be introduced gradually. The time of feeding is largely a matter of the owner's convenience, provided that it is not varied from day to day. As eating is a major event in the life of most pets, mealtimes should be adhered to as closely as possible for the sake of the dog's digestion and household peace. If the dog is well fed, numerous additional supplements should not be necessary—apart, perhaps, from one or two natural substances such as vegetable oil and seaweed powder which are beneficial to the dog's condition. A small amount of green vegetable and parsley, chopped finely and fed raw, can also be given as these contain important vitamins. Carrots given whole, for the dog to gnaw like a bone, are usually eaten with relish.

Grass-eating is common in dogs and unless excessive is quite harmless. It does not indicate a nutrient deficiency, and is far more likely to be a symptom of minor digestive disturbances. Clean, fresh drinking water should always be freely available. A shortage of water leads to illness because it is necessary for many different bodily functions.

Exercise

Oddly enough the only time in their lives that dogs do not *want* unlimited exercise is the time when most of them get it! Puppies are naturally active and generally exercise themselves by playing games and running about the garden. The usual pattern is that after sleep they wake up and play, run around, dig, burrow, jump, get into mischief then promptly fall asleep. At this stage it is most important not to overtire a puppy. Violent exercise can be harmful to his bone formation in that it imposes stresses and strains.

As young dogs mature, formal exercise may be gradually introduced and short walks daily on the lead should be carefully and properly taught. The West Highland adapts to most domestic situations, town or country, but because he belongs to the sporting group, he prefers the outdoor life. So when he is adult, suitable and regular exercise is essential. Ideally this should consist of a combination of lead walking and free galloping in field or parkland. Make the dog walk smartly and briskly to heel on the collar and lead, discouraging all stopping and sniffing until he can run free in open ground. A gallop at the midway point gives an objective to the dog's outing. Letting him have freedom in the local park, open countryside or farmland will see him in his element, running through the brambles looking for his prey, though this should only be allowed if he is sufficiently well-trained and under control not to get either of you into trouble. Most dogs will enthusiastically tackle a mile or two a day without tiring and still have energy left to play.

Even if your dog is well trained to walk to heel, always keep it on the lead in traffic. An unexpected noise which causes him to jump, or a sudden dash after a cat or another dog makes him a potential danger to drivers. Always walk your dog on the inside of the pavement on a short lead, just sufficient length for you to keep control at all times. Dogs have to perform their natural functions, and rather than antagonise the anti-dog lobby, a responsible owner will either kerb-train a dog or clean up after it. Carry a few plastic bags, large enough to accommodate the hand, then any mistakes in public places can soon be removed by placing the hand inside the bag, picking up the mistake and turning the bag over the faeces and knotting it. The bag can then be dropped into the nearest rubbish bin.

Dogs and the Law

Owning a dog not only entails a moral obligation but is also governed by manmade laws. These laws are designed to protect the dog itself from cruelty and misuse, safeguard livestock and wild animals from dogs, and protect people from the dog when it creates a nuisance by attacking or annoying animals or persons. The dog is required to wear a collar with details of the owner's address attached. This is a very sensible precaution as pets do on occasion get lost.

You can be held liable if your dog causes damage to others—for example by a traffic accident—or if it harasses livestock such as sheep or poultry. Therefore you must keep your dog under control at all times. The prudent owner will always keep his pet on a lead when near other animals. Certain public places, parks, playgrounds and buildings may be declared out of bounds to dogs, and in many places town ordinances prohibit dogs from beaches and public places. An offence is committed if your dog fouls the pavements or grass verges. Food shops and restaurants are encouraged by the Food Hygiene Regulation 1970 to ban dogs from their premises.

You may be held liable if your dog creates a nuisance by barking for prolonged periods and annoying your neighbours. It is also an offence for your dog to trespass on private property or to threaten or attack any person in a public place.

Your responsibility to your dog extends to providing it with proper care and attention. This includes food and water, and adequate shelter. You must provide proper veterinary care for its illnesses or injury. Failure to do any of these things is deemed 'causing unnecessary suffering' and is punishable in law by a fine and/or imprisonment.

It is possible to purchase insurance cover for your dog which will take care of the cost of any accidental damage it may cause to property or persons. However it goes without argument that a well-trained and cared-for animal will be unlikely to cause any problems for you or itself.

Summer Care

A sudden spell of warm weather, so welcome to most humans, can cause problems for dogs largely because their owners are unaware of their needs.

Some people believe that because they themselves enjoy stripping off in the sunshine, it is kind to clip their dog's coat right down to the skin, but this is really very cruel as it exposes the skin to the heat, causing considerable pain and possibly heat stroke. Unlike us, dogs do not perspire through the skin but through the tongue, which is why they pant when they get hot. The coat acts as an insulation and it is nature's way of protecting the dog from the elements. It's almost needless to add that a daily summer inspection is essential, and extra precautions should be taken to protect the skin from fleas, ticks and other insects, as hot weather brings these pests out into the open in large numbers. At this time of the year, dust pollen or grass seeds may cause eye and ear irritation, so remove any foreign matter at once.

During a hot spell dogs tend to eat more lightly so the diet may be adjusted. Foods containing carbohydrates should be limited or *completely eliminated* and extra vegetables substituted. White meat such as chicken, fish or tripe may be given in preference to red meat.

Exercise in modified form is still important; it should be in the morning when it is cool and again in the evening when the sun's heat has abated. In hot weather beware of soft asphalt, tar and oil and keep a wary eye open for summer litter when visiting rural areas.

Before taking your dog for a day's outing, make quite sure the trip won't be disastrous from his point of view. You may want to go sightseeing and leave him in the car, but even when parked in the shade with windows open, the inside can become stiflingly hot. Shade is not static and you may find on your return even after a short absence, the car in full sunshine and quite literally a death trap for any animal inside. Sadly one learns of tragedy striking some beloved pet this way every year—so the warning cannot be repeated too often. It is not advisable to let your dog participate in the family's sojourn at the seaside. Much bathing in the sea and rolling in the sand is apt to cause problems and it is well for this reason to supplement the salt bath with a rinsing of fresh water. Beaches afford little shade to lie in, and seaside towns (indeed all towns) are, to a dog, just places where you get trodden on, and where nose-level exhaust pipes squirt petrol fumes in your face. If you do take your dog with you, see that his part of the car is well ventilated, but never let him ride with his head peering out of the window as the wind or dust can cause a serious eye injury. Always take a bottle of fresh water and a drinking bowl, and stop at regular intervals to let him relieve himself.

The Perils of a Swimming Pool

The joys of owning a swimming pool can suddenly be dampened if the life of your beloved pet is lost in a drowning accident. There are commonsense rules that you should apply, to prevent such a disaster happening. The most sensible method is to stop your pet gaining access to the pool unless under strict supervision, by securely fencing off the area.

Although many dogs have the ability to swim, swimming in a chlorinated pool is not beneficial to their welfare, especially to their coats, and usually their introduction to the water is unintentional! Chasing a ball or a bird, seeing a reflection or merely just being inquisitive and—splash, they are in the water. As the sides of the pool are straight and most have a ladder rather than steps into the water, there is nowhere for the dog to gain a foot-hold, so it paddles around aimlessly looking for an exit. The big problem is getting the dog out before exhaustion takes over. Obviously, prevention is better than cure but should you find a dog drowning, rescue it, remove foreign matter from around the nose and mouth, and hold the animal up by the hindlegs for a few seconds to allow water to drain from the nostrils. Artificial respiration should be applied immediately until recommencement of normal breathing, when the body should be well dried.

Winter Care

The West Highland, as the name implies, was bred to be a hardy, outdoor dog, expected to withstand the rigours of a blustery, cold, and wet Highland winter. However, as with most pedigree dogs, the modern style of life has tended to soften the breed and as a result it is necessary to provide more care and attention to their welfare in the winter.

Proper feeding is of prime importance. Food should be provided that is nutritious and it is advisable to include a little cod liver oil or similar supplement to assist in maintaining body heat. It is a good policy to give a warm feed rather than cold, and perhaps also, in very severe conditions, offer a drink of warm milk.

Exercise is most important; short sharp walks and/or free runs if possible are usually enjoyed more than one long marathon-type walk. If you walk your dog on ice and snow make certain that its feet are washed and cleaned when you return home, because various chemicals used, for example by local authorities, to melt the ice may irritate and burn a dog's feet.

Rain does not seem to do any harm. There is a certain amount of oil in the hair which repels moisture and the undercoat is impervious to rain and snow. Of course the dog should be well rubbed down with a towel when he comes indoors. A combination of cold and wet, though, is a different matter, as it is miserable for the dog and could lead to chills or rheumatism if the animal is shut away in a damp condition. If a dog has to travel or sit around in a car during treacherous weather, a coat—the snugly-fitting jersey type—is recommended.

Boarding Kennels

Sometimes a temporary parting is necessary, whether due to your going on holiday abroad or to some personal incapacity. Do not get a guilt complex over this. It is better to make proper arrangements with a professional than to entrust your pet to the amateur 'good Samaritan'. A dog left with friends is a huge responsibility; the embarrassment and distress suffered by a guardian if the dog strays or becomes sick or injured while you are away could be enormous. The experiment may not be a happy one for the dog and it may lead to an estrangement between owner and temporary guardian. Should you decide on this method, however, remember to leave your veterinary surgeon's name and address, plus your authority to call them should a disaster happen. Kennel staff are trained to receive valuable and valued dogs for long or short periods as paying guests and appreciate that each one may be some owner's favourite pet. Under the Animal Establishment Boarding Act 1963, every boarding kennel is licensed by the local authority and is inspected by an Environmental Health Inspector.

Make certain the kennel you plan to use is safe and clean. Use eyes, ears and nose as well as commonsense when visiting the premises. No reputable kennel will object to your viewing the accommodation prior to booking. However, do not turn up out of the blue trying to catch them unprepared. The kennel staff are not about to spring clean just for your benefit. The tour of inspection should be made well in advance of your holiday, by appointment, and not at peak holiday times. I am sure, if your pet were one of the guests, you would rather its welfare took priority over showing prospective clients around. Many kennels restrict the number of people viewing to two, which is sensible as the visit should not be treated as a day out for the family.

Most kennels offer heated accommodation, operate an insurance scheme and cater for bitches in season. Generally staff are willing to administer medications such as eye ointment or pills, so long as the dog is not suffering from an infectious ailment.

Dogs obviously have their own way of communicating with each other, and because the Westie has a friendly nature they are generally happier paired together in kennels. Although most are delighted to welcome their owners when they return with great leaps of joy and wagging tails, there are some dogs who miss their canine companions when they go home, particularly if they are the only dog in the household.

9

Trimming

The art of trimming a West Highland White Terrier is not acquired easily. The tenacity of purpose of the owner decides whether the complete mastery of the job is achieved in one year or several. With some people it presents no problems, and with a little guidance from a few friendly experts some make a pretty good job of a show trim in a very short period. A few, however, lack the necessary patience or real interest and would rather leave the job to others.

To the real enthusiast, bringing a coat to perfection at the right time for a show (or shows) is one of the more fascinating aspects of preparing his dog. It is not a chore that is just endured but a task to which the owner or handler gives much time and thought before deciding to trim or even remove just a few hairs. Coats vary a good deal from dog to dog, and it is only by studying each individual coat and treating it accordingly that the best effect will finally be achieved at the desired time. It is not a thing anyone can just learn in a few lessons; real determination to compete with the best has to be there.

From the time the young puppy has its first tidy-up to the moment it is taken into the ring in all its glory at its first show, every art that the expert knows has been used to achieve near-perfect presentation. When a West Highland White Terrier is finally prepared for show it should look smart and neat but without any obvious signs of having been trimmed. It should have a certain ruggedness, and no attempt must be made to make it look like a Wire Fox Terrier. A few newcomers to the breed sometimes make the mistake of overtrimming, especially with clippers down the neck, which is quite the wrong approach.

Firstly, I would like to quote the breed standard on coat. 'Colour pure white, must be double coated. The outer coat consists of hard hair about two inches long, free from any curl. The undercoat, which resembles fur, is short and close. Open coats are objectionable.'

Those who truly appreciate good texture in coat would never resort to cutting it. If the hair is cut in any way the roots are left in the skin, thereby choking the growth of new hair and causing irritation. Consequently, the coat which comes through is fine, soft, has no texture and will also cause a skin irritation. If the stripping is done by pulling the hairs with the finger and thumb, you are getting it out by the roots. Where each root comes out, there is room for new hairs to grow through. This encourages a good, hard, thick coat to grow.

Today there is a tendency for necks to be overtrimmed, shoulders shaved down, furnishings cut straight, ears clipped and heads apparently barbered with a pudding basin as a pattern. Westies are not a carved out breed, so do not chop and hack at their coat. Scissors are useful tools but do not become addicted to them. Use them sparingly and never leave any scissored lines. Once you get used to *hand trimming* it will not take any longer. Try it and see! A properly trimmed Westie is a work of art and once this has been achieved, a great deal of personal satisfaction rewards the effort. A scissored and clipped Westie is really upsetting to the eyes of those who, over many years, have taken the trouble to trim and care for the coats correctly. Various assortments of tools can be bought and are useful but the best tools of all are the fingers and good strong fingernails. Though, of course, there must be a selection of necessary implements, such as:

Blunt stripping knife with coarse teeth
Fine toothed penknife
Hairdressing scissors—Ama 999 blue steel 7"
Serrated scissors—Ama blue steel 23 teeth
Rounded end and curved scissors
Steel combs—Hindes No 70 and No 71
Bent claw pin slicker brush
Terrier Palm Pad
Nail clippers
Nail file
Chalk or Bob Martin's Cleansfur
Rubber office finger or finger stalls to help grip the hair and also protect the blisters!
PATIENCE—the most important thing of all.

Trimming should preferably be done by daylight rather than artificial light and on a good solid table of suitable height, so that you can work on your dog easily and not strain your back. Have a piece of rubber matting attached to the table to keep the dog from slipping and sliding around while you work (a rubber car mat will do). Whether keeping a puppy for potential show purposes or as a pet, it is essential that it learns to be groomed regularly. Start grooming the puppy at six to eight weeks old. There is, of course, little coat to groom at this stage but it accustoms the puppy to being handled. If the coat is allowed to get tangled, combing will hurt the puppy, who naturally resents it. Particular attention should be paid to the hair under the armpits, thighs, down the legs and around the feet where matted clumps are liable to form. It is very unkind to let a dog's coat get matted and if groomed regularly, it takes barely five minutes to do it thoroughly. The comb must go right though the coat down to the skin and not just over the top of the hair. The head furnishings should be combed forward over the face and the leg hair combed down. A good grooming does a lot for the comfort of the puppy as it gets older, as it removes dead hair, scurf and dirt, stimulates the blood circulation and helps prevent skin trouble. As dogs are unable to tell you if they are in pain, your first warning of any skin problems will be during grooming sessions.

First Trim

At eight weeks the puppy is ready for its first trim. If you have bought the puppy from a breeder this will have been done when you collected him. If you have bred him yourself, then this is the time for you to start work. The long fluffy hair should be pulled off the top third of both the inside and outside of the ears, under the throat in the region of the Adam's apple, in a triangle down to the breast bone and around to the points of the shoulder (you will be able to feel these bones quite well). The easiest way to do this is to rub a little chalk into the hair, making it easier to grip, but being careful that none goes into the ears as this will cause irritation. Then with the index finger and thumb or fine-toothed penknife, pull out the long hairs, just a few at a time until it is nice and even. Next cut out the hair between the pads. Curved scissors are used so that if the puppy moves, the points will not dig into its foot. Comb the hair down around the feet and neaten the long hairs that extend beyond the pads on both front and back feet, being very careful not to cut too high and make an indentation between the legs and feet. Scissor around the anus, cutting the hair close to keep the puppy clean, and blend in the rest of the hair on the hindquarters with the side furnishings, using the stripping knife to give a nice flat bottom. Finally, neaten the tail, pulling the long hairs first and then finishing with straight scissors to point the end.

Great care must be taken at all times to avoid hurting or upsetting puppies when trimming; they have good memories, will remember for a long time if they have been hurt, and fear going on the trimming bench. Never let the puppy lose confidence in you. Hold it firmly, and never let it fall or jump off the table.

The first puppy fluff which begins to stand out and look untidy on the back should be removed when the puppy is around three-and-a-half to four months old. It is always easier to trim after rubbing a little chalk on the puppy's hair as you will get a better grip on the coat. Next, grip the skin of the puppy firmly with the left hand holding slightly above the area being stripped to keep the skin taut. With the right hand, thumb and index finger, pull out a few long hairs at a time with a quick plucking action. It will be found that underneath this first baby hair is a good new straight coat. This first trim makes a vast amount of difference to the puppy's appearance and it is easier to assess its good points when the fluff is removed. Start just behind the ears and back of the head and work along the back to the tail, from the top of the front leg above the elbow to the base of the tail, and under the throat down the chest. If the puppy objects at all it will be when the more tender parts are reached, such as the throat. Here it is permissible to use thinning scissors, but it should be stressed that ordinary scissors must not be used, otherwise the puppy will end up with steps and ridges in its coat. If there are lots of fluffy furnishings some of these may be pulled out as well, enabling the new coat to come through harder. Trim the tail, keeping it thick at the root and then tapering it to a point, which can be shaped with thinning scissors. The time taken for the coat to grow varies slightly from one dog to another but if the puppy fluff has been taken out at this stage a new hard coat should be through by the time the puppy is six months old. Once or twice a week go over the body coat and lightly thin it by pulling out the long ends. New hair is growing in all the time, keeping the dog in coat continually. If the hair is left too long without attention it will grow straggly and dead and look extremely shaggy. In this case a complete strip is the only answer. Wait for a new coat and then start again. Although this will spoil the appearance temporarily, it will be worth it in the long run. A very hard-coated puppy may lack furnishings at this age but they will come later.

Keeping the Coat in Shape

Always give the dog a thorough cleaning with Cleansfur or a good white chalk. Brush and rub it thoroughly into the coat, allow the dog to have a good shake, and then comb well all over to remove every last tangle. It is always easier to trim after the coat has been chalked.

Now the body coat is through and getting thick, the rest of the dog must be put into shape. The head resembles a chrysanthemum, being nice and round and having thick furnishings. Place the fingers behind the ears and the thumbs under the throat, making a circle. This gives you a guideline to shaping the head. Hair behind the fingers should be stripped out and those in front left to be shaped into the head. The ears show about half an inch above the head furnishings. Trim the hair at the top of the head first; this will give you a line to start the shaping. Very carefully, hair by hair, pull out the long ends all over the head until you have achieved a nice round shape. If the head hair is rather thin and straggly at six months or so it is well to shorten it fairly drastically. The benefit will show in a month or two when the hair will have grown close and thick. A well-furnished head greatly improves appearance. The hair on the ears should be short, smooth and velvety with no fringes, and the furnishings should be left on the lower parts to blend in with the head hair. To keep them tidy the ears require to be plucked approximately every week. The eyes should be just visible under heavy eyebrows.

The area from a point under the throat through the chest down to the breast bone, extending to the width of the shoulder, should be stripped fairly close, and be blended into the longer hair on the neck and over the shoulders without leaving any obvious lines or ridges in the different length of hair. This is often more difficult to achieve than it sounds, but persistent attention to the coat over many weeks gets the best results. The inexperienced owner will sometimes try to manage in a couple of days what a more expert groomer will take weeks to accomplish.

The trimming of the front legs and elbows needs to be tackled with some care. The aim is to produce a comparatively straight line from the point of the shoulder down to the toes. The tufty hair on the elbow is a tricky part to trim because if you remove too much hair it will hollow out the elbows, and if you leave too much it will make the dog look out of line at the elbow. Pull a few hairs, brush into place and then view; this way you will see when it is just right. When you are standing in front of the dog, its elbows should seem to lie snugly against the body. Hair on the back of the front legs is combed outwards from the leg and any straggling ends pulled out. This helps the furnishings to thicken and improves texture. If the dog is heavily boned the leg hair can be kept fairly short, but if he is lacking in bone leave the furnishings as thick as possible. Now the feet. Fore feet are larger than hind feet. Trim all the hair out from between the pads on the underfoot, being careful not to trim between the toes. The feet are supposed to be round, so trim them to accentuate their roundness, presenting a clean neat appearance. Shaping the feet should be done gradually. It is so easy to cut too high and emphasize the ankles; the feet are a continuation of the legs and should not look as if they have been put on afterwards.

The neatness of the foot is enhanced by well-kept nails. It is quite a fascinating job trying to trim a front to one's entire satisfaction; a few hairs off here and there. Examine your work from the front and side until the final result is correct from all angles. It is, however, very easy to remove too much hair and regret it later, for there is no going back, at least not for a good many weeks. Hair grows very slowly on the legs, so it behoves one to trim them with very great care.

The line of the neck must flow into the back and not be at right angles to it. A level top-line is desired and the coat should be kept at least two inches long on the back and sides of the body, blending into longer furnishings. Body furnishings can be too profuse, giving the illusion that the dog has barrel shaped ribs or is ultra-low to ground. To rectify these false impressions some of the fullness should be reduced. Selectively strip some of the excessive hair to create a pleasing and correct outline. Likewise, any wispy ends should be levelled as they detract from a smart appearance. Viewed from the rear the hindquarters are quite wide across the top; in fact it should be impossible to see past them. They should continue in a comparatively straight line down the sides of the quarters to the feet. Any ragged ends or bulges of hair should be carefully thinned, until the proper shape is achieved.

At the rear, however, the coat should be taken short. Trim directly under the tail and approximately three-quarters of an inch either side of the anus, cutting the hair short with curved scissors. This also makes for a cleaner, more hygienic dog. The rest of the hair is graduated towards the outer sides of the quarters until it is blended in with the longer hairs on the thighs. This is done using the stripping knife until the dog looks neat and tailored behind, visually shortening the length of the dog and generally improving the profile. A small proportion of furnishings is left on the lower part of the rear to blend with the hair on the inside of the back legs. Viewed from the side the stifles must be well bent. Shorten the hair by pulling out the long ends hanging down to the ground from the stifle and eliminate the thickness on the inside of the hocks until you have a good shape so the dog looks 'right on its toes'. The hind feet should be trimmed in a manner similar to the fore feet, cutting round them and removing the hair between the pads.

Last but by no means least in importance is the tail, as a badly trimmed tail makes a considerable difference to the dog's balance and overall appearance. It should be set well on top of the back and the ideal shape is that of an inverted carrot, being thick at the root and tapering to a point. Stripping the hair is the best policy as it helps the texture of coat but this must be done rather cautiously or holes may appear. It may be necessary to use serrated scissors on the underside of the tail and, for the tip itself, to use hairdressing scissors to form the point. Move the scissors around the tail so as to avoid giving the dog a flat tail. Be careful to let the hair from the body and quarters merge into the tail so that it does not look as if it was put on as an afterthought.

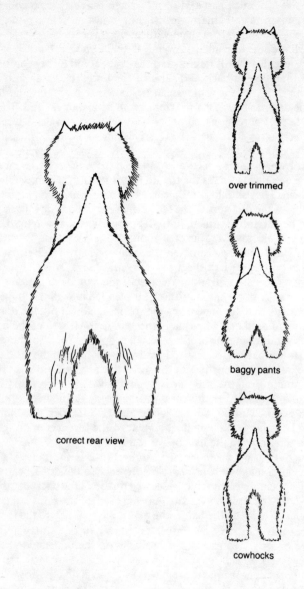

over trimmed

baggy pants

cowhocks

correct rear view

Figure 6 Trimming – hindquarters

Show Coat

Rome wasn't built in a day and nor is a show trimming done in a day!
Once the dog is in good, hard coat it is possible to keep it so indefinitely.
The technique of maintaining a coat in show condition is a simple
process which involves staggering the coat growth by plucking out

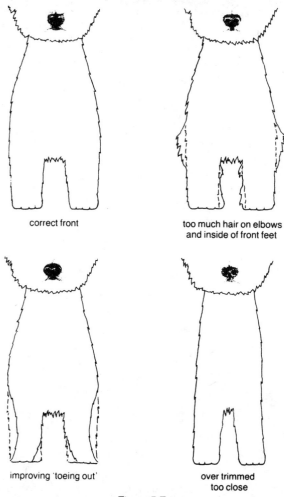

correct front

too much hair on elbows
and inside of front feet

improving 'toeing out'

over trimmed
too close

Figure 7 Front

85

limited amounts on a regular schedule. While the coat is still close-lying, thick and live, the body coat should be brushed back from tail to head, and the long hairs which project beyond the main growth pulled out. Do this several times until individual hairs no longer rise up conspicuously. This system will establish a pattern of continual growth, with new hair coming through replacing the old coat as it is removed. This process should be repeated two or three times a week for optimum results. Now that the dog is in a 'showable' coat you must observe it objectively. Stand the animal on the table and watch him playing and

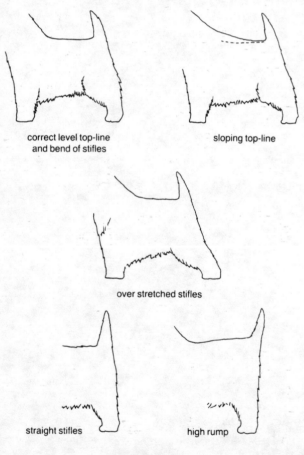

correct level top-line
and bend of stifles

sloping top-line

over stretched stifles

straight stifles

high rump

Figure 8 Body

moving—this way you will discover what minor alterations are required. Every dog is different, no dog is perfect, each one is a new challenge, and you must study the physical conformation and assess the dog honestly before you attend to the finer details. Remove hair where doing so improves appearance and leave hair where it will create the more perfect illusion. Enhance all the good features and minimise the faults. Naturally any alert judge will not be fooled by your artistic efforts but may give your dog the edge over a rival of comparable merit in the final placings.

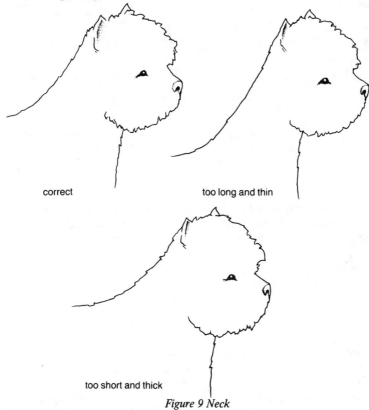

correct   too long and thin

too short and thick

Figure 9 Neck

Pet Trimming

It is unnecessary to study the faults and pay as much attention to detail as in show trimming, but the method employed is the same. However, if you would like to keep your dog smart and still a credit to the breed

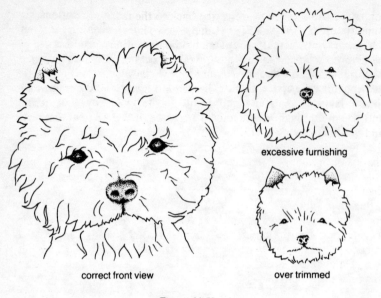

excessive furnishing

correct front view

over trimmed

Figure 10 Head

without so much work, you give it a complete strip when the coat has 'blown', thereby transforming a shapeless, shaggy bundle into a neat, trim and artistic package. Regular grooming will be even more important because, as the coat is longer, it is more likely to become tangled and food particles will clog the whiskers causing the dog to smell.

The time of the year when the dog is stripped is immaterial; do it when the coat is really dead. Some people believe that, in hot weather, dogs' coats should be clipped down to the skin to keep them cool, but the skin can easily get sunburnt, causing the dog considerable pain. 'Do not take the coat off or it will catch cold' is the common cry in the winter; this again is untrue as the protective undercoat that is left acts as insulation. A correctly coated Westie should withstand all kinds of weather, hot or cold, wet or dry. The top wiry harsh coat is not shed like that of smooth-haired breeds, so when the coat is 'blown', it must be pulled out by the roots. The puppy is usually about eight months when it is ready for its first complete strip. Commence by giving the dog a thorough grooming, brushing first to loosen any tangles, then comb through every inch. Finish by giving the dog a good chalking, rubbing it well into the coat. Now you are ready to start stripping. Make an imaginary line from behind the ears and back of the head down to the top of the shoulders, and down the back to the tail, and round to the other shoulder; all the hair between these two lines is stripped off. Grip the puppy firmly with the left hand, holding it slightly above the area to be stripped to keep the skin taut. If this is not done the skin is pulled with the hair and causes discomfort to the dog. With the right hand gather a tuft of hair 'topcoat' between the index finger and thumb, grasp firmly and give a sharp jerk. If the coat is ready it will come away freely and does not hurt the dog. Only a few hairs should be pulled at a time and the pull must always follow the growth of the hairs. This method is the most advantageous for the beginner, as it completely eliminates the chance of breaking or cutting the hairs instead of pulling them out. Alternatively a blunt stripping knife may be used, keeping the wrist firm. If you twist the wrist at all, this will definitely result in cutting rather than plucking the coat. At first, progress may seem slow but speed comes with practice and you will soon have a 'hole' in the coat leaving the soft furry undercoat. The coat is always tougher round the tail and on the back of the neck, so if you do not want to do the dog all in one day these are the places to leave for later. Draw another imaginary line from the base of the ears around the throat to where the lower jaw joins the neck; place your fingers behind the ears and the thumbs under the throat thereby making a circle—hair behind the fingers is stripped out and hair in front left to be shaped into the head. Strip down the chest to the points of the shoulders. The legs and head need to be shaped in the same way as a show dog. Strip the tail before the final shaping with the scissors. If the body furnishings are thick and hang down, pull out the long ones. Do not pull too far down the sides as the furnishings should start on the side of the rib cage, not underneath the body. In the fold on the side of each lower lip, there will usually be a tuft of discoloured hair. Cut this away with the curved ended scissors, taking care not to cut the lip or other face hair.

The dog may become very smelly if he is not kept clean underneath. There is a tuft of hair in front of the penis which gets wet with urine—keep this tuft trimmed but not too close or the dog will get sore. The bitch is apt to wet the long hairs as she 'squats'. This has the same result and can be the source of a strong 'doggy' odour, so it is as well to wash this area from time to time and, when dry, shake on a little talcum powder.

Bathing

The more the Westie is bathed, the dirtier it becomes as shampoos tend to soften the texture of the coat and remove the natural oils, thus making it more liable to pick up dirt and dust. However, there are occasions when baths are necessary—for example after the dog has had a complete strip or if it has external parasites (fleas, lice, ticks, harvest mites etc). A medicated bath may be needed if the dog has a skin irritation. Never give your Westie a bath without first combing him out to the skin on every part of his head and body. If you bath him in a matted condition it cannot be rinsed properly or dried thoroughly. As a result the clumps and snarls can become mildewed, with accompanying offensive odour, and the coat will be stained. So, groom first, then wet the dog with tepid water. Shampoo—you should use a dog shampoo as their skin is much more sensitive than our own—being careful it doesn't go in his ears and eyes. Rinse really well, squeeze out as much water as possible, rub well with warm towels, and then comb into place while the dog is drying. If a medicated bath has been given, generally the preparation used must be allowed to dry into the coat to be fully effective, therefore the dog should be kept in a warm atmosphere to dry, only the surplus moisture being wrung out and the towel used as little as possible.

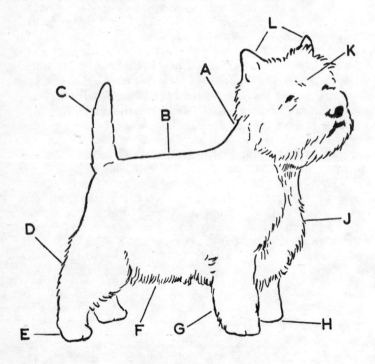

Figure 11 Trimming chart

A   Starting just behind the head, remove the untidy hair until there is a fairly tight top coat. Use the trimming knife or, if you are clever enough, the finger and thumb, a method that is less likely to damage the coat.

B   Continue this along the back and, to a lesser degree, down the sides. Taper the trimming of the neck and shoulders into the body coat.

C   Trim the tail so that it is thick at the base, tapering it to a point and leaving no feather hanging down the back of the tail.

D   Next, carefully tidy up the long hair over the back legs, being careful not to remove too much or, on the other hand, to leave big baggy pants. A Westie's legs should not have the same appearance as a Sealyham's back legs or a cowboy wearing chaps—this is seen too often.

E   Now get the feet in nice shape. The hair should be short and thick and well neatened all round.

F   Leave the skirt deep and full, only removing straggly hairs that may spoil the appearance.

G   Do not remove the feather on the back of the front legs but even up any untidy ends.

H   Tidy around the front feet and see that the nails are short, using nail clippers and a file if necessary.

J   Strip the hair below the throat and down the front fairly closely, carefully blending into the longer hair on the shoulders.

K   The head furnishings should be thick and full. Just even up the ruff to make a good frame for the face.

L   Remove the long hairs from the ears with finger and thumb, gently but firmly, with quick plucking movements until the top half of the ear is smooth and velvety. The hair on the lower half of the ear should *not* be removed but allowed to blend into the head furnishings.

A well-turned-out West Highland White Terrier should look smart without appearing to be trimmed, showing a good neck and shoulders and body shape, and not being shaved in some parts and ridiculously over-furnished in others.

It is essential at all times to keep in mind the points shown in the Standard of the Breed.

10

Preparation for Show

Whether you start showing activities with a puppy or a young dog it is necessary to allow plenty of time in which to prepare it in every way. The training or education may sometimes be completed in a few weeks but some dogs require months before they have gained the necessary confidence that will ensure their making the best of themselves when they appear for the first time in the ring.

So much depends on the amount of attention that has been given to the puppy from babyhood. If it has spent a lot of time with the family in the house and learned to meet strangers without any sign of nervousness or shyness then the task is much easier. A puppy that has had completely happy surroundings all its short life is hardly ever dismayed by unusual happenings and is likely to be a natural showman and need very little extra training for its first outing to a show. If a dog has been kept exclusively in a kennel, however, even with plenty of companions of its own kind, it will be a great ordeal the first time it has to meet strangers, and you may have to concentrate all your efforts and exercise a great deal of patience before it responds as well as you could wish.

If you are to have a six-months-old puppy ready to show by the time it is nine or ten months old there is no time to be lost in making preparations for the great day. Conditioning, grooming, and training, all should be a daily occurrence. Give the dog as much attention as possible so that it really feels important. Always be consistent in your training programme so that the puppy will quickly know what to expect. The whole time spent in training should be a pleasure to which both you and the puppy look forward each day. Keep the puppy happy and it will want to please you.

First is the daily grooming on the table, after which you will persuade it to stand quietly, posed in a correct but easy manner. After a few lessons an adaptable dog will soon learn that you wish it to remain in the same position for a while. While it is so posed go over the dog with your hands, as a judge will do, feeling its head, neck and shoulders, and particularly its feet as some dogs dislike their feet touched. Look at its teeth each day so that it becomes just routine and there will be no fuss or nonsense when the judge wishes to see its teeth. More than one dog has been known to throw away its chances of a prize by refusing to let the judge handle its mouth. Next comes a short daily lesson in walking and standing. Use the same sort of lead that you will use when showing the dog. With the lead in your left hand, walk the dog at a fairly smart but comfortable speed. Restrict the length of your walk before turning about twenty yards from your starting point, the average length of a show ring. Move the dog back and forth across the imagined ring several times. Then make a circular tour, still with the lead in your left hand. At frequent intervals stop and speak encouragingly and gain its attention so that it stands looking towards you in an expectant manner. This is the time to reward it with a piece of liver or some other tit-bit that you have concealed in your pocket. If the liver is kept in a piece of paper that rustles the dog will soon connect the sound with the liver it hopes to receive. Try to get the dog used to moving on a fairly loose lead and to walk close by your side. Stop before you feel that the dog is becoming bored. Always try to keep the dog interested and bright. The very tone of your voice can be important. If you are bored, the dog will be too. It is better to have short sessions twice a day than longer periods. Don't give up in despair if the dog seems to be responding more slowly than you had hoped. There are very few dogs that cannot be trained with patience and kindness. Always praise your dog when it has behaved well.

Once the dog is really responding to its training seek the co-operation of your family and a few friends. If you can muster half a dozen people, and their dogs, you can have the semblance of a private dog show. Someone can be asked to play the role of judge while others take all available dogs, mongrel or otherwise, round the ring. This introduces your dog to the niceties of good behaviour and will stop it from being anti-social when it gets to its first show. It is a good thing for the dog to show a lively interest in the other dogs without wanting to fight them. It gives a wrong image of West Highlands as a whole if some seem to be looking for a fight all the time. Unfortunately, it is thought by some that a terrier lacks spirit if it is not trying to get involved in fights but, of course, this is not so. West Highlands are friendly creatures and usually greet other dogs in an interested but amiable manner.

It is a good thing to accustom all dogs to a travelling box. Some may always be able to travel loose in a car to a show but there are many more that travel in boxes. If they are accustomed to a box they make no fuss and travel comfortably and happily. Start by shutting the dog in its travelling box at home for half an hour at a time. When it finds that it is to be let out again it soon loses all fear of being shut in for longer periods. Dogs should not be kept in cages or boxes for longer than is absolutely essential, but they should be trained to accept it for short periods so that if they must be boxed for any reason they do not become distressed. The box should be large enough for the dog to be able to turn round in it easily and high enough for it to be able to stand up. Ventilation is vitally important. There should be plenty of air holes that cannot in any circumstances get covered up to stop the air circulating freely.

While all this training is going on constant attention to the coat must be maintained, as explained in Chapter 7. At about six months, having kept the dog's coat reasonably tidy and well shaped, all that should be necessary is to give it daily grooming and some trimming, preferably by the finger and thumb method. It is better to keep at it every day since this does away with long hours of preparation on the last day or so before the show and it produces the desired result more easily and painlessly. Constantly plucking away hairs that are loose and spoil the outline will keep the coat tight for an almost indefinite length of time. Pluck any long hairs off the top half of the ears, which should be kept really smooth, and always pluck with the finger and thumb. The back and sides of the neck and the shoulders also need frequent attention. About once a week lightly use the thinning scissors under the throat to keep the hair short and tight. The top of the body and partially down the sides can be kept neat and tidy if a little is removed every day or so, as necessary. If this programme is maintained for three months prior to its first show, in the last two or three days only the final finishing off will be needed: the shaping of the tail, a little neatening round the feet, and the removal of any surplus hair.

See that the teeth are clean. Sticks for removing tartar can be obtained from most chemists and are quite simple to use. Examine the toe nails and, if necessary, cut and file them with a coarse file.

During all this period of training and grooming and trimming the dog must be kept in perfect health and condition. A dog that is not enjoying its food can go out of condition and loose body very quickly. The diet must be balanced, and the food fresh and of the best quality so that it is eaten with relish; for if the dog is not in top physical condition it will not make the most of itself. Good regular food is essential: plenty of meat twice a day and a small quantity of best biscuit. An egg beaten up in milk three or four times a week is appreciated by most dogs and seems to put that little extra zip into them. The meals should be well spaced out and all food dishes removed directly they are empty. Do not over-feed, otherwise the dog will sicken of food and have a stomach upset, the last thing that should be allowed to happen a few days before a show. If the dog becomes bored, keep it on a light diet for a day or two and, at the same time, give it a condition powder each day. This should bring it back into sparkling form quickly. Each dog needs to be treated as an individual, for what suits one does not always suit another. Some will thoroughly enjoy grated carrot and chopped greens mixed with their main meal, but others will sort out all vegetables, however carefully they are mixed in with the meat and biscuit.

Every dog should have at least one complete spell of freedom each day, weather permitting. A dog can cover a lot of ground in fifteen minutes, so whenever possible let the dog out for exercise directly the kennel doors are open. That quick scamper round the garden will liven up the circulation, induce the bowels to move, and give the dog an opportunity of visiting his favourite haunts to see if there is a rabbit waiting to be chased or a mole to be dug out. In bad weather, this very enjoyable exercise may naturally have to be restricted or curtailed altogether, especially just before the show.

Having brought the dog to the peak of condition all that is left is the final clean up. This must be very thorough. Start by washing the stomach, legs and feet and, lastly, the head. Do not wash the dog all over or the hair on the top of the back may become unmanageable. When the dog is dried, finish off by well rubbing all over with chalk; then use brush and comb. When the dog has had a shake and is combed down again you can see if there are any last bits of hair that need to be removed. Never think that you can get away with half cleaning a West Highland; it will stand out a mile if you have not done the job properly.

If the show is a long distance away it will probably be necessary to make an early start, so have everything packed overnight. A capacious holdall will be required to pack all the things that will be needed, which will not be just a brush and comb to tidy the exhibit at the last minute. Once you have seen exhibitors staggering into shows laden with bags, stools, folding table, and everything else that seems necessary for a stay of from six to eight hours, you will soon realise more will be required than those two indispensable items. It is safest to make a list of things that will be needed, and it will be a long one. Bench blankets, bench chains, a tin of cleaning powder, scissors, thinning scissors, trimming knife, all may be needed in case, even at this late hour, a little more trimming is found necessary. Besides these there should be a polythene bottle of water for the dog, and a substantial helping of meat, for it will be a long day, and the dog deserves sustenance as much as its owner. Having made sure that everything the dog needs has been packed, if there is a little room left take a big thermos flask of coffee and a packet of sandwiches for yourself. Beyond that there is no limit to the bits and pieces that you may decide to take along 'just in case': another pair of stockings to replace those you may spoil if you unfortunately fall over a tent-peg, perhaps another pair of comfortable shoes, and toilet requisites for freshening up at the end of the day. There is no end to the list, but it is all part of the fun of getting ready for another dog show.

11

Exhibiting

To have a good dog to show, one that has been bred and reared, trained and prepared by the owner, is one of the most satisfying experiences known to any breeder of dogs. Even if the dog is not destined to reach top honours, the thrill of matching it time and again against some of the top dogs, with varying degrees of success at successive shows, can be highly stimulating. Inevitably, every owner, in the security of his home surroundings, thinks that his own dog is a winner, but there is only one way to have that judgement confirmed, and that is to put it in open competition against others of its kind.

There are four grades or types of shows, which are:

(a) Sanction Shows, open only to members of the society promoting the show and restricted to twenty-five classes. It is unbenched.

(b) Limited Shows, also restricted to members, with a maximum of sixty-five classes and usually unbenched.

(c) Open Shows, in which there are no restrictions on the number of classes and which are open to all, whether members or not. These are invariably benched shows. A breed society is, however, permitted, to hold an unbenched Open Show restricted to twenty classes.

(d) Championship Shows. These are similar to Open Shows except that Kennel Club Challenge Certificates are offered. They are always benched and offer bigger prize money.

It is as well for any intending exhibitor to have visited at least one or more shows to gain some elementary knowledge of what will be expected of him when he makes his début with his dog in the ring. Even if attending the show only as a spectator it is best to arrive in good time to watch all the preparations that each person is making before taking the dogs into the ring, but at this stage it is unwise to pester the exhibitors with all the questions that are begging to be asked. Dog people are always glad to help a beginner by giving him information, but not when they are intent on preparing their own dog for the ring.

Save up all questions until judging is over, when they will get a much better reception, and the most helpful exhibitors may even be prepared to give a free demonstration in trimming and show preparation into the bargain. It is certainly time well spent to have visited one or two shows for the purpose of gaining an inkling of what is required, and show procedure, before venturing out to show a dog for the first time.

Before entering for a show the dog must be registered at the Kennel Club. All the current charges for registering, transfer fees, and so on are printed in Chapter 11.

Until becoming a fairly regular exhibitor at shows, it is necessary to write for schedules from the secretaries of the societies promoting shows that you feel would be a suitable one for starting a dog on its show career. When the schedule is received, read it thoroughly. Having made up your mind to enter the dog for a show it will be a bitter disappointment to find that the final date for entries closed a few days earlier. Secretaries are not permitted, by Kennel Club rules, to accept entries posted after the latest date stated in the schedule.

If you are showing a puppy for the first time it is best not to be too ambitious but to be content with an entry in a puppy class or if there is not a puppy class scheduled, then the next lower class.

Having made the entry, in due course, usually a few days before the show, a pass on which is the dog's number will be received from the secretary. It is essential to take this with you to the show, for without it your dog will not be admitted.

If the entry is for a championship show no effort will have been spared for weeks beforehand to have the dog trimmed to the last hair and in tip-top condition, but even so, the day before the show there is always that final overhaul to ensure that the dog is perfectly clean and looking as well turned out as possible. Even after attending shows for thirty years I still have that feeling of excitement and bustle on the last day as I pack all the necessary equipment to take to the show. Generally, it means an early night ready for setting out at the crack of dawn. Even dogs catch this undercurrent of excitement and are as eager to be up and off as their owners. Those that have been through all the ritual of preparation the day before give tongue directly they hear the first stirrings of the household. The final question before you are driving off is, 'Have we got the tickets?'

Arriving early at the show gives many advantages. One is finding a handy parking site; another, getting inside the show before the vast throng of other exhibitors and their dogs arrive. (Veterinary inspection is no longer required.) Coping single-handed with a couple of dogs and a heavy bag containing all the paraphernalia that always seems so necessary makes early arrival at a show vitally important. Having found

B. Thurse

Ch. Barrister of Branston, 1950

C. M. Cooke

Ch. Bandsman of Branston, 1960

Thomas Fall

Ch. Calluna the Poacher, aged 10½ years

Capt Bower judges Ch. Wolvey Play Girl, shown by Mrs Pacey,
and Ch. Bandsman of Branston, shown by the author.
Bath Canine Society, 1960

American Ch. Rachelwood Raven, 1964

English and Australian Ch. Busybody of Branston, 1963

Anne Cumbers

Ch. Rhianfa's Take Notice and his six week old grandson who became
Australian Ch. Gaywyn Mr Music Man

the bench allotted to your dog, and comfortably settled him, not forgetting to see that he is really securely chained on a chain that prevents him from getting too near the front of the bench, where he might fall off and hang himself, then it is time to relax a little. A bowl of cold water for the dog, and a hot cup of tea or coffee from the thermos flask for yourself, and you will feel like a giant refreshed. Before starting to groom the dog it is advisable to buy a catalogue and find out the number of the ring in which West Highlands are to be judged. If it is a very large show, do some reconnoitring so that you will know in advance how far you have to go from your bench to the ring. It is now time to get to work to remove any travel stains from the dog and to return him to the pristine freshness he had when he left home hours earlier. If he was thoroughly cleaned the previous day, probably only his legs and feet will be soiled, and a rub all over with a little chalk will bring back the shining whiteness. Because he has a white coat it is more than ever necessary that he should be absolutely clean. A half-clean Westie looks dreadful. Once he has been cleaned and well combed out return him to his bench and, settling him comfortably, leave him to rest without further interference until he is required to be taken to the ring. Until judging is over it is unwise ever to be far away. The order of judging may, for some reason or other, occasionally have to be changed. It is your responsibility to be ready and waiting so that when the call 'West Highlands in the ring' comes, you can at least appear to be cool, calm and collected even if your knees are knocking.

It is useful to have in the dress, smock or pants, or whatever is being worn at the time, a large pocket for a piece of liver or some other tempting tit-bit that the dog has been trained at home to expect as a reward for good behaviour. This can be surreptitiously offered to him as and when the need arises, to encourage him to show himself off. A small steel comb or brush carried in the pocket may also come in useful for smoothing down his coat. Sometimes the coat is disarranged by the time the judge has finished his examination, and to do justice to the dog any stray hairs should be slicked down with one or two strokes of the brush or comb.

Directly the stewards call for the first class, if your dog is entered in that class take him into the ring, where the steward will hand you your ring card, which should immediately be attached to some part of your clothing where it can be easily seen by everyone. Club members usually have club badges which are designed to hold the ring card, but failing this a small brooch or pin will suffice to hold the card in place. Once all the exhibits for that class are assembled in the ring the steward will direct the exhibitors to stand in an orderly fashion at one side of the ring and, when he is satisfied that everything is in order, he will tell the judge that all is ready for him. Do not wander about; stay where you have been placed until you are told to move either alone or collectively with the others.

If your dog is not entered in the first class, watch from the ringside to see how quickly judging is proceeding so that when the time comes for your class you will be ready to enter the ring without delay.

From the time you enter the ring concentrate all your attention on your dog. Be calm and self-assured, with confidence in your dog. A West Highland is by nature an assertive dog, ready to greet his nearest rival in an inquisitive manner. It is permissible to allow him to make friendly overtures to other exhibits but he should be restrained from becoming too boisterous or interfering with any dog that does not welcome his attentions. It is considered bad sportsmanship ever to allow one dog to upset another exhibitor's dog. Good manners in the show ring are as essential as in any other walk of life. If showing for the first time, try to place yourself well along the line so that the more experienced exhibitors come before the judge first. This will give you time to adapt yourself to what is going on and then, when your turn comes, you can follow their lead with confidence.

It is usual for the judge to request the exhibitors to go round the ring first. This gives the dogs a chance to settle down and, at the same time, the judge an opportunity for an overall survey of the dogs he is about to judge. Every judge has his own idiosyncrasies about how he likes dogs paraded and brought to him. Some prefer to see each dog move before handling; others want the dog on the table first, and then see its movements. Whatever method is adopted it is up to exhibitors to conform to the judge's directions to the best of their ability.

It is most usual in our breed for the judge to examine each dog on the table, therefore, as soon as the exhibitor preceding you lifts her dog off the table lift yours on to the table, and deftly pose it to the best advantage so that as the judge turns, having by now finished with the previous exhibit, his first impression of your dog is as favourable as you could wish. As the judge starts to examine the dog he will almost certainly ask you its age. Answer clearly and without elaborating in any way. The judge is not interested to know that this is your first show or that someone told you he ought easily to become a champion. Just stand quietly by, keeping your hands out of his way and not touching the dog more than is absolutely necessary.

When the judge is finished he will ask you to move the dog across the ring in a straight line away from him, and then to bring him back again. If he is not satisfied with his movement the first time, he may say 'take him again'. As good movement is so important in a terrier the judge will probably want to see a side view of his action. Never allow yourself to get between the judge and the dog, for however stylish a mover you may be, at that particular moment it is your dog's and not your movement he is concerned with. Always be aware of where the judge has placed himself so that if necessary you can quickly change the lead from the left to the right hand. When moving the dog let him go at the pace that suits him best and to which he has been accustomed when training at home, unless the judge asks you to move either more quickly or slowly. Most Westies like to move at a fairly brisk pace, and a good showman will go gaily and willingly without coaxing. It is best to show them on a fairly loose lead. To string them up on a tight lead is discouraged now far more than it was years back. The dog will move better and much more freely if the lead is loose. The lead should be held so that if any check is necessary the dog will respond immediately to the slightest tightening of the lead. When the judge is finished with you take your place next to the exhibitor that preceded you.

While the rest of the dogs are being seen let your dog relax a little but still remain aware of what the judge is doing, so that when he again turns to the dogs, by now lined up for his final appraisal, your dog is once more on his toes and showing himself to the best advantage to catch the judge's eye. So often, when a lot of good dogs are gathered together and there seems to be little between them, it is the last bit of showmanship that tells. If your dog recognises that tone of encouragement in your voice or hears the faint rustle of paper in your pocket, which indicates a piece of liver or some other tasty morsel coming his way, he may exert that last little extra effort that will make all the difference. If you are one of the few picked out for an award, move at once to the position indicated. Never relax for an instant until the judge has actually marked his book. Many a judge about to mark his book, has taken one last look and found an exhibitor allowing her dog to stand badly in an unguarded moment, thinking that it was all over, and then rearranged his placings.

If you are not among the first three and 'in the money', as the old hands call it, then accept the judge's decision gracefully and find a smile and a cheerful word of congratulation for the winners. Scowling at the judge will do no good to anyone, least of all yourself, and although you are convinced yours was the better dog the judge was probably less biased and saw faults that you were not even aware your dog possessed.

If you are in only one or two classes, return your dog to his bench directly he is finished with and then go back to the ringside to watch the rest of the judging. Watching the more experienced perform is one of the best ways of learning the art of handling. You will see the effortless ease with which they take their dogs through their paces, the dogs seeming to know just what is required of them.

Listening to a group of knowledgeable people discussing the merits or failings of each dog in the ring can also be most revealing. There is so much to see and so much more to learn than the beginner can ever have imagined. There can be a lifetime of the keenest pleasure in showing dogs if the right attitude to it is adopted at all times. Never let disappointments sour you, or success go to your head. It is invariably the lot of the most successful to have their share of reversals, but if you care more for the good of the breed than anything else you will take it all in your stride. Besides all else you will meet the nicest people from all walks of life, all brought together by their love of a good West Highland.

There are more professional handlers than ever before in the Westie rings, and many owners feel at a disadvantage when showing their own against these experts. This is wrong; it should be looked on as a challenge to prepare, and get as much out of, your exhibit as any handler. They know their job but it can be learnt by all. With attention to detail in preparation and an understanding of your dog's temperament nothing is impossible. Time and patience can achieve anything if you have a quality dog to work on. And what a sense of achievement proudly to take your own dog to the top despite the stiffest opposition.

12

Judging

To be invited to judge is a very great compliment and it is not a task to be lightly undertaken. A good judge must have enough confidence to make decisions that may not be too popular but which, on the day, seem right.

An apprenticeship of several years judging at Open Shows used, until recently, to be required by the Kennel Club before anyone could undertake to judge at a Championship Show, but this rule has now been partially relaxed in favour of proof of a breeder's or exhibitor's ability to breed champions and recognise good stock. Before judging a Championship Show the Kennel Club requires the would-be judge to complete a form stating the names and numbers of Champions bred or owned and a detailed summary of judging experience.

To the average person the first engagement to judge at a Championship Show is something of an ordeal. However, it is such an absorbing task that ringside spectators and their comments are soon forgotten.

Naturally, it is expected that the judge should be fully conversant with the standard of the breed, but as no two judges ever quite agree on what is perfection each show brings a fresh thrill or disappointment to some exhibitor.

The approach to judging should be serious, with a full realisation of the responsibility that is to be borne for that particular day. There should be no place for petty-mindedness, and personalities should have no influence on decisions made.

Always arrive in good time. It is not good manners to keep exhibitors waiting; they will have put in a lot of hard work, and travelled long distances, and they will be anxious to get on with the job. In the ring have a few words with your steward, who is a most important person. A good steward will keep everything moving smoothly so that the judge can concentrate solely on the job in hand. The steward will marshal the dogs in the ring, see that none are missing, and that they stand in an orderly manner as required.

Have a method and stick to it for every class so that everyone can be prepared when their turn arrives to be scrutinised.

Terriers always look at their best when moving, and it is as well, if the ring provided is large enough, to begin by having all the dogs move round the ring at a brisk pace. This gives an opportunity for a preliminary sizing up of the dogs and, at the same time, settles them down. Twice round the ring is sufficient; there is no need to keep it up until everyone is giddy.

Set to in a workmanlike manner with a clear mental picture of what you require. Systematically go over each dog in turn. It is the custom in the United Kingdom for a good firm table to be provided so that the dogs may be placed on it. It certainly looks more becoming for a judge to examine a dog while standing erect than almost on his or her knees. At the same time it gives a better view to the ringsiders for whom it can be most instructive in seeing the way each judge goes about his task.

The method by which a judge uses his hands in going over a dog often speaks louder than words. It is almost possible to see into a judge's mind and to know what he is searching for as his hands pass from one salient point to another: the beautiful layback of good shoulders, the quality of bone in the legs and the feet; weighing up a slightly doubtful mouth against the virtue of a good dark eye. Automatically the judge's mind takes it all in. Everything must be considered but at the same time, his mind is searching for the type and quality he hopes to find. Sometimes it seems if one judged each dog solely on the allotted points, they *could* all be equal, but they never are. There is some indefinable quality in the best that makes one dog seem to stand out from all the rest. To award a Challenge Certificate and Best of Breed to a dog that completely satisfies you is something to remember. All judges must surely remember for ever the occasion when an outstanding dog came before them, and what a joy it was to handle that dog. Judging is not quite always so satisfying. There may be times when every dog in a class seems mediocre. It is far more difficult to sort out one poor class than several good ones.

If a judge is faced with a very large class it is better, after each dog has been thoroughly examined and the chances of the best dozen dogs estimated, to allow the remainder to leave the ring. It is less confusing than keeping all of them standing in uncertainty until the final awards are made. Try, if possible, to stick to type and size. If a judge knows his own mind he is not likely to select one that is very heavy bodied and low to ground and the next one high on the leg and quite the opposite in every way from the first. A judge must always be quite firm and definite in making decisions and not be in the least concerned about what the spectators are thinking. It is impossible to please everyone. Because a well known dog comes before you it is not enough to rely on its reputation as a big winner. Have a completely open mind, and if it does not come up to the high standard you expect and you can fault it, do not be influenced by what you know other judges have done. Neither should you seek sensationalism by putting down a good dog just to show that you can be different from everyone else.

Should a dog make a display of temper and refuse to have its mouth examined, a judge is quite justified in placing it in a very low position even though in every other respect it may be a very handsome creature. The same applies if the exhibit refuses to move freely. No matter how perfect it may look when posed by the handler, if it literally has to be dragged across the ring with its tail down it is not showing the characteristic temperament of the breed. The judge may be fully aware that that particular dog is as good a showman as any, on some occasions, but the dog must be judged on its performance on the day.

If one or two dogs take a dislike to each other and persist in trying to fight, the judge should insist that they are firmly controlled and not allowed to upset the rest of the class. The breed has a wonderful reputation for possessing good-tempered dogs, and none should be allowed to destroy it.

Soundness of action is of very great importance. Without it no dog will ever move properly and a judge must therefore pay a good deal of attention to its action both going and coming. Movement, indeed, is often the deciding factor between dogs of almost equal merit in other respects. A really stylish one will take the eye of the judge at once.

Always be most conscientious about giving the same amount of consideration to each dog; on no account give any exhibitor cause for feeling that his dog has been neglected or overlooked. A judge should make clear-cut decisions without hesitation. Just as many, if not more, mistakes are made after weighty consideration than by the swift instinctive decision. When it is all over and you have done your best, never feel that you need apologise to anyone for having placed a dog in a more lowly position than was expected. If judging has been done as conscientiously as one knows how, there should be no reason to make excuses or justify one's placings. Any feeling of disappointment an exhibitor may momentarily feel is usually quickly dissipated as his natural good sportsmanship reasserts itself.

As in most things, judging has its lighter side, as I discovered a few years ago when judging a huge puppy class at Crufts. Deep in thought, and madly concentrating, I slowly became aware that the spectators round the ring seemed to be enjoying a great joke. Hardly daring to move I took a cautious look round. To my great relief I found that a group of pigeons had alighted close behind me and were taking a great interest in the proceedings, and the puppies were showing much animation as they strained at the ends of their leads in the hope of catching a tasty meal.

A judge should try to go about his task as efficiently as possible, remaining unflustered and quite calm at all times, and women judges in particular should be attired in something that allows them to move about in comfort and yet looks neat and tidy after much bending and stooping. Comments overheard from the ringside can be shattering as well as flattering. Skirts that are too tight or too short have been known to cause some amusement, and jangling beads and bracelets can be disturbing to the dogs. It is said that one smart female judge nearly lost her finger when a dog mistook her blood-red nails for a piece of steak.

Never fear criticism; be honest and conscientious, and all will respect you as a judge.

13

The Kennel Club

All shows, except Exemption, are held under Kennel Club Rules and Regulations, copies of which may be obtained from the Secretary of the Kennel Club.

Every dog entered for any show (except Exemption) must be registered, or if already registered when purchased must be transferred to the new owner at the Kennel Club. It is, however, permissible to enter a dog for a show if the Registration or Transfer Cards have not been received back from the Kennel Club by the time entries close, provided that application has been made before that item. In these cases the letters N.A.F. (name applied for) or T.A.F. (transfer applied for), as the case may be, are added after the selected name or registered name.

Registration and transfer forms, and all information may be obtained from the Secretary, The Kennel Club, 1–5 Clarges Street, Piccadilly, W1Y 8AB.

Registration Fees
as from 1 April 1989

	Fees (inclusive of VAT)
REGISTRATION AND DOG NAMING BY BREEDER	**£**
(All the puppies in the litter must be registered)	
Fee (payable in every case)	6.00 per puppy
TRANSFERS:	
Transfer by new owner	6.00
OTHER:	
Re-registration	6.00
Endorsement—Name Unchangeable	6.00
Loan or Use of Bitch	6.00

PEDIGREES:

Export Pedigrees	20.00
Three Generation Pedigree	3.00

AFFIXES:

Registration of an affix by qualification only, see regulations	35.00
Affix Maintenance Fee (Annual)	10.00

The following Regulation was approved by the Kennel Club Show Regulations Committee in January 1961 and appeared in the *Kennel Gazette* in February 1961. It was subsequently incorporated in the Kennel Club Championship Show Regulations pamphlet B(1) as regulation 9(i):

'If an exhibitor reports before the judging of a class or classes that he has entered a dog which is ineligible—
   (1) as regards its breed, colour, sex, weight or height the Show Secretary shall transfer it to the equivalent class or classes for the correct breed, colour, sex, weight or height and, in the event of there being no equivalent class, to the Open Class for the correct breed, colour, sex, weight or height.
   (2) for any other reason other than above the Show Secretary shall transfer it to the Open Class.'

The Committee of the Kennel Club has agreed to endorse registration certificates on request by the owner, i.e. the person who makes the original registration, as follows:

Not Eligible for Export Pedigree

The endorsement can only be removed by the person who made the endorsement or requested it.

14

The Breed Overseas

Each year the number of countries taking up the West Highland White Terrier increases. Distance presents no problem now that transport of livestock has become routine, and in most cases every consideration is given to the dogs' comfort. Now that the virtues of the breed are more fully recognised there seems to be no limit to the number of people determined to possess a West Highland. From far-flung corners of the world enquiries come for, sometimes, just a good companion, but in most instances for a really first-rate dog or bitch to improve present stock or as a foundation for a new kennel.

United States of America

America has long made heavy demands on the breed in the British Isles and many of the best bred in the U.K. cross the water to continue their distinguished careers in other hands.

In so vast a country as the U.S.A., although incredible distances are travelled to the major shows, it is quite possible that some of the best may never meet in competition.

The West Highland White Terrier, when it was still known in America as the Roseneath terrier, was first scheduled at the Westminster Show in 1907, and two years later, in 1909, The West Highland White Terrier Club of America was formed.

The first one of the breed to become an American champion was the English-bred Clonmel Cream of the Skies, bred by the famous Holland Buckley, one of the greatest authorities on the breed in the very early days.

The enthusiasm that is typical of our American friends is very infectious and they spare no effort, time or expense to breed and own the best possible. Many of the imports from Britain have gained the highest honours.

One of the earliest 'greats' to make history was surely the English-bred Ch. Ray of Rushmoor, bred by Miss Smith-Wood in June 1927 and later exported to Mrs John G. Winant, in whose famous Edgerstoune kennel he sired ten champions, all but one bearing the Edgerstoune prefix. Later, many of the best Wolvey champions bred by Mrs Pacey joined the Edgerstounes. Ch. Wolvey Pattern was the first West Highland to go Best in Show at Westminster, a great achievement of which his English breeder was justly proud.

Mrs R. K. Mellon, whose prefix 'Rachelwood' is attached to so many good home-bred Westies, has bred many champions and imported several others, first from the Wolvey kennels and, later, from the 'Hookwoods' owned by the then Miss Ella Wade, who supplied Ch. Hookwood Banneret and Ch. Hookwood Marquis. Still more recently my own kennel has sent out Ch. Bannock of Branston, Ch. Bavina of Branston and, the latest to go to the 'Rachelwoods', Ch. Bardel of Branston and Ch. Briar Rose of Branston.

Other stalwarts of the breed, Mrs Wm Worcester and her daughter Barbara, now Mrs Ed Keenan, have imported several English champions, the most famous and successful undoubtedly being Ch. Cruben Dextor. Dextor, in addition to being a spectacular showman, was also a great stud force, having sired a large number of champions. Barbara also imported the English-bred dog Elfinbrook Simon, who quickly qualified for his title, success culminating in his becoming the second West Highland to go Best in Show at Westminster, America's premier show.

It would be impossible to list all the names famous for breeding good West Highlands in that great country but a few that come readily to mind are Mr and Mrs John T. Marvin's 'Cranbournes', Mrs Brumby's 'Rannockdunes', Mrs Frame's 'Wigtowns', Mr and Mrs Edward Danks's 'Battisons', Mrs C. Fawcett's 'Forest Glen', and Mr and Mrs A. Walters's 'Tyndrum'. There are many, many others all playing their part in keeping the breed to the forefront of dogdom.

The export regulations for sending a dog to the United States of America are quite simple. All that is required is the export pedigree and a certificate of health from the local veterinary surgeon.

Canada

The beginning of the West Highland White Terrier in Canada is very obscure but one of the first breeders must without doubt have been Mr Victor Blochin of the Bencruachan Kennels, Ontario. His introduction to the breed was during the First World War when, as a young Russian officer, he was taken prisoner. Among his fellow prisoners was Angus

Campbell of Dunstaffnage Castle, Scotland, who promised him one of his Westies when it was all over.

In 1922, after the Russian revolution, Mr Blochin came to Scotland and received from Angus Campbell a bitch, which he called Snejka, meaning Little White Snow Flake. When Mr Blochin went to Canada in 1927 he took with him a son of Snejka's, who sired many Bencruachans.

Mr Blochin imported from Miss I. R. Maclean Cowie Rowmore Ardifuir who, in addition to soon becoming a Canadian Champion, was the only West Highland White Terrier to become a Grand Champion, a Canadian award no longer given. It was obtained by winning, in addition to the ten points required for the title of Champion, a further ten points with only champions competing for it.

Mr Blochin had a cemetery for dogs where all their dogs were laid to rest, and for several years it has been open to all Canadian pets. Many well-known names may be seen on the stones.

The Bencruachan Kennels no longer do any exhibiting but they still breed a few litters and carry on the cemetery and boarding business.

Another old kennel is that of Miss Edith Humby and the late Miss Rosamond Billet whose Highland Kennel won their first Best in Show with Edgerstoune Stardust. In 1939 they imported a dog and bitch from the Avonia Kennel in Bristol. Since Miss Billet's death Miss Humby has carried on dog breeding and showing but uses the kennel name 'Humby's' and is strong in Avonia and Shiningcliff lines.

Among the current breeders and exhibitors who have been in the business for many years are:

Mr Fred Fraser of Ottawa, with his Ben Braggie Kennel. He has a long family association with the breed, for his grandfather, Daniel Fraser, bred them in Scotland before going to Canada, and his father Harry Fraser showed and bred them for 50 years. Mr Fraser imported Ch. Stoneygap Sugar Candy of Manraff and Ch. Stoneygap Bobbin of Gillobar, both from Mrs Barr.

Mrs J. H. Daniel-Jenkins (of the Rouge, 1947) imported Ch. Shinning – cliff Sprig from Mrs Finch, winner of Best in Show and Groups. She has bred and made several U.S. and Canadian champions.

Mr and Mrs J. Neill Malcolm (Malcolms, 1948) are not very active in showing at present but they are still breeding. Mr Malcolm is a grandson of Colonel Malcolm of Poltalloch.

Mr and Mrs Albert A. Kaye (Dreamland, 1948) imported a number of young dogs from England, mostly puppies.

Mr and Mrs T. S. Adams (Roseneath, 1949), bred Amer. and Canad. Ch. Roseneath White Knight, winner of several Best in Shows and Groups. They imported Canad. Ch. Cruben Rhoda and Canad. Ch.

Shiningcliff Sunflower. They are breeders of numerous U.S. Champions.

Mrs Sally Hudson of Vancouver imported from Mrs Beer Amer. and Canad. Ch. Whitebriar Journeyman, who was winner of four Best in Show All Breeds, and three Best in Show All Terriers. He was the top winning West Highland in U.S. in 1963, being shown 26 times there and never defeated in the breed. During his U.S. show career Journeyman was in the temporary ownership of Mrs Barbara Sayers.

Amer. and Canad. Ch. Highland Ursa Major, bred by Miss Rosamond Billet and now owned by Mr Perry Chadwick, U.S., became the first West Highland to win the West Highland White Terrier Club of America Speciality Show and, as a stud dog, has made a very great contribution to the breed on the North American continent.

The West Highland White Terrier Club of Canada was formed in 1951 and has held a Speciality Show every year since. There are, currently, between 50 and 60 members. Some of the most active breeders and exhibitors are:

Mr and Mrs T. S. Adams, Roseneath Kennels, Ontario.
Mr and Mrs Victor Blochin, Bencruachan Kennels, Ontario.
Mrs J. A. Bradley, Westlea Kennels, Alberta.
Mr and Mrs Eric Cox, Ervi Kennels, British Columbia.
Mrs J. H. Daniel-Jenkins, Kennels of the Rouge, Ontario.
Mr and Mrs H. N. Flannagan, Manderley Kennels, Ontario.
Mr and Mrs Albert A. Kaye, Dreamland Kennels, Ontario.
Mrs J. Neil Malcolm, Malcolms Kennels, Ontario.
Mr and Mrs R. S. McNicoll, Lochanside Kennels, Quebec.
Mr Fred Fraser, Ben Braggie Kennels, Ontario.
Mrs N. Freemantle, Remasaia Kennels, British Colombia.
Mrs S. J. Navin, Shipmates Kennels, British Columbia.
Mr and Mrs Ed. Payne, Dina-Ken Kennels, Nova Scotia.
Mr and Mrs Walter Stewart, Whinbrae Kennels, British Columbia.
Miss Edith Humby, Humby's Kennels, British Columbia.
Mr and Mrs James Scott, Macmoor Kennels, Ontario.
Col. D. and Miss Helen Seabrook, Stowe Kennels, Ontario.
Mrs Sally Hudson, Sallydean Kennels, British Columbia.

Such is the progress in the breed here that I am informed by Mrs Daniel-Jenkins that there are now over 400 Championship Shows where Westies are usually shown. Great pride is taken in the achievement of Sally and John Bremner's Am. Can. and Bda Ch. Whitebriar Juryman as the top terrier in the 'showcase' of dogs in Canada for 1976.

A great interest is shown in training Westies for obedience. They are, as we all know, a very adaptable and intelligent breed and they are having a lot of success in open competition with other breeds.

The death of Victor Blochin of Bencruachin fame will have been deeply felt. He had been a devoted admirer and breeder of Westies since 1922. He served on the committee of the W.H.W.T. Club of Canada until 1977.

The import regulations are very similar to those of the United States of America.

Australia

On 22nd September 1963 the first West Highland White Terrier Club in Australia was formed, with headquarters in Sydney. After nearly three years of existence, it boasts a membership extending from New South Wales to Queensland, Victoria, South Australia and to New Zealand. The first show was held on 15th November 1964, and for this occasion a beautiful trophy was donated by the West Highland White Terrier Club of Illinois, U.S.A., for Best in Show. The judge was Mr R. Burnell of Sydney, who awarded the top honour to English Ch. Busybody of Branston, with another importation, Wolvey Puritan, the C.C. winning dog.

Mr F. Luland of Sydney judged the second show in April 1965, and a perpetual trophy was donated by the Club President, Mrs E. Kohen. Best in Show again went to Busybody, the C.C. winning dog being her son Langsyne Philibeg by Baxter of Branston. At this show badges given by the 'of England' Club were awarded to class winners, proof indeed that the older clubs in England and America were extending a welcoming hand to the junior member of the clan.

The breed has been known in Australia for many years, even as far back as the beginning of the century, and has enjoyed considerable popularity before the Second World War and during the 1940s, but little was done to improve the breed for many years. There was some interchange of stock with New Zealand, but it was not until about 1960 that the breed began to be noticed at the shows. An analysis of entries for the Sydney Royal Easter Show gives an indication of the increasing popularity of Westies in recent years: 1961 (4), 1962 (3), 1963 (7), 1964 (15), 1965 (21).

Other statistics of interest are that in New South Wales in 1964, 15 litters were registered, 12 champions were made, and there were 5 exports, all to New Zealand.

It is reasonable to predict that the entries will increase for several years to come, gaining impetus through the medium of a very progressive specialist club, and by the undisputed fact that more effort has been spent on this breed than on any other in the terrier group in New South Wales for some time.

In recent years some quality stock has been imported from England to New South Wales. Mr Peter Brown of Goulburn chose Pollyann of Patterscourt, Wolvey Provest, and two Famecheck bitches, Nimble and Delibes, to augment his 'Peteraffles' kennel. Mrs McEachern of Wagga, owning the 'Hielan' dogs, imported Wolvey Puritan. Then, in quick succession, Famecheck Serenade, Baxter of Branston and the English Ch. Busybody of Branston joined Miss B. Faulk's 'Langsyne' kennel.

Mr Phil Cunningham, in South Australia, has founded his strain of 'Pilelo' Westies on a strong team of English dogs and bitches, which include English Ch. Buttons of Helmsley, Famecheck Lucrative and Stonygap Freddie, all well known at English shows.

The impact of this imported blood is beginning to be felt, resulting in increased success at the shows, and a demand by show people for quality stock. The majority of breeders are anxious to maintain quality, which policy, it is hoped, will eventually give Australian West Highland White Terriers world recognition.

Now that air travel is so commonplace in this vast country the prospect of sending a bitch by air anything between one and three thousand miles will not deter them from choosing and using the most desirable stud dog.

In Australia although they are very thankful for their glorious sunshine, they admit that it is a handicap to those who have to cope with white dogs. Importations from England are never again quite as white as when they arrived in that sundrenched land. This is applicable to any white or white-marked dog and the creamy colour that soon appears need not necessarily be a breed fault. This is perhaps a point that overseas judges, and particularly those from England, should bear in mind.

The Regulations for the Importation of Dogs into Australia are very strict but quite simple.

Since the early 1970s dogs can be flown into Australia. The times vary considerably depending on destination. Perth, Western Australia, on a direct non-stop flight takes nineteen hours while to Sydney, on the East Coast, twenty-four to twenty-eight hours is normal. Although this seems an awful long time for dogs to be crated, it is not nearly such a traumatic experience as shipping them, and they appear to arrive in good form.

Summary of regulations controlling the importation of dogs from Great Britain:

1. Permit
   No dog may be imported into Australia, except in accordance
   with the terms of an import permit issued by the Chief Medical
   Officer, Canberra House, London.

   The import permit will state the place of departure from Great
   Britain and the place of entry into Australia dependent upon
   whether the animal is travelling by ship or by aircraft.

2. Documentation
   (i) A declaration by the owner:
       stating that for twelve months preceding the date of export
       or since date of birth, if less than twelve months of age, the
       animal was kept in the country of export, and that during
       this period it had been free from disease and had not been in
       contact with any animal suffering from disease; and that for
       six months preceding export it had not been in official
       quarantine kennels. This must be sworn before a magistrate
       or Commissioner for Oaths.

   (ii) A certificate from a local veterinary inspector of the
        Ministry of Agriculture, Fisheries and Food stating that
        within the period of fourteen days prior to shipment, the
        dog has been subjected to a blood test for leptospirosis and
        a negative result obtained. Agglutination (50%) at titre of
        1:100 is considered to be a positive result. However, a dog
        which has been vaccinated against leptospirosis and which
        shows agglutination at 1:100 but not at greater dilutions
        may be certified as giving a negative result if a second blood
        test twenty-eight days later (the second test being within
        fourteen days of shipment) shows no increase in titre.

        Copies of laboratory reports should be attached to the
        certificates from the local veterinary inspector of the
        Ministry of Agriculture, Fisheries and Food.

   (iii) A certificate from a local veterinary inspector who has been
         approved for examination at the port or air terminal of
         departure, certifying that the animal is free from disease and
         fit to travel.

   The certificate mentioned in 2 (ii) must be signed by a local
   veterinary inspector of the Ministry of Agriculture, Fisheries and
   Food.

   It is the responsibility of the exporter or his agent, if the animal
   is being trans-shipped through London (Heathrow) Airport, to
   ensure that the airline arranges for the animal to be inspected,
   crated and sealed immediately prior to shipment by the

      approved local veterinary inspectors who will be responsible for the completion of part III of the form ED.1.

3.   Quarantine

    Dogs are subject to quarantine in Australia as follows:

    (i) Sixty days quarantine for animals travelling by approved container ships not calling at intermediate ports.

    (ii) Ninety days quarantine for animals travelling by air which have not been unloaded from the aircraft en route.

    (iii) Nine months quarantine for animals travelling on a ship calling at intermediate ports, or by aircraft when their kennel or container has been removed from the aircraft en route. Where crate seals have been broken in transit, the animal will be refused entry into Australia.

4.   Failure to obtain an import permit or to comply with its requirements will result in the dog being refused entry into Australia.

New Zealand

We are indebted to Mrs Harr, the secretary of the New Zealand Kennel Club, for the following information.

The history of dog showing in New Zealand goes back to my knowledge to around about 1886, and no doubt there were earlier Shows than this. In 1886 dog showing was conducted on an inter-provincial basis, and about this time the now New Zealand Kennel Club was first formed in Christchurch and in the early 1900s was transferred to Wellington.

One of the oldest present-day clubs is the Canterbury Kennel Club, formerly known as the Christchurch Dog Club, the Canterbury Club being formed in 1905 in Christchurch and holding its first Show in Hagley Park during the 1906 Exhibition year. This Club has now been operating for 82 years.

Until some years ago dog showing was operated on a four-group basis but some shows now operate on a six-group basis, as is done in Australia.

Today there are approximately 38 dog clubs throughout New Zealand, and once every year every club is invited to send delegates to the New Zealand Kennel Club Conference, and from these delegates the nucleus of the New Zealand Kennel Club Executive is elected as the governing body for the dog fanciers of New Zealand. The rules and regulations for the registration of pure-bred dogs and for the conduct of shows are decided here, and permission obtained for the selection of judges to adjudicate at shows applied for by all dog clubs throughout New Zealand. This organisation has the distinction of being one of the few clubs affiliated to the Kennel Club of England.

Like every other country New Zealand has its problems for the dog fancier who wishes to import stock from overseas to improve his or her particular breed. Dogs imported from any other country except Australia must undergo a quarantine period of six months in Great Britain and a further six months' residency from time of quarantine release.

Facilities for despatch by sea are seldom available, and now it is possible to make shipment direct by air on certain specified flights. The shorter the journey the easier it will be on your dog. In order for space to be booked the airline needs dimensions and combined weight of dog and box.

Prior permission for importation must be obtained from the Animal Health Division, Ministry of Agriculture, New Zealand.

The following is a summary of the various documents necessary to accompany the dog (full details may be acquired from the Ministry of Agriculture, Tolworth, Surrey, England):

Statutory Declaration—dog has been domiciled in Great Britain for one year, or since birth. This is required to be sworn before a Commissioner of Oaths.

Rabies Certificate—vaccinated 30–180 days prior to departure.

Tapeworm Certificate—wormed within 21 days of shipment and no evidence of tapeworm.

Leptospirosis Certificate—blood test within 21 days of shipment to requirements of New Zealand Dept of Agriculture.

Health Certificate—examined within 96 hours prior to leaving.

All the above documents must be delivered at the point of embarkation to an appointed Veterinary Officer, who will check the dog is fit to travel before fastening the special box with an official seal.

Once in New Zealand the dog will be transferred to an approved kennel and there detained in isolation for 30 days.

Hydatids (a type of tape worm peculiar to New Zealand) are the greatest worry of the dog fancier at present. Though not prevalent in show dogs, the fact that dogs have, in some areas, to be dosed three or four times a year causes a lot of worry. In the main cities dosing is once a year and is done on a house-to-house basis; other areas use a dosing strip!

According to Peggy Skey, of New Zealand, the first West Highland White Terriers imported into that country appear to have been by a Mr Hewitt, a chemist of Christchurch, in 1925–30. Later he sold some stock to Mr G. McKay of Somerfield, Christchurch. In 1931 Mr and Mrs Voice purchased a dog puppy from Mr McKay and in 1932 a bitch puppy from Mr Baylis of Auckland. In 1934 they also imported a dog and bitch from Mrs McCracken of Sydney, Australia.

Among other early breeders were Mr John Macdonald of Timaru, Mr Williams of Hawks Bay, Mr T. O'Connor of Dunedin, and in 1935 Mr A. B. Cook of Christchurch started his well-known Avalon Kennels.

Sweden

In 1912 the first West Highland White Terrier was imported from Scotland—a bitch called Bubbles—and was quickly followed by a dog and another bitch, Bubbly under the Steeple, but it appears that no breeding was done.

In 1930 breeding was started by Mrs Marna Boothy-Philip who imported the bitch Clint Chieftainess and, a year later, made the first homebred champions with Dinomin Drabant and Dinomin Surprise.

This started interest in the breed, and the next breeder was Miss Marta Olsson, quickly followed by Mrs Lalla Hoglund and Mrs Elin Svensson, the latter with the prefix 'av Mariedal'. Both founded their kennels on the Dinomin blood lines and each imported stud dogs: Mrs Hoglund, Brean Kivvan, and Mrs Svensson, Wolvey Planter. It was the blood lines from these dogs, and Mrs Boothy-Philip's earlier import, Fearless Favourite, that were the stud force during the time of the Second World War. In about 1943 the breed appears to have slumped and Mrs Svensson was virtually alone.

In about 1950, West Highland White Terriers started to pick up when Mr Eric Werner imported several dogs, including Tachrian Petrarch and the bitch Thimble of Deanscourt, and both soon became champions. Also, Mrs Svensson imported Wolvey Pharoah, and Miss Olsson purchased Craig of Kendrum which became an international champion, and sired several champions, including the bitch Ch. Dox Fia, which became the foundation of Mrs Barbro Eklund's MacMahon Kennels. Mated to Wolvey Pharoah's son, Ch. Macky av Mariedal produced International Ch. MacMahon's Vicke Vire, who has sired thirteen champions.

At about this same time, Mrs Hervor Hornfelt started her 'Coras' Kennel and imported Wolvey Pipe, who produced Ch. Coras Pamela. Other imports include Wolvey Party Suit and Wolvey Pierina.

During the past few years Mrs Barbro Eklund has imported many dogs among whom have been Lasara Lennie and Lasara Lutine, both becoming champions, Sollershott Stepson and Joy of Wynsolot.

Among present day well known breeders are Mrs Birgitta Reyman-Hasselgren. Tweed Tartan Maid is probably the best known of her many champions. The Countess Hamilton imported Swedish cham-

pions Benefactor of Branston and Sollershott Sparkle. In the Gothen-
burg area Mrs Britta Roos-Borjeson bred a great many winners from
Swedish champions Bushey of Branston and Blue Pippin of Branston.
In the capable hands of Mrs Inger Benjamin-Marius, Ch. Bradbury of
Branston quickly gained his Swedish title. I am proud to be the breeder
of Int. and Nordic Ch. Gaywyn Dandini, exported by Miss C. Owen to
Miss Ninnie Sjoquist in 1972 at the age of six months. Dandini is by Ch.
Rhianfas Take Notice ex Bambee of Branston. During 1976 under
Scandinavian, British and American judges he won four Best in Shows
and eight Terrier Groups becoming Top Dog all breeds and being
awarded Golden Dog of the Year.

Regulations for importing into Sweden require a licence from the
Swedish Ministry of Agriculture. A blood test for leptospirae and the
usual health certificate are also required.

Western Germany

In the past few years West Highland White Terriers have been exported
to West Germany and I have been informed that their popularity
increases every year. One of the leading exhibitors and breeders is Mr O.
Flerlage of Osnabrücke.

The import regulations require only the Health Certificate and
Kennel Club Export Pedigree. It is, however, imperative that any dog
sent to Germany *must* have a full complement of 42 teeth, as without
this number a dog is debarred from exhibition.

Japan

The Japanese have been showing great interest in West Highlands and
several dogs have been imported from Britain and America, but it is
regretted that very little information is available about breeding,
exhibiting or import regulations.

South Africa

Although the breed in South Africa is still numerically very small
compared with here, there is a definite improvement in the quality of the
dogs being shown. During the late 1970s several dogs have been
imported giving new scope to the breed. Mrs Bell's (Eloff) success is the
result of her 'Arnholme' dogs, exported of course by Mrs Parr. Mrs
Hogg of Longformacus fame has concentrated on Mrs Gellan's
Backmuir strain. The foundation of Mrs de Wet's Kerrysdale kennel
has been built on Mrs Thomson's Ashgate breeding. Another successful

kennel which has made its mark in recent years is that of Mrs Paulus, 'of Ben Ruadh' suffix. In 1978 not only did her S.A. Ch. Gaywyn Huntsman of Ben Ruadh finish best West Highland and short-legged terrier of the year, but the kennel was awarded exhibitor of the year. S.A. Ch. Newtonglen Heidi of Ben Ruadh and S.A. Ch. Glenalwyne Sunny Lad of Ben Ruadh have continued to keep Mrs Paulus's kennel on the map.

Zimbabwe (Rhodesia)

Zimbabwe suffered a severe blow to the breed during 1978, in the tragic death, caused by a road accident, of Mrs Phyllis Campbell (Inverleith) and Ruth and Allan Lines (Winslarke). To lose the most senior and knowledgeable members of the club must have had a devastating effect on the breed in this part of the world. The future now lies in the hands of Mr Jim Russell.

It should be understood that the requirements of individual countries may change without notification, especially if a rabies outbreak occurs. Therefore it is imperative to consult either the Ministry of Agriculture, Fisheries and Food Animal Health Division IB, Hook Rise South, Tolworth, Surbiton, Surrey, KT6 7NF (Telephone 01–337–6611) or the appropriate embassy prior to making shipping arrangements.

15

Some Ailments and Treatment; Care of the Ageing Dog

Every owner of a dog, whether it be one or a dozen, should know where to find a good veterinary surgeon, and have his address and telephone number in the address book. Often prompt professional advice and attention, whether the emergency is caused by illness or perhaps a road accident, is all that can save a dog's life. Most dogs may never need his services except when they are inoculated and have yearly boosters. Today, a large variety of modern drugs and antibiotics can save dogs from suffering, and indeed, from what would have been certain death years ago. Inoculations against distemper and hardpad have reduced the risk of losing a dog from either of these two infectious diseases to a very low level.

The general public tend to blame every kind of illness suffered by a pedigree dog to the fact that it is what they call 'highly bred'. Inbreeding, or being 'highly bred', has more often than not little if anything to do with it. Dogs, like people, are mainly healthy, but they are just as prone to upsets of various kinds for no apparent reason as their owners are to attacks of flu or gastritis. Any owner who really cares for his dog will soon notice if it is off its food, in the same way that a fond mother notices at once if Johnny doesn't relish his porridge. The dog may have merely an upset stomach which a condition powder will soon put right, but the wise owner will be on the alert for more serious developments. It is fairly easy to keep close watch on a pet dog that is a little off colour and to see whether it regains its appetite later in the day and is ready for its usual exercise. With a large kennel of perhaps thirty or forty dogs it is a different matter and needs a practised eye to spot promptly the dog that is not in its usual sparkling form. For this reason, if for no other, it is advisable that the owner or some other responsible person should make a routine check early in the day. The best time of all is first thing in the morning when the kennel doors are opened. With the urge to be up and doing, that is the natural way of a healthy Westie, any dog that emerges from its kennel in a sluggish manner with its tail down calls for a second look. My experience is that as their kennel doors are opened they hurtle out like jet-propelled missiles even on the coldest mornings. If one does appear to be a bit off form, watch how it behaves for five minutes or so. The trouble may be nothing more than a cyst between the toes or an inflamed ear causing discomfort, or constipation, or indigestion. Any of these treated with some simple but appropriate remedy may quickly be relieved. Should the dog, however, be shivery and hump-backed, take its temperature immediately. A clinical thermometer is an absolutely vital piece of equipment and there should always be a spare one in the medicine chest to replace a broken one. The temperature is one of the surest guides to judging the seriousness of your dog's indisposition. The thermometer should be lightly greased with Vaseline and gently inserted about an inch into the rectum, and left for at least one minute.

If the bowels are easily moved and the excreta is normal it is unlikely that the stomach is out of order. But should there be any sign of diarrhoea, take careful note of how frequently the bowels are moved and, if the diarrhoea is excessive, give a mixture of bismuth and chalk, isolate the dog, and keep it warm and comfortable. If it fails to react to this simple treatment do not delay in getting the veterinary surgeon, for it may easily be the beginning of something more serious. If people would learn to keep their eyes open and really 'see' a dog when they look at it, a lot of trouble would be saved, for the dogs and everyone concerned. Never defer, because you are busy, giving attention to an ailing dog. With long-haired dogs, if the hair is not regularly kept short round the anus and parts immediately surrounding it, the long hair becomes soiled and if not attended to the dog quickly gets into an unpleasant state and becomes miserable. Train yourself, or anyone that has the care of the dog or dogs, to see this sort of thing automatically at a glance and to deal with it without delay.

The normal temperature of a dog is 101·5°F. (38·5°C.) but, like humans, it can vary slightly. So, if on taking a temperature the first time the thermometer reads 102°F. (39°C.), don't conclude too hastily that the dog is ill but watch it closely to see if it is off its food, whether it vomits or not, and what its bowel action is like. If the temperature continues to rise and continues upwards over 102·5°F. (39·5°C.) it is time to call for professional advice. Having placed the dog in a warm place, completely isolated from all other dogs, leave it to rest quietly. Do not try to force a dog running a high temperature to eat. Your vet will require to know the case history of each patient so it is extremely important to note all symptoms. Observe the dog's behaviour. What sort of diarrhoea or vomit (colour, does the animal strain or not, etc.)?

Is the appetite voracious or depraved? Urine – colour, frequency or incontinent? Is the dog in pain—is the pain severe, joint weakness or is there inflammation or swelling? What sort of discharge? Duration of the complaint—how long has it been going on? How long has the problem been going on? Past medical history—previous treatment, other complaints, etc. A highly observant owner who ascertains all the details will assist the vet in making the correct diagnosis.

If you keep a number of dogs and have litters of small puppies, never go straight from any dog that is ailing to the young puppies, or anything else if it can be avoided, without first taking the precaution of washing your hands, changing your shoes and changing anything like an overall or top coat that may have come in contact with a sick dog that you have been attending to. It is better to be ultra cautious about spreading any infection in the beginning. In the same way, extra care about disinfecting a kennel in which a sick dog has been housed is of great importance if germs are to be prevented from spreading. Scrub it out using either strong soda water or water with strong disinfectant. Get right into the corners and move everything movable. In the fairly rare event of a virulent infection occurring in kennels, the safest way to sterilise sleeping boxes, etc., if they are too valuable to be burnt, is to use a blow-lamp or to fumigate the whole kennel. For the disinfection of unoccupied rooms, formaldehyde gas may be liberated from the solution by adding potassium permanganate. Fortunately, the degree of immunity now enjoyed, through the benefits of inoculation, from serious outbreaks of distemper, etc., make the more drastic methods very rarely necessary.

If you are not sure of your diagnosis be sure to get professional advice before it is too late.

Post-operative Care

Following a surgical operation your dog will need a little time to recuperate so do not be surprised if he is not himself after a general anaesthetic. All operations do cause some degree of stress so extra special care and attention during the post-operative recovery period is necessary. Most probably an area of hair will have been clipped from one or both front legs. This is where the anaesthetic drug has been injected. Do not be concerned if the dog sleeps more than usual; this is due to the residual effect of the pre-operative sedative and anaesthetic. A little peace and quiet in a nice warm place for the first twenty-four hours will be much appreciated.

Even if your pet seems his normal self, exercise should be very restricted for forty-eight hours or so, and do not allow him to jump or climb the stairs. His co-ordination might not be so accurate, but worse still he could stretch his stitches. In fact no strenuous exercise should be allowed until after the stitches are removed and he is pronounced fit.

Unless otherwise advised, when feeding sick dogs it is recommended to give small meals on a 'little-and-often' basis. It may be a few days before the patient regains his normal appetite, so it is a good idea to keep his diet as light as possible (chicken, fish etc). On the other hand, he may be very hungry following fasting for the operation, and very thirsty too. Large quantities of water at one time should not be allowed, otherwise he may vomit. When you collect your dog from the surgery following an operation ask the vet for any additional instructions. When should you return for his post-operative check? What medication must he receive during convalescence? Will any dressings need removing or changing in the near future?

Care should be taken that the dog does not lick or nibble his stitches. These are generally removed ten days after the operation.

Abscess A collection of pus which may occur in any part of the body as a result of an infection. The condition is painful and should be treated by frequent warm fomentation which draws it to a head when it should burst. If this does not occur, the abscess may be lanced and the contents evacuated. The wound should then be bathed several times a day with warm salt water and kept open until it is quite clean. Antibiotic treatment is sometimes prescribed.

Anal Glands These can be troublesome if neglected. The usual sign that the glands need emptying is evidenced by a dog dragging its hindquarters along the ground. Any intense irritation round the hindquarters of a dog should give rise to suspicion of anal gland trouble. It is often mistaken for worms. The treatment is quite simple. Place the dog on the table, grasping the tail in the left hand. Take a large piece of cotton wool in the right hand and apply pressure, starting from a little more than an inch below the anus and gradually closing the finger and thumb as you press upwards. It is often possible to feel a little hard lump on either side. With firm pressure the secretion can be ejected into the cotton wool. If left unattended this condition can cause an abscess.

Appetite If decreased it is essential to distinguish between actual loss of appetite due to ill-health and the inability to eat despite hunger due to an obstruction or mouth problem. Treatment must depend on the cause. Increased appetite or insatiable hunger may be a sign of internal parasites and should be treated by appropriate methods. The adult dog that shows a craving for dirt and evil-smelling muck may lack mineral salts in its diet. The diet should be supplemented with calcium lactate and seaweed, from which they appear to derive much benefit.

Canine Parvovirus Late in 1978 a new highly infectious disease appeared, a very severe form of gastro-enteritis. This virus condition can be seen in two different types. *Enteritis*— with the usual clinical symptoms of diarrhoea, vomiting, rapid dehydration and often the temperature being subnormal. With treatment many adult dogs recover after a short illness of this type. *Myocarditis*—in very young puppies, the heart can be so damaged that the puppy dies shortly after infection, or the heart can be permanently weakened. In puppies and in adult dogs, the disease can destroy the white blood cells, which are themselves the animals' main defence against infection. In such cases, the dog may become severely ill or die either due to parvovirus itself, or due to secondary infections against which it is now defenceless. Early in 1981 a dog vaccine became available but until then the vaccine prepared against cat parvovirus (Feline Infectious Enteritis) was licensed to control and prevent canine parvovirus disease in dogs. Spread seems to occur not only by dog to dog contact, but also as a result of carriage by dog owners.

Congenital or Hereditary Defects Unfortunately most pedigree dogs are likely to suffer from one or more disorders and the West Highland is no exception. Some of the problems which may occur are mentioned here. It must be pointed out that although it is probable the problems are present at birth they are not detectable when very young and do not become apparent until the dog is older. Fortunately they are not common but it is sensible to know of their existence.

Craniomandibular Osteopathy—C.M.O. for short. The initial symptoms arise when the puppy is three to four months old. First signs are high temperature, refusal to eat, and marked pain when the jaw is opened. A thickening of the bone in the region of the back teeth will be detected. The condition can be suppressed temporarily with cortisone-like drugs and pain-killers, but will recur at intervals while the jawbone formation phase lasts. Providing the puppy has been kept free of pain, once past the growing stage the symptoms will subside and the dog will be able to lead a reasonable life.

Keratoconjunctivitis Sicca—Dry Eye. This is a chronic inflammatory condition affecting the cornea and conjunctiva and resulting from a failure of tear secretion. Sometimes medical control is possible, but fortunately an operation (Parotid Duct transplant) to divert saliva from the mouth to moisten the corneal surface can be extremely helpful in many patients. Homeopathic treatment zincum met 30c twice daily has been reported as beneficial.

Legg-Calvé-Perthes or more concisely Perthes disease. The condition starts in young dogs, usually when between five and seven months old. It begins as a mild or intermittent hind leg lameness which, over a period of a few weeks, gradually worsens until, in many cases, the dog will refuse to use the affected leg. Final diagnosis can, however, only be made after an X-ray examination. In Perthes disease, the blood supply to the femoral head (the ball part of the hip joint) for some reason becomes interrupted and, as a result, the bone of the femoral head dies and completely disintegrates. A surgical operation to remove the head of the femoral bone may be successful, but treatment should be left entirely to your veterinary surgeon.

Patella Luxation—The condition affects the stifle or knee-joint. One or other of the ligaments which hold it in position are damaged and the patella keeps slipping in and out of position. The disease in its less severe forms results in variable hindleg lameness that causes the dog to favour the affected leg only on occasions and may spontaneously improve and recur. On manipulating the stifle joint the patella can be felt clicking into position.

Copper Toxicosis—At present this problem seems to be virtually unknown in the UK. Information therefore is from American reports. Diagnosis is made from blood tests to determine liver function and liver biopsy. Copper Toxicosis is the major cause of cirrhosis of the liver and has the following symptoms: a) rapid weight loss, b) jaundice, c) fluid accumulation and enlargement of the abdomen. The disease progresses slowly at the onset but normally is not diagnosed until it has advanced too far for satisfactory treatment. There is some research being undertaken in the USA at present.

Constipation If seen in the early stages of the first day or two it is usually cleared by adding raw, roughly grated carrots and finely chopped raw cabbage to the dog's food and giving a dessertspoonful of liquid paraffin before each meal. In the event of the bowels not being moved easily after a reasonable lapse of time further investigation should be undertaken by a veterinary surgeon to find out if a foreign body is obstructing the intestines.

Ear Canker There are several forms of ear trouble, all often loosely referred to as canker. The most common is usually caused by a microscopic insect that betrays its appearance by a rather sticky, dirty dark discharge. If left unattended the discharge may become very hard, when it is necessary to soften it with warm olive oil before it is possible to clean the ear completely without hurting it. Once the discharge is softened, with cotton-wool round an orange stick, gently lift out all the filth. When the ear is thoroughly cleansed and wiped dry with cotton-wool apply one of the proprietary creams or other products available. A liquid or a cream emollient is better than anything in powder form, which has a tendency to clog the ear. Whatever form the irritation takes it must have daily attention if the condition is to be cleared up. If there is no apparent improvement after a week or so it is advisable to change to some other dressing. The condition, if not cured, can cause acute discomfort.

Eclampsia This occurs usually when a bitch is nursing a litter, but it can happen prior to whelping. It is caused by the excessive drain of calcium from the system. The symptoms are shivering, and rapid panting, and the bitch will stagger around and sometimes collapse completely. There must be no delay in getting veterinary assistance. If treated promptly she will usually return to normal in an hour or so. Any delay in treatment will almost certainly prove fatal within a few hours.

Eczema Rarely found among West Highlands, but where the tendency is present any slight irritation of the skin will, if neglected, eventually develop into eczema. First steps should be to purify the blood and tone up the condition generally by giving a teaspoonful of seaweed powder mixed into the main meal of the day. Dogs usually have no dislike of the seaweed powder and take their food quite readily when it is well mixed in. They may drink a little more water until they become accustomed to taking the seaweed powder, which can be continued indefinitely because it is beneficial to the diet at all times. Chopped raw carrots and cabbage should also be mixed in the food.

Wash the dog with a good antiseptic dog shampoo. See that the bedding is kept scrupulously clean, and if blankets are used they must be changed daily if possible. Any bedding such as wood-wool, straw or hay which might irritate the skin should be avoided.

Enteritis Diarrhoea may be due to the following internal parasites:
1 Worm infestation—Roundworms, Whipworms, Tapeworms, Hookworms or *Coccidiosis*.
2 Bacterial infection caused by food poisoning.
3 Allergies to various foods.
4 Absorbability problems—normally associated with a wheat allergy similar to Coeliac disease in humans.
The dog should be fasted for twelve to twenty-four hours and then given three small meals a day of boiled fish, or chicken and boiled long grain rice for two to three days. If the dog is all right, its ordinary food should

then be reintroduced gradually. The dog should *not* be given milk. At first a dessertspoon of the following mixture—half a pint of boiled water, one beaten egg white, and one tablespoon of honey or glucose should be given every hour, then increase the amount after three to four doses. If the diarrhoea does not clear up within two days, professional attention is required. Acute cases, such as when the dog is passing blood, should receive veterinary attention very quickly.

False Pregnancy Even though a bitch has not been mated, nine weeks later she may exhibit all the signs of pregnancy, making a bed, carrying a toy around (mothering her baby) and even producing milk. Her disposition may change and she may become temperamental. For this reason some treatment is necessary. An $\frac{1}{8}$ teaspoon of epsom salts in water given once a day often helps. Increased exercise may assist in alleviating the 'broody' feeling. Hormone treatment is not recommended especially if a breeding future is planned. The only infallible cure for persistent false pregnancies is to have the bitch spayed.

Gastritis It is natural for dogs to vomit occasionally but if it becomes a daily occurrence despite the dog being bright and eating normally it may be caused by a build-up of acidity in the stomach. One charcoal tablet three times a day may help. If the dog vomits frequently and drinks between vomiting it should be seen quickly by a veterinary surgeon. Meanwhile, remove the water which will prevent the vomiting. The condition is usually due to an allergy to a food the dog has eaten. Mutton and pork are the commonest offenders. However, vomiting may also be a symptom of several serious diseases e.g. Parvovirus, and if the vomit is brown there may be peritonitis or an obstruction.

Gastro-Enteritis If a dog is off its food, vomits and has diarrhoea, veterinary advice should be sought, especially if there is blood in the vomit or diarrhoea as the condition may very rapidly prove fatal. In ordinary cases fast for 24 hours and treat as gastritis.

Haematoma A swelling caused by damage to a blood vessel, it occurs most commonly in the ear flap as a blood blister which forms between the skin layers. The problem usually arises from a self-inflicted injury, scratching or striking the ear against a hard surface. A mixture of white iodine and potassium permanganate applied to the ear daily may reduce the swelling; alternatively a surgical opening may be required.

Heatstroke This condition is the result of the dog being over-exposed to sunlight, or being left in a car without adequate ventilation. (It is a fallacy to believe a West Highland will be cooler with the coat clipped off.) The symptoms include panting, profuse salivation, vomiting, staggering and finally collapse. The body temperature is usually 106°F (41°C) and upwards. Heatstroke itself can be fatal if not treated immediately. The victim should be removed to a cool, shady, airy place and plunged in a bath of cold water, applying water constantly to the head and neck. If available ice should be in the water. Once the temperature is down to 103°F (39°C) remove from water and keep taking the dog's temperature to make sure it does not rise again. Conversely if it drops to sub-normal the dog may need to be warmed up. Take its temperature every ten minutes. Once normal the dog should be dried and encouraged to drink.

Indigestion This may be caused by ingestion of unsuitable food, dry biscuit meal etc. or due to the digestive enzymes not being produced in the correct amount. A 'gurgling tummy' and vomiting yellow bile are the classic symptoms of this problem. Simple antacid tablets such as milk of magnesia will be found helpful.

Inoculations A great deal of anxiety about contagious disease has in the last decade been removed from all dog breeders. The very efficient vaccines now commonly in use have given all vaccinated dogs a greater expectation of life. The perils of taking valuable dogs to shows and, in particular, large indoor winter shows has been removed by the use of the various vaccines available. Every dog breeder when selling a puppy that has not already been immunised against hardpad and distemper should obtain a promise from the buyer that the puppy will be kept away from any chance of becoming infected by any other dogs until such time as it is old enough to be immunised, which is usually accepted as no younger than twelve weeks old. It is possible to inoculate at an earlier age than twelve weeks, but the dose needs to be repeated to ensure satisfactory immunity.

It is now possible to have dogs inoculated against the seven following diseases: *Distemper and hardpad, leptospira canicola infection* (bacteria which attack the kidneys), *leptospira icterohaemorrhacaciae infection* (related to leptospira canicola but causing jaundice), an infection usually transmitted by rats, *contagious virus hepatitis* (Rubarth's Disease), a virus infection that attacks the liver, Parvovirus and Parainfluenza, a form of kennel cough.

Interdigital Cysts A painful, fluid-filled swelling between the toes. They should be treated by placing the foot in warm epsom salt water which tends to draw the swelling to a head. Once ruptured and the fluid removed they clear up rapidly. There is a tendency for them to recur regularly, in which case six Brewers' Yeast tablets and the homoeopathic treatment 'Graphites 6X' daily have been found beneficial.

Pyometra Inflammation of the uterus. This often develops after a season—the bitch goes off colour and drinks excessively. There are two types: 'open' and 'closed' pyometra, the only difference being that in the former the pus or fluid is able to flow away from the bitch as a vaginal discharge. The only satisfactory treatment is a hysterectomy.

Skin diseases It is not feasible to go into great detail on this complex subject; there are numerous forms of irritation affecting the skin and these can manifest themselves in various ways and in some cases it is not possible to be sure which is actually responsible. Roughly they can be separated into two groups—internal and external, each group being subdivided into different categories: endoparasites (e.g. worms), ectoparasites (e.g. fleas, lice, ticks, harvest mites, cheyletiella, mange mites), allergic reactions (e.g. due to chemical fertilizers, insecticides*), infections (e.g. bacterial, fungal), hormone imbalance (e.g. thyroid), dietary problems (e.g. due to feeding excess carbohydrates), neglected grooming or incorrect clipping instead of stripping.

The prime concern is always to remove the cause of the irritation, as self-mutilation from nibbling, licking and scratching will only make matters worse and lead to secondary infection. The actual diagnosis is not always simple but thorough routine investigations will help pinpoint troubles as they occur. Medicated baths are normally prescribed to eliminate any livestock. However it may be necessary for your veterinary surgeon to take a skin scraping for laboratory tests to determine the exact cause. The non-parasitic, un-identified spots, rashes, lesions (whether acute or chronic) and wet or dry patches present the biggest problem. There is a vast range of preparations available claiming to be skin cures, but finding the right treatment is not always easy. Where the cause is clear the correct remedy should be applied, but where it is not, try to break down the vicious circle of itch-scratch-itch. The first step is to gently cleanse the affected area and then apply an anti-inflammatory preparation. Benzyl Benzoate has been found successful in clearing some conditions.

It is also advisable to alter the diet. White meat, fish, brown rice and

*Most fertilizers and insecticides, although supposedly harmless to animals, are irritants, therefore dogs permitted to exercise in areas contaminated by these products should immediately be bathed. Sore eyes and skin troubles will undoubtedly erupt if this ritual is neglected.

Elaine Paige with Rum Tum Tugger

Two four-month old puppies

Ch. Pillerton Peterman, 1966

Partners in the funny business! Popov the clown from the Moscow
State Circus with seven-month-old Gemma, 1971

C. M. Cooke

Mrs Pacey judging Ch. Brenda of Branston, shown by Mr G. B. Dennis,
and Ch. Sollershott Soloist, shown by Mrs J. Kenny Taylor.
Southern Counties Canine Association, 1962

Rosern

Miss Cook's Ch. Famecheck Secret, the kennel's thirty-seventh
home-bred champion

Ch. Cedarfell Merry N'Bright, 1970

Ch. Whitebriar Jonfair, 1971

a good proportion of vegetables may be found helpful. A teaspoonful of vegetable margarine or oil, Brewers' Yeast tablets, Seaweed powder and Sulphur tablets, which help to clear the blood of impurities, may be given daily as a supportive treatment. In severe cases veterinary advice may be advisable but the all-too-common use of steroid therapy should be embarked upon with caution as there can be side-effects. It is important for you to understand that cortisone does not actually 'cure' skin diseases, but in some cases provides relief from itching. If in doubt, do consult your veterinary surgeon.

Tracheobronchitis The aggravating condition popularly known as kennel cough, because it spreads most easily where dogs are grouped together, is rarely serious and dogs show few, if any, systemic signs of illness. This disease can be caused by several different viruses and bacteria among which is Bordefella. Generally, infected dogs do not run a fever, maintain their appetite, stay bright and alert, and recover without problems. The cough which appears to come from deep down in the chest can last for a two to three week duration. Common 'cough mixtures' are often employed as part of the treatment. Dogs suffering from kennel cough should be isolated and never taken to places where they can meet other dogs as it quickly passes from one to another. Antibiotics may be administered by a vet to prevent any secondary infections such as bronchitis or pneumonia.

Worms The two types most frequently found in the UK are round worms and tapeworms. Puppies are particularly susceptible to round-worms and as mentioned in a previous chapter the regimen for de-worming begins at ten days. Subsequent doses at six-month intervals probably provide adequate control. This routine de-worming is advisable because dogs can become re-infected at any age, particularly if they hunt rodents. Present-day medicines are safe and easy to administer and do not upset puppies.

Tapeworms are less frequently found, and very rarely in puppies. Dogs kept clean and free of fleas, which are the host of the intermediate stage of the tapeworm, are unlikely to become infected. Successful destruction of the parasite can be difficult to achieve as the head is embedded in the bowel and only segments are expelled. Until the whole of the tapeworm is expelled it will simply grow again. Effective drugs are available from the veterinary surgeon.

Hookworm is occasionally seen in British dogs and is usually not serious, but the form which occurs in other countries may cause anaemia. Whipworm has been found in this country and may become more widespread. These two types of worm are not usually visible to the

131

naked eye, so a faecal sample will be required to determine their presence. So that no other dogs may become infected always burn, at once, expelled worms or any excreta that may contain worms.

Care of the Ageing Dog

Compared with humans, the lifespan of dogs is relatively short, and the elderly friends are the closest and dearest. There are many ways in which the quality of life may be improved, keeping the older dog healthy, happy and contented, and often it is just by a little forethought and consideration. Life expectancy varies but on average the West Highland usually enjoys about twelve to fourteen years. Many surpass this by several years.

Leaving aside accidents and non-preventable or incurable disease, there are many factors which help to ensure a long, healthy life: good management, hygiene, veterinary treatment, housing, adequate exercise and, most important, correct feeding throughout the years. Regular check-ups by the veterinary surgeon at the time of the annual vaccination boosters are another aid to longevity. But the gradual degenerative process is inevitable.

It is sensible to make some dietary adjustments during the latter years as the dog becomes less active and therefore needs fewer calories. Two smaller meals given daily, rather than one large one, help to alleviate the pangs of hunger. Red meat is probably best omitted from the diet. Easily digestible high-quality foods such as cooked eggs, fish, rabbit, chicken or Healthmeal (tinned natural white meat recipe) will be more acceptable. The biscuit part of the diet should also be reduced and substituted with boiled rice or Allbran. Complete invalid diets such as Complan are also invaluable. There are, however, specific illnesses which necessitate substantial changes in the diet. The veterinary surgeon will often give dietary advice during treatment.

It is no kindness to allow any dog to become grossly overweight. Every bodily function is handicapped, and there is a high risk of respiratory problems, heart disease, arthritis and diabetes mellitus. Obesity with all its complications is a very unpleasant condition and it is worth making a strenuous effort to prevent it. Encourage the dog to be active, without expecting too much. Exercise should not be abandoned altogether in the ageing dog, as this is often the highlight of its day even though it may not be as active as before. The dog will still enjoy a daily walk at his own pace and over a distance which stops short of tiring him.

Ageing usually impairs the dog's eyesight and hearing. A pet which is partially or even completely blind has little or no problem in its own territory; however care should be taken not to move the furniture around too much, as in strange surroundings the dog may bump himself and injure that fragile body. Loss of hearing is not a great disadvantage either, provided the owner bears the disability in mind and protects the deaf animal from possible dangers. The dog will not respond to your call but may well pick up vibrations if you clap your hands. Neither infirmity will prevent the dog living a contented life.

From every point of view it is important that teeth and gums should be clean and healthy. Fragments of food may lodge and decompose between the teeth and an extremely offensive smell results. Dogs shed teeth as they age and total extraction is no problem. Providing food is not presented in large chunks, they can cope very well without teeth.

Kidney problems are common in old age, often heralded by an increase of thirst. If the dog seems to be drinking water by the bowlful and urinating in apparently the same quantity, the owner's first impulse might be to reduce the water supply, which is detrimental to the condition. Veterinary treatment and a protein-reduced diet will often postpone the inevitable progress of the disease.

The bowel, like the dog itself, is less active with increasing years. Some foods will ferment and produce gas, which in turn causes flatulence. Charcoal tablets are thought to be helpful. Dietary deficiency, or lack of exercise causing the muscles in the intestine to become more sluggish, may be the source of constipation.

Bones become more brittle and arthritis of the joints is common. As the years go by the dog will become more susceptible to cold, so special measures should be taken to guard him from damp and chills. Exposure to cold depresses the circulation so it is particularly important to provide him with a warm, draughtproof bed. Lameness, or inability to move about with the customary agility, may signal the onset of rheumatism. Treatments that will give relief from the acute pain are obtainable from your veterinary surgeon.

Regular grooming becomes even more essential in old age, as scurf and debris rapidly accumulate on the skin and the hair can become a tangled mess. Coats should be kept trimmed, and nails, which appear to grow at an accelerated rate, require more frequent clipping.

Take care to avoid infectious diseases, because when these hit an elderly dog they can debilitate him to an alarming degree. Subjecting him to stressful situations can make him more prone to illness. Far too often the owner does not seem to realize when something is wrong, and the dog may suffer unnecessarily. Old dogs may become incontinent. They may lose their sense of security or become disorientated. These are common symptoms of senility. Other ailments include tumours, warts, heart, kidney and liver disease, as well as prostate or womb problems.

These should all receive prompt attention.

The utmost patience and forgiveness will be needed for some of the weakness that old age brings. Take care not to startle the elderly dog when in a deep and prolonged sleep, as he may respond with a growl or snap which was not really intended. It is now your turn to repay the love and affection that has been bestowed on you through the many years of trustfulness and a little extra love and care will go a long way to give that happiness that now is so essential.

There comes a time, though, when life becomes a burden to your dog. He is pitiful in his weakness, with no future. Then there is one last service which can be performed to spare him unnecessary suffering. It is always a painful and difficult decision, but wrong to allow a dog to linger on when there is no pleasure in life for him. In the end your conscience must be your guide. Do not let your old dog be sent or taken to the veterinary surgeon to die, perhaps frightened and bewildered in an unfamiliar place among strange people. Ask the vet to visit. Let your old friend be gently helped on his way in his own home with his owner beside him in the swift and merciful way which modern medicine has made possible.

Every kennel should have a medicine cupboard. Different lotions, powders and pills will be collected as the need arises but a few essentials are in almost daily use. They are cottonwool, Dettol, T.C.P., olive oil, liquid paraffin, worm tablets, Pulvex, and, of course, a thermometer or, better still, two. If pills or medicines are prescribed, always see that the directions and purpose for which they are intended are clearly written on the bottle or box.

16

The Breed in the 1970s

by Catherine Owen

With a certain amount of trepidation I embark on this new chapter for the sixth edition, an undertaking bestowed on me by Mrs D. Mary Dennis who, after so many years being actively involved in every aspect of the West Highland, has now retired from the dog world and has settled for a quieter life.

A new chapter on the 1970s seems a fitting inclusion in this book as, during the last decade, the breed has not only increased in popularity as a house pet, maintained its position as top terrier in Kennel Club registrations, but has also become the top contender for group and best in show honours at all breed championship shows. Unfortunately, invariably when a breed becomes popular the indiscriminate breeders take over, the breed suffers badly and the quality begins to fall. Over the years the breed has changed enormously, but the standard has stayed the same. Fads and fancies should be forgotten and the aim of breeding well-balanced, sound West Highlands of the correct type and size should be continued. With so many newcomers appearing in the show ring it is even more important that the older, established breeders should set a high standard in preparing their dogs for show also. It is no use misleading beginners by letting them think show dogs are prepared overnight with a pair of scissors. Educate them to work on the coats regularly. Keeping a dog in show coat should be looked on as a challenge.

Now having said the future of the breed should be watched carefully, I will go back over the last ten years. There are many in the breed with successful show records, combined with top producers which deserve the credit for the increase in popularity. However, it will not be possible to give every individual a mention in a limited space so I trust that my omissions will be forgiven.

In 1970 the nearest a West Highland came to top honours for several years was when Mr and Mrs Paintings' Ch. Cedarfell Messenger Dove went reserve Best in Show at the National Terrier. This could be called beginner's luck as Dove was the first dog the Paintings had ever owned. Not content with this win, she finished the year by winning the most challenge certificates in the breed.

The following year the biggest and most important win was the Best in Show All Breeds at Bath with Ch. Checkbar Tommy Quite Right, owned by Mrs J. Taylor; but it was the late Myra Sills who piloted him through to this honour. Babychamps was the new word in dog terminology and was used for those precocious youngsters who win their three challenge certificates but, because they are under twelve months, may not carry the title of champion. This Kennel Club ruling was proved to be ridiculous very quickly but still it exists. A great deal to promote interest in pedigree dogs and shows was achieved by the introduction of the *Daily Express* Pup of the Year Competition. Although the sponsors have changed, the competition continues and the number of all breed puppies challenging for the coveted title runs into hundreds each year.

Two West Highlands claimed group wins during 1972; firstly, at the Birmingham National Centenary, Mrs Coy's Ch. Cedarfell Merry 'n' Bright took the honour. A few shows later at Chester it was the turn of Ch. Sarmac Heathstream Drummer Boy, owned by Mrs Millen, to take the privileged spot. Topping the bitches this time was Int. Ch. Famecheck Busybody who managed to head the breed in England, USA and Canada all in the same year. Busybody was exported by her breeder Miss Cook in the July and joined Mr and Mrs Keenan in New Jersey. Her Canadian title was won in just twenty-three hours, and for good measure she made it a Best in Show win. Int. Ch. Famecheck Hallmark, her sire, still dominates many pedigrees today.

The year 1973 marked the hundred years' existence of the Kennel Club, and to commemorate this a specially commissioned bronze medallion was presented to all Cruft's Best of Breed winners. Mrs Abbey's Kristajen Crackerjack was our lucky dog. The West Highland flag was kept flying at the Welsh Kennel Club by Ch. Ardenrun 'Andsome of Purston winning the group. This dog completed his title at fourteen months of age; he was campaigned by his owner Mr Collings before joining Dr Hunt in the USA where he continued his winning ways to become top of the breed.

The introduction of the Breeding of Dogs Act came into force April 1974 and, despite a dramatic rise in the rate of inflation, no decline was evident in the exhibition of dogs. During the year no less than four different dogs won groups. Mr Herbison's Ch. Milburn Mandy, expertly handled by Ernie Sharpe, topped the group in Scotland, Best in Show in Belfast and also the National Terrier. Ch. Dianthus Buttons, owned by Mrs Newstead and so ably handled by Geoff Corish, headed two more groups at Malvern and Peterborough. At the Welsh show it was the turn of Ch. Birkfell Silver Thistle of Clanestar, bred by Miss Cleland and handled by her owner Mrs Lancaster. The L.K.A. must have been a historic day for Mrs Lees who took her homebred Carillyon Cadence right through from winning her first challenge certificate to being awarded the terrier group, a great thrill for her owner.

1975 saw Olac Moonbeam owned by Mr Tattersall as the first West Highland to qualify for the finals of the Pup of the Year, when she won her round at Edinburgh. Ch. Glenalwyne Sonny Boy, another of Ernie Sharpe's charges, owned by Miss Herbert, finished Best in Show at Leicester—just a start to his many such wins. However, it was Mrs Torbet's Glengordon Hannah that topped the poll by winning most challenge certificates throughout the year.

Ch. Dianthus Buttons carried off 1976's most prestigious award when he was declared by top international all-round judge, Mr J. Braddon, supreme champion of Cruft's. For jubilant Mrs Newstead and new co-owner Mrs D. Taylor it must have been a dream come true. After this win Buttons's appearances were far more spasmodic. West Highlands the world over basked in his reflected glory, and demand for puppies just like 'Bertie Buttons' was never ending. The temptations were great for the get-rich-quick to jump on the bandwagon. What a terrible thought that our lovely breed should be spoiled just for the sake of making money.

One could assume that after this great win no other West Highland would stand a chance in the show ring during the year, but this was not so as three others shared the limelight. Mr Tattersall's Ch. Olac Moonbeam fulfilled her early promise by adding two groups and reserve Best in Show to her credit. Ch. Glenalwyne Sonny Boy claimed another three, while a new boy, Mr and Mrs Gellan's Backmuir Noble James, took another. Seven groups in one year. What an achievement for any breed!

Britain was not the only country to be experiencing the year of the West Highland as Ch. Gaywyn Dandini was dominating the Swedish shows. I was fortunate enough to attend the Göteborg show so had the pleasure of seeing Dandini, whom I had exported at six months, presented with the coveted Golden Dog award that is given to Sweden's top dog each year.

It was interesting also to learn that two West Highlands were in England, after becoming international champions. They were seeking the English title to add to their laurels. Miss J. Kabel, who is now in partnership with Mrs B. Graham (Lasara) brought her Int. and Dutch Ch. Lasara Lots of Fun home after a very successful career on the

Continent; Fun claimed his English title in 1978. The Swedish bred Int. and Nordic Ch. Tweed Tartan Caledonier, bred and owned by Mrs B. Hasselgren, was the first Scandinavian bred West Highland to win in England. After an unfortunate start, Geoff Corish applied the professional touch to his preparation and presentation and it was not long before he gained his crown and returned to his homeland.

Ch. Glenalwyne Sonny Boy made 1977 another year to remember in his three-year career by collecting another fourteen challenge certificates. It was no surprise that, being top terrier for two consecutive years, Sonny Boy participated at the Contest of Champions, a competition by special dispensation of the Kennel Club for the thirty-two top dogs of all breeds, held in aid of the Animal Health Trust Small Animals Centre. When Sonny Boy eventually took a rest from the show ring he had collected thirty-three c.c.s, more than any other dog in the breed.

In 1978 Pedigree Petfoods announced a new competition, this time for the veterans, and again our breed featured well, as both Ch. Whitebriar Jonfair and my own Ch. Alpinegay Sonata won their way through to the final. Sonata, at twelve years five months, was the oldest by twenty-one months of the ten finalists. In the breed classes, Ch. Domaroy Saracen, owned by Mr and Mrs Wilshaw, dominated the scene, collecting nine challenge certificates during the year, and also won the terrier group at Bournemouth. Back to the puppies for 1979, where it was the turn of Miss Cook's Famecheck Silver Jubilee to become one of the year's top ten puppies. Miss Cook celebrated her kennel's silver jubilee year by making Ch. Famecheck Extra Special the thirty-first homebred champion. Geoff Corish was again the important member of the team to take Extra Special through to his title in just twelve days.

More publicity was given to our breed when the British Post Office designed stamps with dogs, to be issued at the time of Cruft's, February 1979. The Scottish breed chosen for the 11p stamp was the West Highland. In retrospect our breed has certainly created some notable achievements and made its presence felt in the show ring. Now entering the 1980s I can only reiterate the caution to be selective with your breeding programme. Study the breed standard closely, accept it as your blue print and then try to emulate it. Remember foundation stock for many a country has been based primarily on imports from our top producing kennels. The future lies in the hands of the knowledgeable breeders of today; it is for them to continue breeding the correct type and temperaments.

One more word of warning: there is an increasing tendency for exhibitors who chalk dogs at shows indiscriminately to use too much chalk. The result will be the unnecessary loss of venues, and the Kennel

Club committee has recently (February 1981) introduced new regulations defining the use of chalk (in block form only) in preparation of dogs for exhibition.

The Kennel Club

With the tremendous increase in the number of pure-bred dogs owned in the country, it became necessary for the Kennel Club to revise the registration system to enable the large number to be handled more efficiently. The preliminary change came into effect on 1 April 1976, and involved the introduction of three main stages of registration: (a) Recording of each litter, (b) Basic Registration, (c) Advancement to an Active Register for those dogs which were (i) bred from (ii) exhibited or entered for competition and (iii) exported. By the end of the year, the revised system was still very much in the 'running in' stage with some modification being considered, and another 'pilot scheme' was conducted the following year. This experiment continued to present problems, until finally an amended system—a more simple form of single registration—was put into action on 1 October 1978 and this eliminated a lot of the earlier problems. The Basic Register was discontinued and all subsequent registrations were accepted as Active.

An application to register or transfer a dog must be made on the appropriate official form obtainable from the Kennel Club. The procedure now is quite straightforward. Recording the litter is essential if any of the puppies are to be registered at any time. This is done by the breeder (owner of the dam at the time of whelping) completing the K.C. Form 1, "Application for puppy registration and litter recording by the breeder". All relevant information such as the registered name and number of the sire and dam, date of mating and puppies' birth, number and sex of litter must be included. The declaration has to be signed by both the breeder and the owner of the sire before the document, together with the correct fee, is returned to the Kennel Club. Application can be made for the puppies' registration on the same form or the appropriate certificates will be sent to you for the new owners to register at a later date.

The owner of a dog is entitled to have any or all of the following endorsements placed on the records of the dog and to have the relevant registration and/or transfer certificate marked accordingly:

(a) Not eligible for entry at shows, Field Trials or Working Trials held under Kennel Club rules.

(b) Progeny not eligible for registration.

(c) Not eligible for the issue of an Export Pedigree.

(d) Name unchangeable (on payment of additional fee).

Any endorsement shall only be lifted at the written request of the individual imposing it.

Another amended regulation affects the eligibility of dogs for entry at shows:

'In estimating the number of prizes won, all wins up to seven days before the date of closing of entries shall be counted when entering for any class and the date published in the schedule. Wins in Variety Classes do not count for entry in Breed Classes.' In calculating the last date to which awards will count for eligibility for entry in classes, seven clear days should be allowed prior to the announced date for the closing of entries.

New regulations governing the use of a registered affix are also in force and, with very few exceptions already sanctioned by the Kennel Club, the affix must be used as a prefix when the dog has been bred by the owner and is solely and unconditionally his property or was bred from parents each of which was bred by him. Otherwise, it must be used as a suffix, that is to say, the last word in the name.

There was a change too in the qualification required for entry into the Kennel Club Stud Book. The following dogs are entitled: Dogs winning Challenge Certificates, Reserve Challenge Certificates, or First, Second or Third, in Open Class where Kennel Club Challenge Certificates are competed for when such Classes are not subject to any limitation as to weight, colour or other description.

The few variations in regulations mentioned here are by no means all of the changes which have taken place, so all breeding and exhibiting enthusiasts are strongly advised to purchase a copy of the Kennel Club Year Book which is published annually and which is a mine of information.

WORLD BREED CLUBS

West Highland White Terrier Club. Formed 1905
  Secretary: Mrs Irene Gellan, Mayfield, Carnock Road, Dunfermline,
  Fife.
    Telephone—Dunfermline (0383) 21698

West Highland White Terrier Club of England. Formed 1905
  Secretary: Mrs Jean Abbey, 7 Pottery Lane, Woodlesford, Leeds,
  Yorks LS26 8P.
    Telephone—Leeds (0532) 821047

Southern West Highland White Terrier Club. Formed 1980
  Secretary: Mrs Marjorie Dickinson, 42 Southview Drive, Upminster,
Essex RM14 2LD.
    Telephone—Upminster (040 22) 28658

North of Ireland West Highland White Terrier Club. Formed 1959
  Secretary: Mrs M. Johnston, 24 Corkhill Road, Sesinore, Co.
  Tyrone, N. Ireland.
    Telephone—Fintona (0662) 841618

West Highland White Terrier Club of Ireland. Formed 1946
  Secretary: Mrs Ethel Morrow, 3 Taney Road, Dundrum, Dublin 14,
  Ireland.
    Telephone—Dublin (0001) 983195

Westie Rescue Scheme.
  Secretary: Mrs B. Graham, Kiln Farm, Oxford Road, Stokenchurch,
  Bucks.
    Telephone—Kingston Blount (0844) 52303

West Highland White Terrier Club of Nederland. Formed 1978
  Secretary: Miss L. Meerwijk, Katijdeweg 14, 4153 RG Beesd,
  Holland.

West Highland White Terrier Club of Sweden. Formed 1965
  Secretary: Gunhild Werner, Verdandivägen 11, 13146 Nacka,
  Sweden.

West Highland White Terrier Club of Norway.
  Secretary: Reidun Aril, Bjornvagen 23, 0307 Oslo 3, Norway.

West Highland White Terrier representative of Danish Terrier Club
  Inge Marie Ravn, Tingvej 36, Vejerslev, 8881 Thorsø, Denmark
    Telephone—Arhus (6) 871455

West Highland White Terrier Club of America. Formed 1909
  Secretary: Mrs Betty Williams, 3524 Kirby Lane, Louisville, Ken-
  tucky, 40299, USA.

West Highland White Terrier Club of California
Secretary: Miss Cathleen Blattler, 1146 Petra Way, Alpine, California 92001, USA.

West Highland White Terrier Club of Greater Baltimore
Secretary: Gwendolyn S. Law, 8248 Riviera Drive, Severn, Maryland 2114, USA.

West Highland White Terrier Club of Greater Denver
Secretary: Ms Hazel Norris, 3427 Grape Street, Denver, Colorado 80207, USA.

West Highland White Terrier Club of Greater New York
Secretary: Ms Carolyn Macri, 2517 Natta Blvd., Bellmore, New York 11710, USA.

West Highland White Terrier Club of Indiana
Secretary: Mrs Nora Niermeyer, 10679 Highland Drive, Indianapolis, Indiana 46280, USA.

West Highland White Terrier Club of Northern Illinois
Secretary: Mrs Patti Lockman, 349 Pearson Circle, Naperville, Illinois 60540, USA.

West Highland White Terrier Club of Northern Ohio
Secretary: Mrs Mina Moses, 29159 Chardon Road, Wickliffe, Ohio 44092, USA.

West Highland White Terrier Club of Greater Washington
Secretary: Mrs Colleen Pettis, 10260 New Hampshire Avenue, Silver Spring, Maryland 20930, USA.

San Francisco Bay West Highland White Terrier Club
Secretary: Mrs Linda Cooley, 5147 South Front Road, Livermore, California 94550, USA.

West Highland White Terrier Club of Southern Michigan
Secretary: Ms Mary Lynne Bell, 3720 Woodland, Royal Oak, Michigan 48073, USA.

West Highland White Terrier Club of South-East Texas
Secretary: Kay M. Kelley, 8868 Cedarspur, Houston, Texas 77055, USA.

Trinity Valley West Highland White Terrier Club
Secretary: Ms Nelda Lane, 1412 Highland Road, Dallas, Texas, USA.

West Highland White Terrier Club of Western Pennsylvania
Secretary: Mrs Lois Drexler, 2410 Hahntown-Wendel Road, N. Huntington, Pennsylvania 15642, USA.

William Penn West Highland White Terrier Club
Secretary: Mrs Martha W. Black, Box 198 River Road, R.R.1,

Washington Crossing, Pennsylvania 18977, USA.

Canadian West Highland White Terrier Club. Formed 1951
Secretary: Mrs Renee Good, 63-270 Timberbank Blvd., Scarbo-
rough, Ontario M1W-2M, Canada.

The West Highland White Terrier Club of South Africa. Formed 1983
Secretary: Mrs Marge Heine, P.O. Box 781510, Sandton 2146, South
Africa.
Telephone—782-9301

The West Highland White Terrier Club of Australia. Formed 1963
Secretary: Mrs V. Regner, 4 Sutton Street, Blacktown, New South
Wales 2148, Australia.

The West Highland White Terrier Club of Victoria.
Secretary: Mrs M. Bradshaw, 17 Brixton Street, Bon Beach, Victoria
3196, Australia.

West Highland White Terrier Club of South Australia
Secretary: Mrs L. Mackness, 15 Brolga Avenue, Glenalta 5052,
South Australia

Note: It may be advisable for anyone wishing to contact any of the
American Westie clubs to check the name and address of the current
secretary with the West Highland White Terrier Club of America or the
American Kennel Club, 51 Madison Avenue, New York 10010.

WEST HIGHLAND WHITE TERRIER CHAMPIONS 1947 to 1988

Name	Sex	Sire	Dam	Owner	Breeder	Born
1947						
Betty of Whitehills	B	Garvie O'The Hills	Say Nought	Mrs V. Swan	Mrs F. Barr	27-2-44
Freshney Fiametta	B	Melbourne Mathias	Freshney Felicia	Miss E. E. Wade	Mrs M. McKinney	10-12-43
Shiningcliff Simon	D	Ch. Leal Flurry	Walney Thistle	Mrs J. Finch	Mrs J. Finch	10-5-45
Timoshenko of the Roe	D	Irish Ch. Tam O' Shanter of the Roe	Whisper of the Roe	The Hon. Torfrida Rollo	Mrs E. M. Ganett	23-3-45
1948						
Baffle of Branston	B	Freshney Frinton	Baroness of Branston	Mrs D. M. Dennis	Mrs D. M. Dennis	13-9-46
Brean Dearrsach	B	Brean Young of Lochinvar	Brean Everoch	Mrs E. O. Innes	Mrs E. O. Innes	1-4-43
Cruben Crystal	B	Freshney Andy	Cruben Miss Seymour	Dr & Mrs A. Russell	Dr & Mrs A. Russell	9-3-46
Deirdre of Kendrum	B	Roddy of Whitehills	Gyl of Kendrum	The Hon. T. H. Rollo	The Hon. T.H. Rollo	23-8-46
Hookwood Mentor	D	Furzefield Piper	Bonchurch Bunty	Miss E. E. Wade	Mr A. Brown	14-5-47
Macairns Jemima	B	Ch. Leal Sterling	Macairns Jeannie	Mr C. Drake	Mr C. Drake	1-8-43
Pygmalion of Patterscourt	D	Ch. Melbourne Mathias	Pola of Patterscourt	Mr W. Patterson	Mr W. Patterson	19-12-45
Wolvey Prospect	D	Ch. Wolvey Prefect	Wolvey Poise	Mrs C. Pacey	Mrs C. Pacey	14-10-44
1949						
Athos of Whitehills	D	Freshney Andy	Julie of Whitehills	Mrs V. M. Swam	Mrs V. M. Swam	18-12-45
Binnie of Branston	B	Freshney Andy	Belinda of Branston	Mrs D. M. Dennis	Mrs D. M. Dennis	28-8-45
Furzefield Pax	D	Furzefield Piper	Cassette of Eastfield	Mrs D. P. Allom	Mrs D. P. Allom	11-11-47

Lorne Jock	D	Freshney Andy	Fuff Ici	Messrs McEwan & McVicar	Messrs McEwan & McVicar	10-7-46
Macconachie Tiena Joy	B	Ch. Shiningcliff Simon	Macconachie Pearlie	Mr A. H. Salsbury	Mr A. H. Salsbury	27-10-47
Shiningcliff Storm	D	Leal Pax	Walney Thistle	Mr H. S. Hallas	Mrs J. Finch	13-11-46
Wolvey Penelope	B	Wolvey Parole	Wolvey Poise	Mrs C. Pacey	Mrs C. Pacey	5-11-45
Wolvey Prudence	B	Wolvey Premier	Wolvey Plume	Mrs C. Pacey	Mrs. C. Pacey	15-5-45
1950						
Barrister of Branston	D	Ch. Hookwood Mentor	Bloom of Branston	Mrs D. M. Dennis	Mrs D. M. Dennis	1-12-48
Brisk of Branston	D	Ch. Hookwood Mentor	Bloom of Branston	Mrs J. G. Winant	Mrs D. M. Dennis	11-7-49
Furzefield Preference	B	Furzefield Piper	Casette of Eastfield	Miss E. E. Wade	Mrs D. P. Allom	28-5-49
Heathcolne Roamer	D	Am. Ch. Cruben Silver Birk	Heathcolne Peggy Walker	Mrs N. M. Baxter	Mrs N. M. Baxter	14-1-44
Isla of Kendrum	B	Furzefield Piper	Ch. Deirdre of Kendrum	The Hon. T. Rollo	The Hon. T. Rollo	8-5-49
Maree of Kendrum	B	Furzefield Piper	Ch. Deirdre of Kendrum	The Hon. T. Rollo	The Hon. T. Rollo	8-5-49
Shiningcliff Sprig	D	Ch. Shiningcliff Simon	Freshney Folly	Mrs J. Finch	Mrs J. Finch	3-8-47
1951						
Cruben Dextor	D	Ch. Hookwood Mentor	Am. Ch. Cruben Melphis Chloe	Dr & Mrs Russell	Dr & Mrs Russell	17-1-50
Crystone Chatterer	B	Cruben Faerdele	Heathcolne Frolic	Mrs E. Anthony	Mrs E. Anthony	30-5-49
Chrystone Cherry	B	Ch. Heathcolne Roamer	Crystone Crystal	Mrs E. Anthony	Mrs E. Anthony	7-9-49
Furzefield Provost	D	Furzefield Piper	Calluna Nike	Mrs D. P. Allom	Miss A. A. Wright	30-10-48

Name	Sex	Sire	Dam	Owner	Breeder	Born
Hookwood Sensation	D	Ch. Hookwood Mentor	Ch. Freshney Fiametta	Miss E. E. Wade	Miss E. E. Wade	11-2-49
Lynwood Branston Blue	B	Ch. Hookwood Mentor	Bloom of Branston	Mrs M. G. Ellis	Mrs D. M. Dennis	2-12-48
Mallaig Silver Empress	B	Cruben Silver Birk	Mallaig Pola Maid	Miss E. E. Wade	Mr E. Bagshaw	22-6-47
Mark of Old Trooper	D	Ch. Shiningcliff Simon	Dainty Dinkie	Mr E. Ward	Mr E. Ward	17-1-48
Shiningcliff Snowcloud	B	Ch. Shiningcliff Simon	Shiningcliff Snow White	Mrs J. Finch	Mrs J. Finch	15-3-47
Shiningcliff Sultan	D	Ch. Melbourne Mathias	Walney Thistle	Mrs J. Finch	Mrs J. Finch	21-11-48
Staplands Shepherd	D	Shiningcliff Shardy	Cestrian Kilty	Mr & Mrs H. T. Walsh	Mr & Mrs H. T. Walsh	27-2-49
1952 Brush of Branston	B	Int. Ch. Brisk of Branston	Binty of Branston	Mrs D. M. Dennis	Mrs D. M. Dennis	3-10-50
Cotsmor Crunch	B	Hookwood Mentor	Cotsmor Crisp	Mrs R. Capper	Mrs R. Capper	26-3-50
Furzefield Pilgrim	D	Furzefield Piper	Furzefield Purpose	Mrs D. P. Allom	Mrs D. P. Allom	27-1-51
Hasty Bits	D	Claregate Benjamin of Branston	Walfield Fleur	Mrs G. M. Barr	Mrs G. M. Barr	13-12-50
Heathcolne Gowan	B	Ch. Heathcolne Roamer	Heathcolne White Sprig	Mrs F. M. Brown-ridge	Mrs N. Baxter	16-6-48
Perchance of Patterscourt	B	Petronius of Patterscourt	Perrow of Patterscourt	Mrs R. M. Jones	Mr W. J. Patterson	9-5-48
Shiningcliff Dunthorne Damsel	B	Shiningcliff Shardy	Pathton of Patters-court	Mrs J. Finch	Mrs G. Thorneycroft	18-2-49
Staplands Spitfire	D	Ch. Staplands Shepherd	Staplands Saint	Mr & Mrs H. T. Walsh	Mr & Mrs H. T. Walsh	9-7-50

146

Wolvey Piquet	B	Wolvey Presto	Wolvey Patsy	Mrs C. Pacey	Mrs C. Pacey	9-8-50
Wolvey Poster	D	Ch. Wolvey Prospect	Wolvey Phrolic	Mrs C. Pacey	Mrs C. Pacey	27-3-50
1953 Calluna the Poacher	D	Calluna Bingo	Calluna Vermintrude	Mrs A. Beels	Mrs A. Beels	27-3-52
Cotsmor Cream Puff	B	Ch. Barrister of Branston	Cotsmor Crisp	Mrs R. K. Capper	Mrs R. K. Capper	20-8-51
Cruben Moray	D	Int. Ch. Cruben Dextor	Cruben Fancy	Dr & Mrs Russell	Dr & Mrs Russell	8-9-51
Hookwood Gardenia	B	Ch. Hookwood Mentor	Barassie Bright Beam	Mrs G. M. Barr	Mr H. Galt	25-1-50
Lynwood Blue Betty	B	Furzefield Piper	Ch. Lynwood Branston Blue	Mr & Mrs G. Ellis	Mr & Mrs G. Ellis	21-7-50
Lynwood Timothy	D	Furzefield Piper	Ch. Lynwood Branston Blue	Mr & Mrs G. Ellis	Mr & Mrs G. Ellis	28-1-52
Rosalan Rogue	D	Ch. Hookwood Sensation	Rosalan Regina	Miss E. E. Wade	Mrs D. A. Phillips	13-5-51
Shiningcliff Donark Decision	D	Ch. Shiningcliff Simon	Donark Determined	Mrs F. Finch	Mrs L. Dwyer	17-4-50
Shiningcliff Sugar Plum	B	Ch. Shiningcliff Simon	Thalia of Trenean	Mrs F. Finch	Mrs G. Frost	1-4-51
Wolvey Peach	B	Wolvey Presto	Wolvey Patsy	Mrs C. Pacey	Mrs C. Pacey	9-8-50
Wolvey Poppet	B	Wolvey Paramount	Ch. Wolvey Peach	Mrs C. Pacey	Mrs C. Pacey	24-12-51
1954 Bannock of Branston	D	Ch. Barrister of Branston	Binty of Branston	Mrs D. M. Dennis	Mrs D. M. Dennis	11-6-52
Biretta of Branston	B	Ch. Barrister of Branston	Ch. Baffle of Branston	Mrs D. M. Dennis	Mrs D. M. Dennis	30-5-52
Cotsmor Creambun	B	Ch. Barrister of Branston	Cotsmor Crisp	Mrs R. Capper	Mrs R. Capper	20-8-51

Name	Sex	Sire	Dam	Owner	Breeder	Born
Eoghan of Kendrum	D	Ch. Barrister of Branston	Ch. Isla of Kendrum	Hon. T. Rollo	Hon. T. Rollo	3-7-52
Famecheck Lucky Charm	B	Ch. Shiningcliff Sultan	Famecheck Paddy Scalare	Miss F. M. C. Cook	Miss F. M. C. Cook	5-2-53
Laird of Lochalan	D	Ch. Rosalan Rogue	Susan of Northcliff	Mrs R. W. Scott	Mrs R. W. Scott	29-12-52
Mairi of Kendrum	B	Ch. Barrister of Branston	Ch. Isla of Kendrum	Miss J. Herbert	Hon T. Rollo	21-1-51
Tulyar of Trenean	D	Int. Ch. Cruben Dextor	Heathcolne Thistle	Mrs W. Dodgson	Mrs W. Dodgson	2-7-52
Wolvey Pageboy	D	Wolvey Paramount	Ch. Wolvey Peach	Mrs C. Pacey	Mrs C. Pacey	24-12-51
1955 Brendalee	B	Fruin of Kendrum	Dainty Brenda	Mrs H. M. Jeffrey	Mrs H. M. Jeffrey	18-11-53
Famecheck Viking	D	Ch. Calluna the Poacher	Famecheck Fluster	Miss F. M. C. Cook	Miss F. M. C. Cook	7-10-53
Lynwood Marcia	B	Ch. Wolvey Poster	Ch. Lynwood Branston Blue	Mr & Mrs G. Ellis	Mr & Mrs G. Ellis	10-2-53
Nice Fella of Wynsolot	D	Fan Mail of Wynsolot	Shiningcliff Starturn	Mrs E. A. Green	Mrs E. A. Green	24-5-53
Quakertown Quality	B	Ch. Calluna the Poacher	Calluna Miss Phoebe	Mr & Mrs H. Sansom	Mr & Mrs H. Sansom	13-2-54
Raventofts Fuchsia	B	Ch. Cruben Moray	Raventofts Periwinkle	Mrs N. Whitworth	Mrs N. Whitworth	10-1-53
Rowmore Brora of Kennishead	D	Int. Ch. Cruben Dextor	Cinda of Kennishead	Miss I. Maclean Cowie	Miss I. Maclean Cowie	10-6-52
Slitrig Solitaire	B	Ch. Furzefield Pilgrim	Slitrig Sequin	Mrs C. M. Kirby	Mrs C. M. Kirby	19-9-53
1956 Banda of Branston	B	Ch. Barrister of Branston	Binty of Branston	Mrs D. M. Dennis	Mrs D. M. Dennis	16-8-54
Bramhill Patricia	B	Calluna Big Wig	Bramhill Beatrix	Mr J. H. Gee	Mrs J. H. Gee	9-11-53

148

Name	Sex	Sire	Dam			Date
Broomheater Fianna	B	Int. Ch. Cruben Moray	Broomheather Flora	Mrs E. Hay	Mrs E. Hay	21-8-54
Famecheck Gay Crusader	D	Ch. Famecheck Happy Knight	Ch. Famecheck Lucky Charm	Miss F. M. C. Cook	Miss F. M. C. Cook	7-9-54
Famecheck Happy Knight	D	Ch. Calluna the Poacher	Famecheck Fluster	Miss F. M. C. Cook	Miss F. M. C. Cook	7-10-53
Slitrig Shandy	D	Ch. Barrister of Branston	Ch. Slitrig Solitaire	Mrs C. Pacey	Mrs C. M. Kirby	22-3-55
Wolvey Patricia	B	Ch. Wolvey Poster	Ch. Wolvey Peach	Mrs C. Pacey	Mrs C. Pacey	30-8-54
Wolvey Philippa	B	Ch. Wolvey Poster	Ch. Wolvey Peach	Mrs C. Pacey	Mrs C. Pacey	30-8-54
Wolvey Pied Piper	D	Furzefield Pilgrim	Wolvey Padella	Mrs C. Pacey	Mrs C. Pacey	14-4-55
1957						
Banker of Branston	D	Ch. Barrister of Branston	Binty of Branston	Mrs D. M. Dennis	Mrs D. M. Dennis	8-5-56
Cruben Chilibeam	B	Ch. Calluna the Poacher	Cruben Cutie	Dr & Mrs M. Russell	Dr & Mrs M. Russell	16-8-54
Crystone Cressina	B	Calluna Big Wig	Crystone Charming	Mrs E. Anthony	Mrs E. Anthony	12-12-55
Famecheck Ballet Dancer	B	Ch. Famecheck Viking	Famecheck Silver Dollar	Mrs G. Bingham	Miss Cook	26-12-55
Famecheck Comet	B	Ch. Famecheck Gay Crusader	Ch. Famecheck Lucky Mascot	Mr A. Berry	Miss F. M. C. Cook	20-7-56
Famecheck Lucky Mascot	B	Ch. Shiningcliff Sultan	Famecheck Paddy Scalare	Miss F. M. C. Cook	Miss F. M. C. Cook	5-2-53
Kirmbrae Symmetra Sailaway	D	Int. Ch. Cruben Moray	Denmohr Gay Girl	Miss J. Brown	Miss J. Brown	15-10-53
Mistymoor Andrea	B	Ch. Furzefield Pilgrim	Mistymoor Deirdre	Miss M. M. Batchelor	Miss M. M. Batchelor	2-11-54
Wolvey Pirate	D	Ch. Wolvey Pageboy	Wolvey Playmate	Mrs C. Pacey	Mrs C. Pacey	5-10-55

Name	Sex	Sire	Dam	Owner	Breeder	Born
1958						
Brindie of Branston	B	Ch. Banker of Branston	Bono of Branston	Mrs D. M. Dennis	Mrs D. M. Dennis	22-4-57
Calluna the Laird	D	Ch. Laird of Lochalan	Calluna Sheenagh	Miss A. A. Wright	Miss A. A. Wright	1-12-56
Famecheck Gaiety Girl	B	Ch. Famecheck Gay Crusader	Ch. Famecheck Lucky Mascot	Miss F. M. C. Cook	Miss F. M. C. Cook	24-1-56
Famecheck Lucky Choice	B	Ch. Shiningcliff Sultan	Famecheck Paddy Scalare	Miss F. M. C. Cook	Miss F. M. C. Cook	24-9-53
Famecheck Jolly Roger	D	Ch. Famecheck Happy Knight	Int. Ch. Famecheck Lucky Charm	Mr. A. Berry	Miss F. M. C. Cook	7-9-54
Freshney Fray	B	Ch. Barrister of Branston	Freshney Flute	Mrs P. M. Welch	Mrs M. McKinney	25-8-54
Joseydean Minuet	B	Ch. Furzefield Pilgrim	Bonchurch Bud	Mrs J. W. M. Martin	A. Brown	10-2-54
Quakertown Questionaire	D	Ch. Eoghon of Kendrum	Quakertown Questionmark	Mrs K. Sansom	Mrs K. Sansom	8-8-55
Rivelin Rustle	B	Rivelin Renown	Cruben Margaret	Mrs M. W. Pearson	Mrs M. Tazzyman	16-12-55
Shiningcliff Sheela	B	Shiningcliff So-So	Miss Prim	Mrs F. Finch	Miss Holland	9-7-55
Sollershott Sun-up	D	Ch. Nice Fella of Wynsolot	Cotsmor Crack O' Dawn	Mrs D. J. Kenney Taylor	Mrs D. J. Kenney Taylor	27-4-57
Stoneygap Commodore	D	Slitrig Skipper	Stoneygap Twig	Mrs G. M. Barr	Mrs G. M. Barr	23-5-57
Wolvey Piper's Son	D	Ch. Wolvey Pied Piper	Wolvey Pennywise	Mrs C. Pacey	Mrs C. Pacey	10-3-57
Wolvey Postmaster	D	Ch. Wolvey Poster	Wolvey Paulina	Mrs C. Pacey	Mrs C. Pacey	29-5-56
1959						
Banessa of Branston	B	Ch. Nice Fella of Wynsolot	Baffin of Branston	Mrs D. M. Dennis	Mrs D. M. Dennis	3-6-56

Name	Sex	Sire	Dam	Owner	Breeder	Date
Broomlaw Brandy	D	Eriegael Fabian O' Petriburg	Crystone Constance	Mrs M. B. Law	Mrs M. B. Law	21-1-57
Citrus Warbler	D	Ch. Famecheck Jolly Warrior	Famecheck Cygnet	Mrs M. Lemon	Mrs M. Lemon	14-1-57
Cruben Happy	B	Calluna Big Wig	Cruben Elsa	Dr & Mrs A. Russell	Dr & Mrs A. Russell	11-5-57
Eriegael Mercedes	D	Ch. Kirnbrae Symmetra Sailaway	Eriegael Andrasda	Miss J. Brown	Miss J. Brown	8-3-56
Famecheck Jolly Warrior	D	Ch. Famecheck Happy Knight	Int. Ch. Famecheck Lucky Charm	Miss F. M. C. Cook	Miss F. M. C. Cook	25-2-55
Furzefield Pickwick	D	Wolvey Postboy	Furzefield Picture	Mrs D. P. Allom	Mrs D. P. Allom	3-9-57
Phrana O' Petriburg	B	Calluna Big Wig	Phil O' Petriburg	Mrs A. Beels	Mrs A. Beels	23-6-58
Wolvey Palor	D	Ch. Wolvey Pirate	Wolvey Padella	Mrs C. Pacey	Mrs C. Pacey	23-5-57
Wolvey Pipers Tune	D	Ch. Wolvey Pied Piper	Ch. Wolvey Peach	Mrs C. Pacey	Mrs C. Pacey	23-6-57
Wolvey Postgirl	B	Ch. Wolvey Postmaster	Slitrig Spangle	Mrs Kirby	Mrs Kirby	30-9-57
1960 Bandsman of Branston	D	Ch. Banker of Branston	Ch. Banessa of Branston	Mrs D. M. Dennis	Mrs D. M. Dennis	27-9-58
Broomheather Freesia	B	Ch. Famecheck Jolly Roger	Ch. Broomheather Fianna	Mrs E. Hay	Mrs E. Hay	15-11-57
Eriegael Storm Child	B	Ch. Kirnbrae Symmetra Sailaway	Eriegael Martinette	Miss J. Brown	Miss J. Brown	11-1-59
Famecheck Gay Buccaneer	D	Ch. Famecheck Gay Crusader	Ch. Famecheck Lucky Mascot	Miss F. M. C. Cook	Miss F. M. C. Cook	12-4-59
Famecheck Joy	B	Int. Ch. Famecheck Viking	Ch. Famecheck Lucky Choice	Miss F. M. C. Cook	Miss F. M. C. Cook	9-1-55

Name	Sex	Sire	Dam	Owner	Breeder	Born
Famecheck Musketeer	D	Ch. Famecheck Gay Crusader	Ch. Famecheck Lucky Mascot	Miss F. M. C. Cook	Miss F. M. C. Cook	20-7-56
Glengyle Tapestry	B	Ch. Famecheck Gay Crusader	Ch. Freshney Fray	Mrs P. Welch	Mrs P. Welch	10-7-57
Stoneygap Flash	B	Ch. Furzefield Provost	Sheila Delight	Mrs G. M. Barr	Mr Hewett	12-7-59
Symmetra Skirmish	D	Tulyers Boy	Famecheck Lucky Star	Miss J. Brown	Mr & Mrs H. Mitchell	24-4-56
Wolvey Pavlova	B	Ch. Wolvey Palor	Wolvey Peewit	Mrs C. Pacey	Mrs C. Pacey	20-1-57
Wolvey Playgirl	B	Ch. Wolvey Pirate	Wolvey Padella	Mrs C. Pacey	Mrs C. Pacey	23-5-57
Workman of Wynsolot	D	Ch. Nice Fella of Wynsolot	Sally Ann of Wynsolot	Mrs E. A. Green	Mrs E. A. Green	17-10-58
1961 Brenda of Branston	B	Ch. Sollershott Sun-up	Ch. Brindie of Branston	Mrs D. M. Dennis	Mrs D. M. Dennis	1-2-60
Broomheather Fleur de Lis	B	Ch. Kirnbrae Symmetra Sailaway	Ch. Broomheather Fianna	Mrs E. Hay	Mrs E. Hay	20-6-58
Buttons of Helmsleigh	B	Ch. Furzefield Pickwick	Snowey Fee	Mrs G. M. Barr	Mr Rowland	4-3-59
Glengyle Thistle	B	Ch. Eriegal Mercedes	Ch. Glengyle Tapestry	Mrs P. M. Welch	Mrs P. M. Welch	23-5-58
Phancy O' Petriburg	B	Phryne O' Petriburg	Junyer Julie	Mrs A. Beels	Mr & Mrs A. Thomson	29-12-59
The Prior of Raventofts	D	Ch. Calluna the Laird	Pippa of Raventofts	Mrs N. Whitworth	Mrs N. Whitworth	7-3-60
Wolvey Permit	D	Ch. Wolvey Pipers Tune	Wolvey Pennywise	Mrs C. Pacey	Mrs C. Pacey	23-6-59
Wolvey Pickwick	D	Ch. Wolvey Pipers Tune	Wolvey Padella	Mrs C. Pacey	Mrs C. Pacey	13-2-59

1962						
Alpin of Kendrum	D	Quakertown Quizzical	Pixie of Kendrum	Hon T. H. Rollo	Hon T. H. Rollo	13-4-61
Banner of Branston	B	Ch. Banker of Branston	Bono of Branston	Mrs D. M. Dennis	Mrs D. M. Dennis	4-9-59
Banny of Branston	B	Ch. Banker of Branston	Bono of Branston	Mrs D. M. Dennis	Mrs D. M. Dennis	18-10-60
Birkfell Sea Shanty	B	Ch. Famecheck Jolly Roger	Birkfell Schottische	Miss S. Cleland	Miss S. Cleland	29-10-59
Birkfell Solitaire	B	Ch. Famecheck Jolly Roger	Birkfell Snowstorm	Miss S. Cleland	Miss S. Cleland	10-4-59
Famecheck Madcap	B	Ch. Famecheck Gay Crusader	Ch. Famecheck Lucky Mascot	Miss F. M. C. Cook	Miss F. M. C. Cook	20-10-59
Slitrig Sachet	B	Ch. Wolvey Postmaster	Slitrig Spangle	Mrs C. M. Kirby Mr L. Pearson	Mrs C. M. Kirby	28-8-58
Sollershott Soloist	D	Ch. Bandsman of Branston	Citrus Silhouette	Mrs D. J. Kenney Taylor	Mrs D. J. Kenney Taylor	28-6-60
Stoneygap Bobbin Gillobar	D	Bobbin of the Avenue	Stoneygap Rocky	Mr F. W. Fraser	Mrs G. M. Barr	10-8-60
Wolvey Punch	D	Ch. Wolvey Pipers Tune	Wolvey Peewit	Mrs C. Pacey	Mrs C. Pacey	15-6-60
1963						
Billybong of Branston	D	Ch. Bandsman of Branston	June of Braddocks	Mrs D. M. Dennis	Mrs Pickess	11-2-61
Busybody of Branston	B	Ch. Sollershott Sun Up	Ch. Brindie of Branston	Mrs D. M. Dennis	Mrs D. M. Dennis	2-10-61
Lasara Lee	B	Lasara Laddie	Lasara Lassie	Mrs B. Graham & Mrs G. Hazell	Mrs B. Graham & Mrs G. Hazell	9-10-61
Petriburg Mark of Polteana	D	Ch. Calluna the Poacher	Whitebriar Jantie	Mrs A. Beels	Dr M. W. Beaver	22-9-60

Name	Sex	Sire	Dam	Owner	Breeder	Born
Slitrig Shiningstar of Lynwood	B	Ch. Famecheck Gay Buccaneer	Slitrig Sweet Suzette	Mr & Mrs G. Ellis	Mrs C. Kirby	16–12–61
Sollershott Symphony	B	Ch. Bandsman of Branston	Citrus Silhouette	Mrs J. Kenney-Taylor	Mrs J. Kenney-Taylor	28–6–60
Stoneygap Sugar Candy of Manraf	B	Ch. Workman of Wynsolot	Sugar Puff of Manraf	Mr F. W. Fraser	Mrs M. A. Farnham	26–4–62
Waideshouse Woodpecker	D	Waideshouse Wallaby	Waideshouse Wicked-ness	Mr & Mrs B. Thomson	Mr & Mrs B. Thomson	3–4–62
Whitebriar Jimolo	D	Ch. Famecheck Jolly Roger	Whitebriar Juna	Mrs J. E. Beer	Mrs J. E. Breer	22–1–60
Wolvey Paperman	D	Ch. Wolvey Pickwick	Wolvey Pipinella	Mrs C. Pacey	Mrs C. Pacey	14–11–61
1964 Baggage of Branston	B	Ch. Billybong of Branston	Becky of Branston	Mrs D. M. Dennis	Mrs D. M. Dennis	13–6–62
Citrus Lochinvar of Estcoss	D	Ch. Sollershott Sun-up	Famecheck Foxtrot	Mrs V. L. W. Estcourt	Mrs M. Lemon	5–9–59
Kandymint of Carryduff	B	Gillie of Carryduff	Sugarmint of Carry-duff	Mr J. C. Bell	Mr J. C. Bell	18–3–60
Mahgni Wooster	D	Ch. Calluna the Laird	Symmetra Symbol	Mr J. W. Stead	Mr A. Ingram	3–3–60
Rhianfa Rifleman	D	Rhianfa the Rock	Rhianfa Cheyenne Bodie	Mr F. N. Sills	Mrs A. Sagar	15–6–60
Rivelin Rhumba	B	Ch. Famecheck Gay Crusader	Rivelin Ragtime	Mr B. Osborne	Mrs M. Pearson	2–8–59
Snowcliff Spring Song	B	Ch. Calluna the Laird	Sweet Reality	Messrs Pearson & Berry	Mrs W. Pearson	14–3–61
Quakertown Quistador	D	Ch. Alpin of Kendrum	Ch. Quakertown Querida	Mrs K. Sansom	Mrs K. Sansom	26–12–63

Waideshouse Warrant	D	Ch. Petriburg Mark of Polteana	Waideshouse Wickedness	Mr & Mrs B. Thomson	Mr & Mrs B. Thomson	15-12-62
Waideshouse Woodlark	B	Waideshouse Wallaby	Waideshouse Wickedness	Mr & Mrs B. Thomson	Mr & Mrs B. Thomson	3-4-62
1965						
Bardel of Branston	D	Ch. Billybong of Branston	Ch. Banner of Branston	Mrs D. M. Dennis & Mrs R. K. Mellon	Mrs D. M. Dennis	16-6-63
Briarrose of Branston	B	Ch. Sollershott Sun Up	Ch. Brindie of Branston	Mrs D. M. Dennis & Mrs R. K. Mellon	Mrs D. M. Dennis	11-12-62
Glengyle Teasle	B	Ch. Sollershott Soloist	Ch. Glengyle Thistle	Mrs P. M. Welch	Mrs P. M. Welch	13-12-61
Phelo O' Petriburg	B	Ch. Petriburg Mark of Polteana	Phino O' Petriburg	Mrs E. A. Beels	Mrs E. A. Beels	2-2-63
Phluster O' Petriburg	B	Ch. Petriburg Mark of Polteana	Ch. Phancy O' Petriburg	Mrs E. A. Beels	Mrs E. A. Beels	22-9-62
Pillerton Pippa	B	Ch. Petriburg Mark of Polteana	Pillerton Pickle	Mrs S. J. Kearsey	Mrs S. J. Kearsey	15-5-63
Sollershott Freshney Foy	D	Ch. Sollershott Sun-up	Freshney Faggot	Mrs J. Kenney-Taylor	Mrs McKinney	26-8-63
Sollershott Sober	D	Ch. Sollershott Soloist	Sollershott Daybreak	Mrs J. Kenney-Taylor	Mrs J. Kenney-Taylor	14-9-63
1966						
Alpinegay Impressario	D	Warberry Satellite	Warberry Wideawake	Mrs B. Wheeler	Mrs B. Wheeler	20-1-65
Birkfell Summer Sun	B	Ch. Kimbrae Symmetra Sailaway	Ch. Birkfell Solitaire	Miss S. Cleland	Miss S. Cleland	16-8-62
Famecheck Verona	B	Famecheck Romeo	Ch. Famecheck Gaiety Girl	Miss F. M. C. Cook	Miss F. M. C. Cook	19-9-63
Glengyle Blackpoint White Magic	B	Ch. Whitebriar Jimolo	Whitebriar Joris	Mrs P. M. Welch	Mrs P. Bird	11-3-62

155

Name	Sex	Sire	Dam	Owner	Breeder	Born
Incheril Amarylis	B	Ch. Petriburg Mark of Polteana	Raasay Spry	Mr C. W. Berry	Mr C. Berry	27-9-62
Monsieur aus der Flerlage	D	Int. Ch. Barnstormer of Branston	Daggy Hallodri	Miss B. Zakschewski	Mr W. Flerlage	17-11-62
Pillerton Peterman	D	Slitrig Simon of Lynwood	Pillerton Pickle	Mrs S. J. Kearsey	Mrs S. Kearsey	16-5-64
Pillerton Petra	B	Slitrig Simon of Lynwood	Pillerton Pickle	Mrs S. J. Kearsey	Mrs S. J. Kearsey	16-5-64
Waideshouse Wiloughby	D	Ch. Petriburg Mark of Polteana	Waideshouse Wickedness	Mr & Mrs B. Thomson	Mr & Mrs B. Thomson	7-8-63
1967 Birkfell Seafire	B	Ch. Kirnbrae Symmetra Sailaway	Ch. Birkfell Sea Shanty	Miss S. Cleland	Miss S. Cleland	4-10-62
Famecheck Hallmark	D	Famecheck Marksman	Famecheck Caprice	Miss F. M. C. Cook	Miss F. M. C. Cook	16-1-64
Famecheck Bernard	D	Famecheck Hallmark	Famecheck Banshee	Miss F. M. C. Cook and Dr Silfvast	Miss F. M. C. Cook	25-7-65
Famecheck Dainty Maid	B	Ch. Famecheck Hallmark	Famecheck Juliet	Miss F. M. C. Cook	Miss F. M. C. Cook	20-4-65
Glengyle Trader	D	Glengyle Tweed	Glengyle Tansy	Mrs P. M. Welch	Mrs P. M. Welch	3-8-61
Highstile Prank	D	Ch. Sollershott Soloist	Wolvey Puffin	Mrs M. Bertram	Mrs M. Bertram	6-5-64
Highstile Poppet	B	Ch. Quakertown Quistador	Wolvey Puffin	Mrs M. Bertram	Mrs M. Bertram	10-2-66
Lasara Louise	B	Int. Ch. Lasara Liegeman	Lasara Lydia	Mrs B. Graham and Mrs G. Hazell	Mrs B. Graham and Mrs G. Hazell	29-7-64
MacNab of Balmaha	D	Lymehills Rhianfa Viking	Pinkholme Prestige	J. Wilson	Mr & Mrs E. S. Vernon	9-11-65

156

	B/D	Sire	Dam	Breeder	Owner	Date
Masquerade of Bamburgh	B	Warberry Satellite	My Lady of Bamburgh	Mrs M. A. Beesley	Mrs M. A. Beesley	8-9-65
Morenish Geordie	D	Ch. Sollershott Freshney Froy	Morenish Jane	Mrs G. Wallace	Miss E. C. Grieve	21-1-66
Pinkholme Paramount	D	Ch. Citrus Lochinvar of Estcoss	Pinkholme Promise	Mrs I. Dickinson	Mrs I. Dickinson	2-2-63
Slitrig Goshell of Branston	D	Ch. Billybong of Branston	Slitrig Sweet Suzette	Mrs D. M. Dennis	Mrs C. Kirby	15-4-65
Snow Goblin	D	Rivelin Rector	Rayon Mill Penny	Mrs M. Hampson	Mr S. Allen	6-11-61
Strathairlie Swiss Miss	B	Ch. Bandsman of Branston	Strathairlie Starmist	Mrs M. Black	Mrs M. Black	24-9-62
Woodpuddle Bawbee	B	Calluna John O'Gaunt	Woodpuddle Bumble	Mrs C. Ingram	Mrs C. Ingram	20-1-64
1968 Alpinegay Sonata	D	Warberry Satellite	Warberry Wideawake	Miss C. Owen	Mrs. B. Wheeler	11-8-66
Famecheck Trojan	D	Ch. Famecheck Hallmark	Ch. Famecheck Verona	Miss F. M. C. Cook	Miss F. M. C. Cook	3-3-65
Famecheck Maid to Order	B	Ch. Famecheck Hallmark	Famecheck Helen	Miss F. M. C. Cook	Miss F. M. C. Cook	22-7-66
Lindenhall Discord	D	Ch. Citrus Warbler	Rainsborowe Bridie	Miss R. J. Fisher	Miss R. J. Fisher	4-3-66
Renlim Rachael	B	Ch. Pillerton Peterman	Wolvey Pardon Me	Mr and Mrs W. H. Milner	Mr and Mrs W. H. Milner	23-1-66
Rhianfa Up and Coming of Estcoss	B	Ch. Citrus Lochinvar of Estcoss	Rhianfa Rainsborowe Poppea	Mrs V. L. W. Estcourt	Mrs A. M. Sagar	27-7-64
Waideshouse Waterboy	D	Ch. Waideshouse Wiloughby	Ch. Waideshouse Woodlark	Mr and Mrs B. Thomson	Mr and Mrs B. Thomson	23-8-64

Name	Sex	Sire	Dam	Owner	Breeder	Born
Whitebriar Jillan	B	Can. Ch. Whitebriar Jamie	Whitebriar Jatoma	Mrs M. Coy	Mrs J. E. Breer	12–5–63
1968 Glengyle Tuggles	B	Ch. Billybong of Branston	Ch. Glengyle Tapestry	Mrs P. Welch	Mrs P. Welch	23–7–63
Quakertown Querida	B	Quakertown Quarrelsome	Cara of Kendrum	Mrs K. Sansom	Mrs K. Sansom	9–10–60
1969 Birkfell Solace	B	Ch. Pillerton Peterman	Ch. Birkfell Solitaire	Miss S. Cleland	Miss S. Cleland	16–5–66
Birkfell Solitude	B	Ch. Pillerton Peterman	Ch. Birkfell Solitaire	Miss S. Cleland	Miss S. Cleland	10–9–67
Checkbar Remony Rye	B	Broomheather Marksman	Brox Sundae	Mrs J. Taylor	Mrs E. Currie	3–9–65
Checkbar Donsie Kythe	D	Parkendcot Bobby Dazzler	Ch. Checkbar Remony Rye	Mrs J. Taylor	Mrs J. Taylor	23–11–67
Famecheck Sterling	B	Ch. Famecheck Hallmark	Famecheck Banshee	Miss F. Cook	Miss F. Cook	28–6–67
Famecheck Fashion Plate	B	Famecheck Man o'Mark	Famecheck Filibuster	Miss F. Cook and Mr P. Newman	Miss F. Cook	1–6–68
Glengyle Taiho	B	Ch. Bandsman of Branston	Ch. Glengyle Tapestry	Mrs P. Welch	Mrs P. Welch	22–9–62
Highstile Priceless	B	Ch. Alpin of Kendrum	Highstyle Pernickety	Mrs M. Bertram	Mrs M. Bertram	13–4–67
Lorrell Last Legacy	D	The Squire of Cardona	Lorrell Treasure	Mrs M. Duell	Mrs M. Duell	25–12–67
Lindenhall Drambuie	D	Ch. Sollershott Soloist	Rainsborowe Bridie	Mrs Millen	Mrs R. Beaver	15–1–65

158

Name	Sex	Sire	Dam	Breeder	Owner	Date
Lindenhall Donna	B	Ch. Citrus Warbler	Rainsborowe Bridie	Miss R. Fisher & Mr J. Wilson	Miss R. Fisher	4-3-66
Quakertown Quandry	D	Ch. Quakertown Quistator	Quakertown Queen	Mrs K. Sansom	Mrs K. Sansom	9-3-67
1970 Cedarfell Messenger Dove	B	Whitebriar Jackson	Ch. Whitebriar Jillan	Mrs H. Painting	Mrs M. Coy	7-8-67
Famecheck Air Hostess	B	Ch. Famecheck Trojan	Famecheck Rowena	Miss F. Cook	Miss F. Cook	11-7-67
Heath of Backmuir	D	Ch. Sollershott Freshney Foy	Highstile Pick Me Up	Mr & Mrs Gellan	Mr & Mrs Gellan	21-6-67
Rosyles Promise	D	Ch. Quakertown Quandary	Highstile Prim	Mrs S. Wood	Mrs S. Wood	5-10-68
Sumar Glengyle Tucket	B	Ch. Glengyle Trader	Ch. Glengyle Tuggles	Miss S. Jackson	Mrs P. Welch	25-10-67
Thornesian Marquis	D	Rocket Ranrou	Thornesian Cologyne	Mr & Mrs L. Haynes	Mr & Mrs L. Haynes	12-7-68
1971 Bradbury of Branston	D	Bartel of Branston	Blue Velvet of Branston	Mrs D. M. Dennis	Mrs D. M. Dennis	27-8-66
Ballacoar Musetta of Cedarfell	B	Whitebriar Jackson	Ch. Whitebriar Jillan	Mrs S. Morgan	Mrs M. Coy	28-4-69
Birkfell Something Stupid	B	Ch. Macnab of Belmaha	Ch. Birkfell Solace	Miss S. Cleland	Miss S. Cleland	7-1-68
Cedarfell Merry-'n-Bright	D	Cedarfell Man o' Minx	Cedarfell Minuet	Mrs M. Coy	Mrs M. Coy	14-2-70
Famecheck Glamis	B	Ch. Famecheck Hallmark	Shadwin Shanto Bella	Miss F. Cook	Miss F. Cook	8-5-69
Highstile Phidget	B	Ch. Quakertown Quandary	Highstile Pernickety	Mrs M. Bertram	Mrs M. Bertram	30-10-70

Name	Sex	Sire	Dam	Owner	Breeder	Born
Incheril Inge	B	Halfmerke Monarch	Incheril Ilex	Mrs C. Berry	Mrs C. Berry	25-1-69
Pillerton Peterkin	D	Ch. Pillerton Peterman	Pillerton Polka	Mrs S. Kearsey	Mrs S. Kearsey	29-1-68
Sealaw Selena	B	Ch. Macnab of Balmaha	Betsy May of Balmaha	Mr G. Corish	Mr G. Corish	16-12-67
Checkbar Tommy Quite Right	D	Ch. Alpin of Kendrum	Ch. Checkbar Remonay Rye	Mrs J. Taylor	Mrs J. Taylor	20-4-69
Whitebriar Jonfair	D	Whitebriar Johncock	Whitebriar Jeenay	Mr J. Hodsall	Mrs J. Beer	1-6-70
1972 Birkfell Sea Squall	D	Ch. Quakertown Quandary	Birkfell Sea Fury	Miss S. Cleland	Miss S. Cleland	20-11-70
Birkfell Solicitude	B	Ch. Famecheck Hallmark	Ch. Birkfell Solitude	Miss S. Cleland	Miss S. Cleland	18-12-68
Famecheck Busybody	B	Ch. Famecheck Hallmark	Famecheck Wellmaid	Miss F. M. C. Cook	Miss F. M. C. Cook	7-11-70
Lasara Limpet	B	Ch. Pillerton Peterman	Lasara Limit	Mrs B. Graham & Hazell	Mrs B. Graham & Hazell	27-1-67
Melwyn Pillerton Picture	B	Eriegael Storm Warning	Ch. Pillerton Pippa	Mrs R, Pritchard	Mrs S. Kearsey	30-8-68
Medalist of Cedarfell	D	Provost o' Petriburg	Ch. Whitebriar Jillan	Mrs B. Armstrong	Mrs M. Coy	14-10-68
Rhianfa Take Notice	D	Lymehills Birkfell South Pacific	Rhianfa Lady Constance of Estcoss	Miss C. Owen	Mrs A. Sagar	24-2-69
Sarmac Heathstream Drummer Boy	D	Ch. Lindenhall Drambuie	Heathstream Cedarfell Misty Dell	Mrs A. Millen	Mrs Farnes	11-5-69
Tasman March of Time	D	Ch. Highstile Prank	Pillerton Pollyann	Mrs C. Bonas	Mrs C. Bonas	21-9-68
White Rose of Ide	B	Ch. Heath of Backmuir	Gala of Backmuir	Mr P Newman	Mr & Mrs Gellan	26-7-70

160

Tasman Adoration	B	Tasman Temptation	Tasman Beau	Mrs C. Bonas	Mrs C. Bonas	8-8-70
1973						
Gaywyn Gypsy	B	Ch. Alpinegay Sonata	Ch. Phelo O' Petriburg	Miss C. Owen	Mrs E. A. Beels	24-6-69
Famecheck Heirloom	B	Ch. Famecheck Hallmark	Ch. Famecheck Air Hostess	Miss F. M. C. Cook	Miss F. M. C. Cook	25-8-70
Clantartan Chrysanthemum	B	Clantartan Carnog Crest	Clantartan Calla Pippa	Mrs J. Blakey	Mrs J. Blakey	19-6-69
Lasara Linda Belle	B	Ch. Pillerton Peterman	Lasara Lydia	Mrs B. Graham & Mrs G. Hazell	Mrs B. Graham & Mrs G. Hazell	20-10-65
Pillerton Prejudice	B	Ch. Pillerton Peterman	Birkfell Screech Owl	Mrs S. Kearsey	Mr M. Collings	21-4-71
Halfmarke Marina	B	Toibeech White Cockade	Halfmerke Moonbeam	Mr G. D. Green	Mr G. D. Green	9-11-70
Drumcope Dewdrop	B	Ch. Checkbar Donsie Kythe	Drumcope Bonnie	Mrs N. Copeland	Mrs N. Copeland	23-8-70
Nailbourne Nutcracker	B	Ch. Lindenhall Discord	Quakertown Quincella	Mrs H. Davies	Mrs L. B. Bell	6-7-69
Easter Bonnetina	B	Rivelin Jock	Samantha of the Highlands	Mrs B. Pogson	Mr G. Lancaster	2-4-69
Commander of Tintibar	D	Ch. Checkbar Donsie Kythe	Sally of Clyndarose	Mr & Mrs H. S. Brittain	Mrs. E. Brittain	30-4-69
Gaywyn Bradey of Branston	D	Ch. Alpinegay Sonata	Beautiful Biddy of Branston	Miss C. Owen	Mrs D. M. Dennis	27-6-69
Ardenrun Andsome of Purston	D	Ch. Whitebriar Jonfair	Ardenrun Agitator	Mr M. Collings	Mr C. Oakley	18-6-72
Purston Petite	B	Ch. Pillerton Peterman	Birkfell Screech Owl	Mr A. Parr	Mr M. Collings	21-4-71

Name	Sex	Sire	Dam	Owner	Breeder	Born
Glengordon Finearte Prince of Peace	D	Ch. Sarmac Heathstream Drummer Boy	Ch. Cedarfell Messenger Dove	Mrs K. Budden	Mrs H. Painting	14-11-70
Cedarfell Moon Melody	B	Ch. Lindenhall Drambuie	Cedarfell Minuet	Mr R. Armstrong	Mrs M. Coy	3-7-69
1974 Birkfell Soliloquy	B	Ch. Famecheck Hallmark	Ch. Birkfell Solitude	Miss S. Cleland	Miss S. Cleland	16-12-68
Checkbar Finlay MacDougal	D	Ch. Checkbar Donsie Kythe	Happy Sheila Belle	Mrs J. Taylor	Mrs J. Taylor	30-8-71
Milburn Mandy	B	Ch. Quakertown Quandary	Milburn Melody	Mr N. Herbison	Mr N. Herbison	29-10-71
Dianthus Buttons	D	Ch. Alpin of Kendrum	Starcyl Sioux	Mrs Newstead	Mrs Newstead	1-1-72
Furzeleigh Last Edition	B	Ch. Rhianfa's Take Notice	Whitebriar Jeenay	Mr J. Hodsoll	Mr J. Hodsoll	17-11-72
Olac Moonraker	D	Pillerton Perry	Miranda Moon of Olac	Mr D. Tattersall	Mr D. Tattersall	3-4-73
Famecheck Silver Charm	B	Ch. Famecheck Hallmark	Ch. Famecheck Air Hostess	Mr. A. Torbet	Miss F. M. C. Cook	16-4-73
Birkfell Silver Thistle of Clanestar	B	Ch. Birkfell Sea Squall	Ch. Birkfell Solitude	Mrs D. K. Lancaster	Miss S. Cleland	15-1-72
Purston Peter Pan	D	Ch. Pillerton Peterman	Birkfell Screech Owl	Mr. M. Collings	Mr. M. Collings	24-11-72
Eriscort Special Request	D	Ch. Quakertown Quandry	Eriscort Domaroy Debutante	Mr R. Hodgkinson	Mr R. Hodgkinson	2-7-72
Drumcope Teddy Tar	D	Ch. Checkbar Donsie Kythe	Drumcope Bonnie	Mrs N. Copeland	Mrs N. Copeland	23-8-70

Henry C. Schley

American Ch. Lymehills Birkfell Solstice, 1971

Wilhelm Dufwa

Int. and Nordic Ch. Tweed Tartan Maid, 1971

Seven Birkfell Champions, 1972
left to right: Seafire, Summer Sun, Solace, Solitude, Sea Shanty,
Something Stupid, Solicitude

Ch. Dianthus Buttons – Supreme Champion, Crufts, 1976

Ch. Carillyon Cadence, 1975

Anne Roslin-Williams

Ch. Glenalwyne Sonny Boy, 1975 – the breed record holder with 33 CCs

Gerald Foyle

Ch. Glengordon Hannah, 1975

Gustav Adolph Eck

Int. Nordic and Swedish Ch. Gaywyn Dandini,
Golden Dog 1976

Lucky of Loughore	D	Glentromie Peter	Lupin of Loughore	Mr J. S. Madill	Mr J. S. Madill	23-5-70
Highstile Popsy	B	Quakertown Quireboy	Ch. Highstile Poppet	Mrs M. Bertram	Mrs M. Bertram	8-10-70
1975 Candida of Crinan	B	Selig Rustin of Crinan	Highstile Pixie	Mrs B. Hands	Mrs C. Clay	4-9-72
Melwyn Milly Molly Mandy	B	Cedarfell Man O' Minx	Ch. Melwyn Pillerton Picture	Mrs. R. Pritchard	Mrs R. Pritchard	30-12-71
Binate Inveraray	D	Braidholme White Tornado of Binate	Drumcope Starry Mist	Mr & Mrs Haverhand	Mrs Copeland	26-10-71
Robbie McGregor of Wyther Park	D	Nolstar Snowstorm	Nolstar Patine	Miss A. Garnett	Mr Schmidt	9-8-71
Carillyon Cadence	B	Ch. Cedarfell Merry-N-Bright	Whitebriar Jamanda	Mrs. T. M. Lees	Mrs T. M. Lees	24-2-72
Justrite Jacinda	B	Ch. Medallist of Cedarfell	Ch. Cedarfell Moon Melody	Mr & Mrs R. Armstrong	Mr & Mrs R. Armstrong	7-5-73
Ballacoar Samantha	B	Cedarfell Man-O-Minx	Blackpoynt Blythe Spirit	Mrs P. Graham	Mrs S. Morgan	29-9-72
Glenalwyne Sonny Boy	D	Ch. Cedarfell Merry-N-Bright	Clynebury Silver Kilt	Miss J. Herbert	Miss J. Herbert	20-3-73
Glengordon Hannah	B	Ch. Glengordon Finearte Prince of Peace	Glengordon Suzette	Mrs M. Torbet	Mrs H. Budden	8-12-71
Yelrav Spangle	B	Yelrav Gay Marquis	Yelrav Scorcha	Mr & Mrs Brownhill	Mr & Mrs E. Varley	5-10-72
Incheril at Large	D	Ch. Checkbar Donsie Kythe	Incheril Ispedixit	Mr C. Berry	Mr C. Berry	8-1-74

Name	Sex	Sire	Dam	Owner	Breeder	Born
1976						
Olac Moonbeam	B	Ch. Olac Moonraker	Tasman Ovation	Mr D. Tattersall	Mr D. Tattersall	12-10-74
Birkfell Snowbird	B	Ch. Birkfell Sea Squall	Ch. Birkfell Solace	Miss S. Cleland	Miss S. Cleland	5-11-72
Kirkgordon Musical Cowboy	D	Ch. Medallist of Cedarfell	Kirkgordon Meldoy	Mr P. Hyne	Mrs M. Dickinson	4-12-72
Meryt Silver Secret	B	Ch. Rhainfa's Take Notice	Ch. Easter Bonnetina	Mrs B. Pogson	Mrs B. Pogson	9-3-74
Backmuir Noble James	D	Famecheck Major Domo	Backmuir Mary Stuart	Mr & Mrs Gellan	Mr & Mrs Gellan	9-10-73
Ashgate Lochinvar	D	Quakertown Quintar	Tervin Penny of Binate	Mrs S. Thomson	Mrs S. Thomson	6-12-73
Whitebriar Jimmick	D	Ch. Whitebriar Jonfair	Whitebriar Jesca	Mrs J. E. Beer and Miss Murphy	Mrs Beer	20-10-72
Incheril Impudence	B	Ch. Checkbar Finlay MacDougal	Ch. Incheril Inge	Mr C. Berry	Mr C. Berry	24-1-74
1977						
Ashgate Stewart of Greenveldt	D	Tervin Pacey of Ashgate	Ballacoar Simona	Mr & Mrs Green	Mrs Thomson	7-10-74
Domaroy Last Pennyworth	D	Ch. Birkfell Sea Squall	Rhianfa's Eliza For Common	Mr & Mrs Wilshaw	Mr & Mrs Wilshaw	2-8-73
Incheril Say No More	B	Ch. Checkbar Finlay MacDougal	Incheril Isadora	Mr C. W. Berry	Mr C. W. Berry	4-2-75
Pitskelly Tam O'Shanter	D	Ch. Angligate Tom Cobleigh	Pitskelly Hiney	Miss R. E. Ogilvie	Miss R. E. Ogilvie	21-8-75

Millburn Merrymaid	B	Ch. Lucky of Loughore	Ch. Milburn Mandy	Mr M. Collings	Mr H. Herbison	7-3-75
Tasman Elation of Ashgate	B	Ch. Tasman March of Time	Ch. Tasman Adoration	Mrs S. Thomson	L. Bonas	4-8-74
Morenish Fanny MacDougal	B	Ch. Checkbar Finlay MacDougal	Morenish Janie Alison	Miss E. C. Grieve	Miss E. C. Grieve	11-3-74
Domaroy Erisort Serenade	B	Highstile Pirate	Erisort Domaroy Debutante	Mr & Mrs Wilshaw	Mr K. Hodkinson	22-11-73
Gleneyre Sweetbriar	B	Ch. Birkfell Sea Squall	Birkfell Sweet Charity	Mrs K. M. Gallagher	Mrs K. M. Gallagher	6-1-73
Whitebriar Jennymoon	B	Ch. Whitebriar Jonfair	Whitebriar Jesca	Mrs J. E. Beer & Miss M. Murphy	Mrs J. E. Beer	20-10-72
Whitebriar Jaydixie	B	Ch. Whitebriar Jonfair	Whitebriar Jesca	Mrs J. E. Beer & Miss M. Murphy	Mrs J. E. Beer	16-10-74
1978 Angilgate Tom Cobleigh	D	Ch. Whitebriar Jonfair	Angilgate Ready About	Mrs B. Strivens	Mrs B. Strivens	21-7-73
Domaroy Saraband of Whitebriar	D	Ch. Tasman March of Time	Ch. Domaroy Erisort Serenade	Mrs J. E. Beer & Miss M. Murphy	Mr & Mrs R. Wilshaw	24-1-76
Domaroy Saracen	D	Ch. Tasman March of Time	Ch. Domaroy Erisort Serenade	Mr & Mrs R. Wilshaw	Mr & Mrs R. Wilshaw	24-1-76
Lasara Lots of Fun	D	Lasara Lincoln	Famecheck Corinne of Lasara	Miss J. Kabel	Mrs B. Graham & Mrs G. Hazell	17-10-73
Tervin Perigrine At Checkbar	D	Ch. Checkbar Finlay MacDougal	Pied Piper of Tervin	Mrs Jean L. Taylor	Mr & Mrs J. Lowry	1-11-75
Carillyon Caraval of Clarinch	B	Ch. Whitebriar Jonfair	Ch. Carillyon Cadence	Mrs P. M. Buchanan	Mrs T. M. Lees	20-11-75
Famecheck Holy Orders	B	Famecheck Firm Favourite	Famecheck Maid to Order	Mrs B. Graham & Miss J. Kabel	Miss F. M. C. Cook	11-9-75

Name	Sex	Sire	Dam	Owner	Breeder	Born
Glenalwyne Shieldu	B	Ch. Cedarfell Merry-N-Bright	Clynebury Silver Kilt	Miss J. Herbert	Miss J. Herbert	20-3-73
Kirkgordon Morning Song	B	Ch. Medallist of Cedarfell	Kirkgordon Melody	Mrs M. H. Webster	Mrs M. Dickinson	4-12-72
Kristajen Copyright	B	Kristajen Tom Thumb	Kristajen Little Bo Peep	Mr K. & Mrs J. Abbey	Mr K. & Mrs J. Abbey	16-2-74
Norjons Anastasia of Whitebriar	B	Ch. Ashgate Lochinvar	Whitebriar Joskitty	Mrs J. E. Beer & Miss M. Murphy	Mrs L. D. Mitchell	8-9-76
Rotella Royal Penny	B	Ch. Olac Moonraker	Rotella Regal Lady	R. Wright	R. Wright	23-3-75
Tollcross Fiona	B	Ch. Purston Peter Pan	Tollcross Escoss Peggotty	Mrs M. K. Greening	Mrs M. K. Greening	1-1-76
1979 Ashgate Lairg	D	Ashgate Stirling	Ashgate Lingay	Mrs S. Thomson	Mrs S. Thomson	7-8-75
Camphill Kelly	D	Mac's Ryan of Sandyknowes	Camphill Janeayre	N. Simpson	N. Simpson	5-10-77
Famecheck Extra Special	D	Famecheck Royal Binge	Famecheck Special Order	Miss F. M. C. Cook	Miss F. M. C. Cook	17-12-76
Olac Moondrift	D	Ch. Backmuir Noble James	Miranda Moon of Olac	D. Tattersall	D. Tattersall	25-1-76
Tweed Tartan Caledonier	D	Nord. Ch. Tweed Tory	Tweed Tartan Maid	Mrs B. Hasselgren	Mrs B. Hasselgren	13-4-73
Birkfell Sunrise	B	Int. & Eng. Ch. Lasara Lots of Fun	Birkfell So Simple	Mrs J. Abbey	Miss S. Cleland	20-6-77
Erisort Sleighbelle	B	Arnholme Arrogance of Crinan	Ch. Erisort Something Special	Mrs B. H. Hands & Mr K. Hodkinson	Mr K. Hodkinson	24-12-77

Name	Sex	Sire	Dam			Date
Erisort Something Special	B	Ch. Erisort Special Request	Erisort Speculation	K. S. Hodkinson	K. S. Hodkinson	1-9-76
Sumar Sosues	B	Ch. Checkbar Finlay MacDougal	Ch. Sumar Glengyle Tucket	Miss S. M. Jackson	Miss S. M. Jackson	2-2-77
Tasman Impression of Macbec	B	Famecheck Midnite Marauder	Tasman Scintillation	Mrs F. Becquet	C. K. Bonas	19-6-75
Willmay Womble	B	Ch. Olac Moonraker	Arnholme Adorable of Willmay	Mr & Mrs R. Cummins	Mr & Mrs R. Cummins	3-1-77
1980 Ardenrun Merryman of Sarmac	D	Ch. Sarmac Heath-stream Drummer Boy	Ardenrun Northern Light	Mrs A. Millen	Mr Oakley	10-8-75
Furzeleigh Startrek	D	Ch. Whitebriar Jimmick	Ashgate Hightae	Mr J. Hodsoll	Mr J. Hodsoll	11-9-77
Kilbrannon Kid Kurrie Is Justrite	D	Ch. Whitebriar Jimmick	Jayne of Justrite at Kilbrannon	Mr & Mrs Armstrong	Mrs M. Webster	3-2-78
Poolmist Pauchte	D	Ch. Purston Peter Pan	Poolmist Pert Dobbie	Mr J. H. M. Jansen	Mr & Mrs Foulkes	5-10-78
Rotella Mighty Mike	D	Ch. Erisort Special Request	Ch. Rotella Royal Fortune	Mr R. Wright	Mr R. Wright	6-1-79
Whitebriar Jeronimo	D	Lasara Loyal	Ch. Whitebriar Jennymoon	Mrs J. E. Beer & Miss M. Murphy	Mrs J. E. Beer & Miss M. Murphy	3-3-78
Halfmoon of Olac	B	Ch. Olac Moondrift	Arnholme Temperley Tangerine	Mr D. Tattersall	Mr & Mrs Parr	18-9-79
Olac Moondream	B	Eng. & Nordic Ch. Tweed Tartan Caledonier	Ch. Olac Moonbeam	Mr D. Tattersall	Mr D. Tattersall	31-3-78
Rotella Royal Fortune	B	Ch. Birkfell Sea Squall	Ch. Rotella Royal Penny	Mr R. Wright	Mr R. Wright	18-10-76

Name	Sex	Sire	Dam	Owner	Breeder	Born
Whitebriar Jillsown	B	Eng. & N. Z. Ch. Domaroy Saraband of Whitebriar	Ch. Whitebriar Jaydixie	Mrs J. E. Johnson	Mrs J. E. Beer & Miss M. Murphy	28-12-76
Arnholme Ad-Lib	D	Ch. Olac Moonraker	Admiration of Arnholme	Mr & Mrs Gordon	Mr & Mrs A. Parr	31-7-77
Grierson Fancy	B	Ch. Kirkgordon Musical Cowboy	Ardenrun Delilah	Mrs D. De Terry	Mrs V. H. Cook	20-6-76
1981						
Arnholme April Jester	D	Ch. Olac Moondrift	Tancharny Alicia of Arnholme	Mr & Mrs A Parr	Mr & Mrs A Parr	19-4-79
Guilliland Grant	D	Guilliland Glencairn	Guilliland Gael	J. Guthrie	J. Guthrie	22-7-78
Haweswalton Houdini	D	Ch. Cedarfell Merry-N-Bright	*Haweswalton Veiled Venus	Mrs S. Hawes	Mrs S. Hawes	4-3-80
Lasara Loyals Pick	D	Lasara Loyal	Famecheck Corinne of Lasara	Mrs B. Graham & Miss J. Kabel	Mrs B. Graham & Miss J. Kabel	10-4-77
Newtonglen Foot Print	D	Ch. Glengordon Finearte Prince of Peace	Newtonglen Lorna	Mrs M. Torbet	Mrs M. Torbet	24-8-79
Newtonglen Macintosh	D	Ch. Glengordon Finearte Prince of Peace	Newtonglen Lorna	Mrs M. Torbet	Mrs M. Torbet	7-7-78
Strathtay Viking at Domaroy	D	Ch. Domaroy Saracen	Strathtay Roseabelle	Mrs & Mrs R. Wilshaw	Mr & Mrs Lindsay	6-5-78
Ashgate Carnassarie	B	Ch. Ashgate Lairg	Ch. Tasman Elation of Ashgate	Mrs S. Thomson	Mrs S. Thomson	13-9-78
Birkfell Spinning Jenny	B	Ch. Erisort Special Request	Birkfell Something Shy	Miss S. Cleland	Miss S. Cleland	22-9-79

Name	Sex	Sire	Dam	Breeder	Owner	Date
Famecheck Bright Star	B	Ch. Famecheck Extra Special	Famecheck Adamant	Miss F. M. C. Cook	Miss F. M. C. Cook	28-5-78
Famecheck Full O' Beans	B	Ch. Famecheck Extra Special	Famecheck Royal Beano	Miss F. M. C. Cook	Miss F. M. C. Cook	25-12-78
Famecheck Specialist	B	Ch. Famecheck Extra Special	Famecheck Gay Manner	Miss F. M. C. Cook	Miss F. M. C. Cook	1-1-78
Lasara Lend A Hand	B	Eng & Dutch Ch. Lasara Lots of Fun	Ch. Famecheck Holy Orders	Mrs C. Hartmann	Mrs B. Graham & Miss J. Kabel	26-12-77
Whitebriar Jannine at Sumaba	B	Ch. Whitebriar Jimmick	Whitebriar Jasnina	Mrs S. M. Baccino	Miss Kellow	3-7-78
Japple of Whitebriar	D	Lasara Loyal	Whitebriar Jarippa	Mrs J. E. Beer & Miss M. Murphy	Mrs A. Appleby	6-6-76
1982						
Ashgate Claymore	D	Ch. Ashgate Lairg	Ashgate Clola	Mrs S. Thomson	Mrs S. Thomson	23-7-77
Haweswalton Mr Volvo	D	Ch. Domaroy Saracen	Haweswalton Gay Spark	Mrs S. Hawes	Mrs S. Hawes	21-4-79
Kilbrannon Crispin	D	Kilbrannon Curtain Up	Jayne of Justrite at Kilbrannon	Mrs M. H. Webster	Mrs M. H. Webster	24-11-79
Sarmac Big Snob	D	Ch. Domaroy Saracen	Sarmae Silver Sequin	Mrs E. A. Millen	Mrs E. A. Millen	23-11-77
Ashgate Glamis	B	Ch. Domaroy Saracen	Ashgate Cromarty	Mrs S. Thomson	Mrs S. Thomson	22-2-77
Crinan Candee	B	Arnholme Arrogance of Crinan	Crinan Christiana	Mrs B. H. Hands	Mrs B. H. Hands	26-8-77
Incheril Evita	B	Ch. Birkfell Sea Squall	Incheril Say No More	C. W. Berry	C. W. Berry	30-12-77
Lasara Like-A-Lot	B	Eng. & Dutch Ch. Lasara Lots of Fun	Ch. Famecheck Holy Orders	Mrs B. Graham & Miss J. Kabel	Mrs B. Graham & Miss J. Kabel	20-5-79

Name	Sex	Sire	Dam	Owner	Breeder	Born
Trethmore Tom Boy	B	Trethmore Tommy Owt	Trethmore Tartan Dancer	Miss E. M. Wilson	Miss E. M. Wilson	31-7-79
Whitebriar Jaunty	B	Ch. Pitskelly Tam O'Shanter	Ch. Whitebriar Jennymoon	Mrs J. E. Beer & Miss M. Murphy	Mrs J. E. Beer	30-9-76
1983 Highstile Paladin	D	Ch. Domaroy Saracen	Highstyle Party Manners	Mrs M. Bertram	Mrs M. Bertram	8-6-81
Haweswalton Sportsman	D	Ch. Haweswalton Mr Volvo	Whitebriar Jeanette	Mrs S. Hawes	Mrs S. Hawes	14-1-82
Jaimont of Whitebriar	D	Eng NZ & Aust Ch. Domaroy Saraband of Whitebriar	Whitebriar Jayla	Mr & Mrs R. & B. Armstrong	J. Drummond-Dunn	26-3-79
Melwyn Mastermind	D	Cedarfell Masterfull	Melwyn Molly Malone	Mr & Mrs E. L. & J.W. Roylance	Mr & Mrs Pritchard	24-5-78
Arnholme Aphrodite	B	Ch. Arnholme April Jester	Willmay What-a-Lass at Arnholme	Mr & Mrs Bowden	Mr & Mrs Parr	23-5-80
Backmuir Sweetbriar	B	Ch. Heath of Backmuir	Backmuir Nettle	Miss E. M. MacAllan	Mr & Mrs Gellan	20-8-78
Crinan Celtic Song	B	Morenish Just William	Crinan Celtic Ayre	Mrs B. H. Hands	Mrs B. H. Hands	29-10-81
Famecheck Radio Star	B	Ch. Famecheck Extra Special	Famecheck Adamant	Miss F. M. C. Cook	Miss F. M. C. Cook	28-5-78
Famecheck Superlative/ Super-Active	B	Ch. Famecheck Extra Special	Famecheck Super Sonic	Miss F. M. C. Cook	Miss F. M. C. Cook	31-8-80
Olac Moonpoppy	B	Olac Mooncopy of Marank	Ch. Halfmoon of Olac	D. Tattersall	D. Tattersall	21-4-82

170

Snowqueen of Furzeleigh	B	Ch. Whitebriar Jeronimo	Norjons Anthea	J. Hodsoll	Rowe	4-9-79
1984						
Angus of Furzeleigh	D	Furzeleigh Drum Major	Whitebriar Janyetta	J. Hodsoll	Mrs Hepburn	19-4-82
Arnholme A-Cinch	D	Ch. Arnholme April Jester	Arnholme Annalise of Poolmist	Mr A. Gordon & Mrs D. M. Parr	Mr & Mrs Parr	16-10-80
Ashgate Culnacraig	D	Ch. Ashgate Claymore	Ashgate Kylesmorer	S. Thomson & G. Grandfield	S. Thomson	21-11-81
Casstine Magregor at Kilbrannon	D	Ch. Kilbrannon Crispin	Gaelicglory-Gemma	Mrs M. H. Webster	Mrs Codling	3-4-81
Domaroy Suzerain	D	Ch. Domaroy Saracen	Domaroy Starshine	Mr & Mrs R. Wilshaw	Mr & Mrs R. Wilshaw	23-1-83
Midshipman of Haweswalton	D	Ch. Haweswalton Houdini	White Misty of Kenstaff	Mrs S. Hawes	Mr & Mrs Owen	25-12-82
Lasara Lookatim	D	Can. Ch. Haweswalton Man About Town	Ch. Famecheck Holy Orders	Mrs B. Graham & Miss J. Kabel	Mrs B. Graham & Miss J. Kabel	25-1-81
Ashgate Ailsa Craig	B	Ch. Ashgate Claymore	Ch. Tasman Elation of Ashgate	Mrs S. Thomson	Mrs S. Thomson	10-12-77
Domaroy Silver Fern	B	Ch. Erisort Special Request	Strathtay Tamarind of Domaroy	Mr & Mrs R. Wilshaw	Mr & Mrs R. Wilshaw	2-9-79
Justrite Jassie	B	Ch. Kirkgordon Musical Cowboy	Justrite Jenny	Mr & Mrs R. & B. Armstrong	Mr & Mrs R. & B. Armstrong	4-2-81
Newtonglen Miss Muffet	B	Ch. Newtonglen Macintosh	Famecheck Really Special	Mrs M. Torbet	Mrs M. Torbet	18-10-82
Rotella Mighty Miss	B	Ch. Erisort Special Request	Ch. Rotella Royal Fortune	R. Wright	R. Wright	14-1-80

171

Name	Sex	Sire	Dam	Owner	Breeder	Born
Tammy of Gilbri	B	Aust. Ch. Ashgate Tartan Trews	Ashgate Tobermory	Mrs G. A. Broom	Mrs E. Jenkins	19-11-79
Valida Sundae Snowball of Kilbrannon	B	Ch. Haweswalton Mr Volvo	Cedarfell Mockbretia	Mrs M. H. Webster	Mrs M. Ledger	21-6-81
Westmill White Witch	B	Ch. Cedarfell Merry-N-Bright	Westmill White Rose	Miss J. E. Johnson	Miss J. E. Johnson	15-5-80
1985						
Asgate Achnasheen	D	Ashgate Auchenleck	Haweswalton Gemma of Ashgate	Mrs S. Thomson	Mrs S. Thomson	17-12-83
Clan Crinan	D	Morenish Just William	Crinan Celtic Ayre	Mrs B. Hands	Mrs J. E. M. Williams & Mrs B. Hands	9-9-83
Haweswalton Storm Trooper	D	Ch. Haweswalton Houdini	Haweswalton High Society	Mrs M. B. Atkinson	Mrs S. Hawes	26-4-83
Ballacoar Jinny Is Justrite	B	Ch. Haweswalton Houdini	Lasara Little Gem	Mr & Mrs R. Armstrong	Mrs S. R. Morgan	30-8-83
Ballacoar Josey Is Justrite	B	Ch. Haweswalton Houdini	Lasara Little Gem	Mr & Mrs R. Armstrong	Mrs S. R. Morgan	30-8-83
Beebeemi Daisychain At Rithmic	B	Ch. Domaroy Last Pennyworth	Beebeemi Daisy Clipper	Miss Kim Parvin	Mr A. S. & Mrs J. R. Mitchell	11-9-80
Famecheck Full of Hope	B	Famecheck Doubly Special	Ch. Famecheck Full O'Beans	Miss F. M. C. Cook	Miss F. M. C. Cook	24-7-82
Haweswalton Carousel	B	Ch. Haweswalton Houdini	Haweswalton High Society	Mrs S. Hawes	Mrs S. Hawes	26-4-83
Lasara Lady Sue	B	Ch. Haweswalton Houdini	Lasara Liza Jane	Mrs B. Graham & Miss J. Kabel	Mrs B. Graham Miss J. Kabel	11-4-83
Newtonglen Louise	B	Ch. Newtonglen Macintosh	Famecheck Really Special	Mrs M. Torbet	Mrs M. Torbet	1-7-81

Name	Sex	Sire	Dam	Owner	Breeder	Born
1986						
Cameron at Kilbrannon	D	Ch. Casstine Magregor at Kilbrannon	Gaelicglory Girl Friday	Mrs M. H. Webster	Mrs D. I. Martin	28-11-84
Cregneash Candytuft of Rotella	D	Ch. Rotella Mighty Mike	Twinkletoes Trixie	Mr R. Wright	Mr S. Limb	29-1-80
Haweswalton Aye Buster at Olton	D	Arnholme Aye One At Olton	Haweswalton Call Me Madam	Mr R. C. Hill & Dr M. P. Wilson	Mrs S. Hawes	19-1-83
Lasara Love All	D	Ch. Midshipman of Haweswalton	Lasara Lucky Lot	Mrs B. Graham & Miss J. Kabel	Mrs B. Graham & Miss J. Kabel	8-9-84
Newtonglen Scotsman	D	Famecheck Super Star	Ch. Newtonglen Louise	Mrs M. Torbet	Mrs M. Torbet	10-3-84
Pepabby Poacher	D	Ch. Highstile Paladin	Highstile Prose	Mr & Mrs J. M. Edmondson	Mr & Mrs J. M. Edmondson	12-7-83
Brielow Beezneez	B	Ch. Jaimont of Whitebriar	Ch. Arnholme Aphrodite	Mr & Mrs J. Bowden	Mr & Mrs J. Bowden	7-12-83
Domaroy Silver Lichen	B	S.A. Ch. Ashgate Whaslikus	Ch. Domaroy Silver Fern	Mr & Mrs R. Wilshaw	Mr & Mrs R. Wilshaw	28-10-82
Drummersdale Oops A Daisy	B	Morenish Just William	Drummersdale Arabella	Mrs J. Lea	Mrs E. Wright	7-11-82
Famecheck Secret	B	Famecheck Bright Light	Ch. Famecheck Radio Star	Miss F. M. C. Cook	Miss F. M. C. Cook	12-12-83
Gilbri Pippins Pride	B	Erisort Senator of Ashgate	Ashgate Gilbri Su	Miss T. M. Broom	Miss T. M. Broom	26-8-82
Sarmac Silver Secret of Lusundy	B	Ch. Sarmac Heathstream Drummer Boy	Nozomi Sweet Fleur of Sarmac	Mrs H. M. Dangerfield	Mrs A. Millen	9-1-82

Name	Sex	Sire	Dam	Owner	Breeder	Born
1987 Count at Kristajen	D	Ch. Cregneash Candytuft of Rotella	Canestar Clarissa	Mrs J. Abbey	Mrs D. K. Lancaster	14-6-83
Cregneash Crusader	D	Ch. Domaroy Saracen	Birkfell Summer Sky	Mr S. A. Limb	Mr S. A. Limb	26-10-83
Hillsted Sporting Chance	D	Ch. Haweswalton Sportsman	Jopeta Sheena Macpherst	Mr J. & Mrs K. Fox	Mr J. & Mrs K. Fox	24-3-85
Olac Moon Pilot	D	Olac Moonmaverick	Olac Winter Moon	Mr D. Tattersall	Mr D. Tattersall	16-3-86
Peter Pan Is Suebeck	D	Ch. Suebeck Peterlee	Justrite Janis	Mrs P. Mitchell	Mrs M. Jackson	29-12-84
Sarmac Drummers Boy	D	Ch. Sarmac Heathstream Drummer Boy	Nozomi Sweet Fleur of Sarmac	Mrs E. A. Millen	Mrs E. A. Millen	9-1-82
Suebeck Peterlee	D	Ashgate Royal Stewart of Suebeck	Sardon Secondhand Rose of Suebeck	Mrs P. Mitchell	Mrs P. Mitchell	6-7-83
Whitebriar Jolson	D	Ch. Ardenrun Merryman of Sarmac	Whitebriar Jenstar	Mrs J. Crittenden	Mrs J. E. Beer & Miss M. Murphy	16-5-81
Ashgate Donna	B	Erisort Senator of Ashgate	Ch. Ashgate Ailsa Craig	Mr & Mrs Thomas & Miss Cery	Mrs S. Thomson	9-8-82
Ashgate Skara	B	Ashgate Kirkcowan of Poolmist	Ashgate St Kilda	Mrs S. Thomson	Mrs S. Thomson	4-9-83
Cripsey Gemma	B	Gaywyn Limited Edition	Cripsey Victoria	Mr & Mrs W. Havenhand	Mr & Mrs W. Havenhand	4-1-84
Dazzle Me Bridie of Cranella	B	Mansditch Snowman	Shentonfield Prima	Mrs B. E. Bunting	Mr R. Ellison	16-12-82
Glenveagh Giselle	B	Ch. Clan Crinan	Glenveagh Melrose Morag	Mrs M. Johnston	Mrs M. Johnston	16-2-86
Haweswalton Mermaid	B	Ch. Midshipman of Haweswalton	Haweswalton High Society	Mrs S. Hawes	Mrs S. Hawes	31-1-85

Name	Sex	Sire	Dam	Owner	Breeder	Born
1988						
Ashgate Leckie	D	Ch. Ashgate Achnasheen	Ch. Ashgate Sheigra	Mrs S. Thomson	Mrs S. Thomson	12-5-86
Solar Storm of Sunway	D	Ianbar Introduction	Sumway Soliloquy	Mr L. J. & Mrs J. F. Shell	Mrs P. Hooper	4-8-83
Tiellos Toby Jugge	D	Ch. Arnholme Ad Lib	Arnholme April Song	Messrs Gordon & Luty	Mr & Mrs Gordon	19-12-81
Ashgate Sallachy	B	Ch. Ashgate Achnasheen	Ch. Ashgate Skara	Mrs S. Thomson	Mrs S. Thomson	12-12-85
Ashgate Sheigra	B	Ch. Ashgate Culnacraig	Ch. Ashgate Skara	Mrs S. Thomson	Mrs S. Thomson	3-1-85
Birkfell Samite	B	Morenish Just William	Ch. Birkfell Spinning Jenny	Miss S. Cleland	Miss S. Cleland	12-10-82
Birkfell Sunbonnet	B	Birkfell Student Prince	Ch. Birkfell Samite	Mrs D. Fraser Smith	Miss S. Cleland	30-7-85
Brierlow Blazing Sensation	B	Ch. Jaimont of Whitebriar	Ch. Arnholme Aphrodite	Mrs J. Bowden & Mr A. Gordon	Mr & Mrs J. Bowden	12-8-85
Justrite Jixey	B	Ch. Jaimont of Whitebriar	Ch. Ballacoar Jinny Is Justrite	Mr & Mrs R. Armstrong	Mr & Mrs R. Armstrong	11-11-85
Sarmac First Lady	B	Ch. Sarmac Heathstream Drummer Boy	Sarmac What A Cracker	Mrs E. A. Millen	Mrs E. A. Millen	24-1-83
Tasman Admired	B	Exultation of Tasman	Reservation of Tasman	Mrs C. K. Bonas	Mrs C. K. Bonas	9-10-83
Truffles of Holycross	B	Patajohn Playboy	Minerva of Kenwunn	Mr D. & Mrs C. A. Biggs	Mrs P. M. Wilcox	29-1-84

175

Family Tree 'A': Mainly male, all bitches included have the suffix (b)

Ch. White Sylph (b)
1920

Ch. Wolvey Guy
1924

Ch. Dornie Busybody
D 1927

Wolvey Pickle

Wolvey Proctor

Wolvey Poppingay (b)

Ch. Wolvey Prefect
1936

Ch. Clint Constable
1936

Ch. Wolvey Patrician
1926

Clint Crofter

Ch. Rodrick of Rushmoor
1931

Ch. Ray of Rushmoor
1929

Int. Ch. Wings (b)
1932

Ch. Wolvey Pauline
1930 (b)

Wolvey Poppingay (b)

Ch. Wolvey Prefect
1936

Ch. Wolvey Pintail
1936

Ch. Wolvey Pepper
1930

Ch. Wolvey Peacock
1934

Ch. Clint Cocktail
1931

Clint Corinth (b)

Ch. Wolvey Prospect
1948

Ch. Wolvey Poster
1952

Brean Bronnie (b)

Ch. Brean Glunyieman
1934

Ch. Calluna Ruairidh
1937

Ch. Clint Constable
1936

Belinda of Branston (b)

Ch. Wolvey Prefect
1936

Furzefield Provider

Furzefield Piper

Ch. Leal Flurry
1938

Ch. Shiningcliffe Simon
1947

Ch. Melbourne Mathias
1939

Furzefield Penelope (b)

Furzefield Piper
1947

Continued on Family Tree 'C'

Continued on Family Tree 'B'

Family Tree 'B'. Mainly male, all bitches included have the suffix (b)

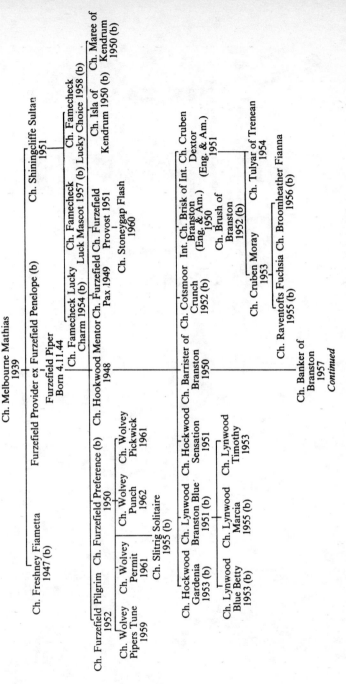

Ch. Barrister of Branston 1950

Ch. Freshney Fray 1958 (b)

Ch. Glengyle Tapestry 1960 (b)

Ch. Mairi of Kendrum 1954 (b)

Ch. Eoghan of Kendrum 1954

Ch. Quakertown Questionaire 1958 (b)

Ch. Cotsmoor Cream bun 1954 (b)

Quakertown Quizzical

Ch. Glengyle Thistle 1961 (b)

Ch. Alpin of Kendrum 1962

Ch. Quakertown Quistador 1964

Ch. Cotsmoor Banker of Branston 1957

Ch. Cotsmoor Creampuff 1953 (b)

Calluna Big Wig 2 C.C.s

Famecheck Fluster (b)

Phryne O' Petriburg

Ch. Phrana O'Petriburg 1959 (b)

Ch. Phancy O'Petriburg 1961 (b)

Ch. Famecheck Happy knight 1956

Ch. Famecheck Viking 1954

Ch. Famecheck Jolly Warrior 1958

Ch. Famecheck Gay Crusader 1956

Ch. Famecheck Ballet Dancer 1957 (b)

Ch. Famecheck Gay Buccaneer 1960

Ch. Famecheck Musketeer 1960

Ch. Glengyle Tapestry 1960 (b)

Ch. Rivelin Rhumba 1964 (b)

Ch. Brindie of Branston (b)

Am. Ch. Rainsborowe Redvers 1963

Ch. Bandsman of Branston 1960

Ch. Brenda of Branston 1961 (b)

Ch. Busybody of Branston Eng. & Aust. 1963 (b)

Ch. Biarrose of Branston 1965 (b)

Ch. Banner of Branston 1962

Ch. Banny of Branston (b) 1962

Ch. Bavena of Branston 1959 (b) Eng. & Am.

Ch. Bardel of Branston 1965

Ch. Billybong of Branston 1963

Ch. Sollershott Symphony 1963 (b)

Ch. Sollershott Soloist 1962

Ch. Sollershott Sober 1965

Ch. Glengyle Teasle (b) 1965

Ch. Bardel of Branston 1965

Sw. Ch. Benefactor of Branston 1965

Ch. Baggage of Branston 1964

Ch. Slitrig Goshell of Branston 1967

Family Tree 'C'. Mainly male, all bitches included have the suffix (b)

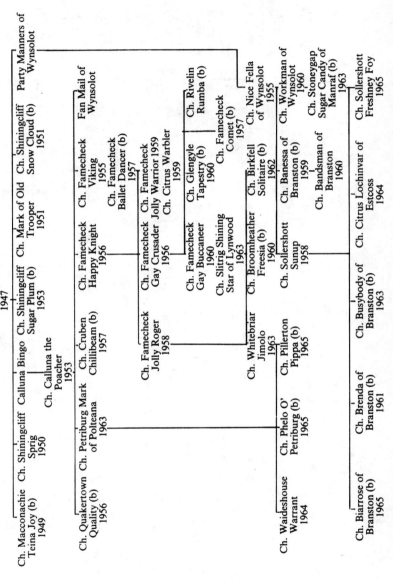

Eng. & Aust.: CHAMPION BUSYBODY OF BRANSTON AND CHAMPION BRIARROSE OF BRANSTON

Sire
Ch. Sollershott Sun-Up

- Ch. Nice Fella of Wynsolot
  - Fan Mail of Wynsolot
    - Party Manners of Wynsolot
      - Ch. Shiningcliff Simon
      - Snowcloud of Wynsolot
    - Freedoms Fortune
      - Heathcolne Mischief
      - Queen of the Night
  - Shiningcliff Starturn
    - Ch. Shiningcliff Sultan
      - Ch. Melbourne Mathias
      - Walney Thistle
    - Ch. Shiningcliff Dunthorne Damsel
      - Shiningcliff Shardy
      - Pathton of Patterscourt
- Cotsmor Crack O' Dawn
  - Ch. Furzefield Pilgrim
    - Furzefield Piper
      - Furzefield Provider
      - Furzefield Penelope
    - Furzefield Purpose
      - Ch. Furzefield Pax
      - Calluna Siren
  - Cotsmor Crusty
    - Ch. Wolvey Poster
      - Ch. Wolvey Prospect
      - Wolvey Phrolic
    - Ch. Cotsmor Crunch
      - Ch. Hookwood Mentor
      - Cotsmor Crisp

Dam
Ch. Brindie of Branston

- Ch. Banker of Branston
  - Ch. Barrister of Branston
    - Ch. Hookwood Mentor
      - Furzefield Piper
      - Bonchurch Bunty
    - Bloom of Branston
      - Brigadier of Branston
      - Baroness of Branston
  - Binty of Branston
    - Brigadier of Branston
      - Ch. Melbourne Mathias
      - Buzz of Branston
    - Beau of Branston
      - Bobby of Branston
      - Belinda of Branston
- Bono of Branston
  - Ch. Barrister of Branston
    - Ch. Hookwood Mentor
      - Furzefield Piper
      - Bonchurch Bunty
    - Bloom of Branston
      - Brigadier of Branston
      - Baroness of Branston
  - Cheeky Cherubim
    - Baron of Branston
      - Bobby of Branston
      - Belinda of Branston
    - Stort Bedelia
      - Freshney Mac Ruairidh of Tiriosal
      - Freshney Fragaria

CHAMPION FAMECHECK COMET, CHAMPION FAMECHECK MADCAP, CHAMPION FAMECHECK GAIETY GIRL, CHAMPION FAMECHECK GAY BUCCANEER and CHAMPION FAMECHECK MUSKETEER

Sire
Ch. Famecheck Gay Crusader

- **Ch. Famecheck Happy Knight**
  - Ch. Calluna the Poacher
    - Calluna Bingo
      - Ch. Shiningcliff Simon
      - Cruben Miss Rustle
    - Calluna Vermintrude
      - Furzefield Piper
      - Calluna Nike
  - Famecheck Fluster
    - Ch. Barrister of Branston
      - Ch. Hookwood Mentor
      - Bloom of Branston
    - Freshney Futurist
      - Freshney Frisk
      - Freshney Fairy
- **Ch. Famecheck Lucky Charm**
  - Ch. Shiningcliff Sultan
    - Ch. Melbourne Mathias
      - Ch. Leal Flurry
      - Leal Chieftainess
    - Walney Thistle
      - Ch. Wolvey Prefect
      - White Sheen of Wick
  - Famecheck Paddy Scalare
    - Freshney Fatmah
      - Freshney MacRuairidh of Tiriosal
      - Freshney Farel
    - Freshney Futurist
      - Freshney Frisk
      - Freshney Fairy

Dam
Ch. Famecheck Lucky Mascot

- **Ch. Shiningcliff Sultan**
  - Ch. Melbourne Mathias
    - Ch. Leal Flurry
      - Ch. Calluna Ruairidh
      - My Riviera Rose
    - Leal Chieftainess
      - Ch. Clint Chief
      - Clint Cullette
  - Walney Thistle
    - Ch. Wolvey Prefect
      - Ch. Wolvey Peacock
      - Wolvey Popinjay
    - White Sheen of Wick
      - Dougald
      - Cora
- **Famecheck Paddy Scalare**
  - Freshney Fatmah
    - Freshney MacRuairidh of Tiriosal
      - MacNab of Tiriosal
      - Security of Tiriosal
    - Freshney Farel
      - Ch. Melbourne Mathias
      - Freshney Felicia
  - Freshney Futurist
    - Freshney Frisk
      - Freshney Niall
      - Freshney Farel
    - Freshney Fairy
      - Wolvey Padlock
      - Victoria of Kenbury

CHAMPION DOMAROY SARACEN and Eng. Aust. & N.Z.
CHAMPION DOMAROY SARABAND OF WHITEBRIAR

Sire
Ch. Tasman March of Time

- Ch. Highstile Prank
  - Ch. Sollershott Soloist
    - Ch. Bandsman of Branston
      - Ch. Banker of Branston
      - Ch. Banessa of Branston
    - Citrus Silhouette
      - Ch. Sollershott Sun-up
      - Famecheck Cygnet
  - Wolvey Puffin
    - Ch. Wovey Piper's Tune
      - Ch. Wolvey Pied Piper
      - Ch. Wolvey Peach
    - Wolvey Peewit
      - Ch. Wolvey Pirate
      - Wolvey Paulina
- Pillerton Pollyann
  - Ch. Pillerton Peterman
    - Slitrig Simon of Lynwood
      - Ch. Famecheck Gay Buccaneer
      - Slitrig Sweet Suzette
    - Pillerton Pickle
      - Ch. Calluna The Poacher
      - Blainy of Branston
  - Pillerton Polka
    - Ch. Bandsman of Branston
      - Ch. Banker of Branston
      - Ch. Banessa of Branston
    - Blainy of Branston
      - Ch. Nice Fella of Wynsolot
      - Ch. Banda of Branston

Dam
Ch. Domaroy Erisort Serenade

- Int, Ch. Highstile Pirate
  - Ch. Birkfell Sea Squall
    - Ch. Quakertown Quandary
      - Ch. Quakertown Quistador
      - Quakertown Queen
    - Birkfell Sea Fury
      - Eriegael Storm Warning
      - Ch. Birkfell Sea Shanty
  - Ch. Highstile Poppet
    - Ch. Quakertown Quistador
      - Ch. Alpin of Kendrum
      - Ch. Quakertown Querida
    - Wolvey Puffin
      - Ch. Wolvet Piper's Tune
      - Wolvey Peewit
- Erisort Domaroy Debutante
  - Famecheck Knight Errant
    - Ch. Famecheck Jolly Warrior
      - Ch. Famecheck Happy Knight
      - Int. Ch. Famecheck Lucky Charm
    - Famecheck Rowena
      - Am. Ch. Famecheck Romeo
      - Ch. Famecheck Gaiety Girl
  - Rhianfa's Eliza for Common
    - Am. Ch. Lymehills Birkfell South Pacific
      - Int. Ch. Macnab of Balmaha
      - Ch. Birkfell Solace
    - Rhianfa Lady Constance of Estcoss
      - Estcoss Beaucaire of Greenlodge
      - Ch. Rhianfa Up-and-Coming of Estcoss

CANADIAN CHAMPION HIGHLAND URSA MAJOR

Sire
Belmertle Aldrich

- Can. Ch. Robinridge MacBeth
  - Eng. & Am. Ch. Ray of Rushmoor
    - Ch. Wolvey Patrician
      - Ch. Wolvey Guy
      - Ch. Wolvey Clover
    - Binny of Rushmoor
      - Ch. Gwern Wilfrid
      - Noreen
  - Edgerstoune Rarity
    - Clint Courtier
      - Wolvey Patron
      - Eriska Bhan
    - Clint Creena
      - Ch. Clint Cocktail
      - Clint Caltha
- Can. Ch. Robinridge Cherie
  - Am. Ch. Edgerstoune Roughy
    - Eng. & Am. Ch. Ray of Rushmoor
      - Ch. Wolvey Patrician
      - Binny of Rushmoor
    - Can. Ch. Clint Casserole
      - Ch. Clint Cocktail
      - Clint Caltha
  - Am. Ch. Wolvey Pace of Edgerstoune
    - Ch. Wolvey Patrician
      - Ch. Wolvey Guy
      - Ch. Wolvey Clover
    - Wolvey Promise
      - Wolvey Pickle
      - Wolvey Priscella

Dam
Edgerstoune Stardust

- Am. Ch. Edgerstoune Roughy
  - Eng. & Am. Ch. Ray of Rushmoor
    - Ch. Wolvey Patrician
      - Ch. Wolvey Guy
      - Ch. Wolvey Clover
    - Binny of Rushmoor
      - Ch. Gwern Wilfrid
      - Noreen
  - Can. Ch. Clint Casserole
    - Ch. Clint Cocktail
      - Clint Crofter
      - Medusa of the Creek
    - Clint Caltha
      - Positive Under the Steeple
      - Thistle Under the Steeple
- Am. Ch. Edgerstoune Starlet
  - Am. Ch. Edgerstoune Royalty
    - Wolvey Phantom of Edgerstoune
      - Ch. Wolvey Poacher
      - Ch. Wolvey Pintail
    - Edgerstoune Raith
      - Am. Ch. Edgerstoune Wallie
      - Ch. Edgerstoune Rhea
  - Edgerstoune Joyce
    - Am. Ch. Wolvey Prophet of Edgerstoune
      - Ch. Wolvey Poacher
      - Rosalie of Rushmoor
    - Can. Ch. Clint Casserole
      - Ch. Clint Cocktail
      - Clint Caltha

CHAMPION CALLUNA THE POACHER

Sire
Calluna Bingo

Ch. Shiningcliff Simon

- Ch. Leal Flurry
  - Ch. Calluna Ruaridh
    - Eng & Am. Ch. Ray of Rushmoor
    - Calluna Cranreuch
  - My Riviera Rose
    - Ch. Skelum of the Roe
    - Peek-a-Boo of the Roe
- Walney Thistle
  - Ch. Wolvey Prefect
    - Ch. Wolvey Peacock
    - Wolvey Popinjay
  - White Sheen of Wick
    - Dougald
    - Cora

Cruben Miss Rustle

- Am. Ch. Cruben Cranny
  - Cruben Flash
    - Eogham Ban
    - Cruben Flame
  - Cruben Miss Seymour
    - Macconochie Seymour
    - Ban-Righ Na Fhraoiche
- Cruben Odditty
  - Cruben Chief
    - Am. Ch. Cruben Silver Birk
    - Cruben Cronee
  - Ban-Righ Na Fhraoiche
    - Ch. Calluna Ruaridh
    - Calluna Fancy Free

Dam
Calluna Vermintrude

Furzefield Piper

- Furzefield Provider
  - Ch. Wolvey Prefect
    - Ch. Wolvey Peacock
    - Wolvey Popinjay
  - Ch. Placemore Prosperity
    - Furzefield Prosper
    - Flinders Melly
- Furzefield Penelope
  - Ch. Melbourne Mathias
    - Ch. Leal Flurry
    - Leal Chieftainess
  - Furzeleigh Prunella
    - Furzefield Provider
    - Furzefield Print

Calluna Nike

- Ch. Melbourne Mathias
  - Ch. Leal Flurry
    - Ch. Calluna Ruaridh
    - May Riviera Rose
  - Leal Chieftainess
    - Ch. Clint Chief
    - Clint Callette
- Calluna Victory Wings
  - Closburn Clonhie
    - Ch. Calluna Ruaridh
    - Wolvey Prickle
  - Calluna Carry On
    - Rodrick Dhu
    - Calluna Taudie

184

CHAMPION WHITE SYLPH (BITCH) 1920

Sire
White Don

- Ch. Highclere Rhalet (1920)
  - Ch. Moreso (1914)
    - Ch. Morova (1911)
      - Dunvegan Chief
      - Newtonmore
    - Mingle
      - Cannoch
      - Mingarry
  - Highclere Rival
    - Dunollie Chief
      - Dunollie Alaister
      - Dunollie Morag
    - Blanche Flower
      - The Chiel
      - Promise
- Lady White
  - White Prince
    - Hillsman Sands
      - Alistair Sands
      - Wiseful Sands
    - Judy (unreg)
      - —
      - —
  - Biddy
    - Ch. Cairn Nevis (1911)
      - Ch. Morven (1907)
      - Corrymona
    - White Belle
      - White Jock
      - White Daisy

Dam
White Belle

- White Jock
  - Hielan Conqueror
    - Ch. Lagavulin (1911)
      - Ossian
      - Baroness
    - Hielan Lass
      - Don
  - Model Supreme
    - Chawston Garry
      - Cornhill Jessie
      - Ch. Oronsay (1908)
    - White Lodge Swinger (unreg)
      - Carna
      - —
- White Daisy
  - Inverailort Roy
    - Ballach Bhan
      - —
      - Conas
      - Feorach
    - Inverailort Speirrag
      - Ch. Morven (1907)
      - Inverailort Judy
  - Dornie
    - Carron Marvel
      - Glenmhor White Prince
      - Dyce Beauty
    - Newtonmore
      - Brockdair
      - Heather

CHAMPION RHIANFA TAKE NOTICE

Sire
Am. Ch. Lymehills
Birkfell South Pacific

- Eng. & Am. Ch.
  MacNab of Balmaha
  - Lymehills Rhianfa Viking
    - Ch. Sollershott Soloist
      - Ch. Bandsman of Branston
      - Citrus Silhouette
    - Cotsmoor Crackling
      - Ch. Workman of Wynsolot
      - Cotsmor Cosset
  - Pinkholme Prestige
    - Ch. Glengyle Trader
      - Glengyle Tweed
      - Glengyle Tansy
    - Pinkholme Promise
      - Pinkholme Purpose
      - Estcoss Gomac
- Ch. Birkfell Solace
  - Ch. Pillerton Peterman
    - Slitrig Simon of Lynwood
      - Ch. Famecheck Gay Buccaneer
      - Slitrig Sweet Suzette
    - Pillerton Pickle
      - Blainy of Branston
      - Ch. Famecheck Happy Knight
  - Ch. Birkfell Solitaire
    - Ch. Famecheck Jolly Roger
      - Ch. Famecheck Lucky Charm
      - Ch. Eoghan of Kendrum
    - Birkfell Snowstorm
      - Birkfell Schottishe
      - Ch. Nice Fella of Wynsolot

Dam
Rhianfa Lady Constance
of Estcoss

- Estcoss Beaucaire of
  Greenlodge
  - Ch. Citrus Lochinvar
    of Estcoss
    - Ch. Sollershott Sun-up
      - Cotsmor Crack O'Dawn
      - Famecheck Saturn
    - Famecheck Foxtrot
      - Famecheck Gypsy
      - Ch. Famecheck Happy Knight
  - Famecheck Vivacious
    - Ch. Famecheck
      Gay Crusader
      - Ch. Famecheck Lucky Charm
      - Ch. Shiningcliff Sultan
    - Ch. Famecheck
      Lucky Charm
      - Famecheck Paddy Scalare
      - Ch. Nice Fella of Wynsolot
- Ch. Rhianfa Up and
  Coming of Estcoss
  - Ch. Citrus Lochinvar
    of Estcoss
    - Ch. Sollershott Sun-Up
      - Cotsmor Crack O'Dawn
      - Famecheck Saturn
    - Famecheck Foxtrot
      - Famecheck Gypsy
      - Ch. Banker of Branston
  - Rianfa Rainsborowe
    Poppa
    - Ch. Bandsman of Branston
      - Banessa of Branston
      - Ch. Famecheck Musketeer
    - Rainsborowe Michala
      - Rainsborowe Treasure

186

CHAMPION BIRKFELL SEA SQUALL

Sire
Ch. Quakertown Quandary

Ch. Quakertown Quistador
- Ch. Alpin of Kendrum
  - Quakertown Quizzical
    - Ch. Quakertown Questionaire
    - Ch. Quakertown Quality
  - Pixie of Kendrum
    - Hamishj of Kendrum
    - Gean of Kendrum
- Ch. Quakertown Querida
  - Quakertown Quarrelsome
    - Ch. Quakertown Questionaire
    - Ch. Quakertown Quality
  - Cara of Kendrum
    - Rory of Kendrum
    - Rona of Kendrum

Quakertown Queen
- Quakertown Quarrelsome
  - Ch. Quakertown Questionaire
    - Ch. Eoghan of Kendrum
    - Quakertown Questionmark
  - Ch. Quakertown Quality
    - Ch. Calluna the Poacher
    - Calluna Miss Phoebe
- Quakertown Quickstep
  - Ch. Famecheck Gay Crusader
    - Ch. Famecheck Happy Knight
    - Int. Ch. Famecheck Lucky Charm
  - Quakertown Quicksilver
    - Ch. Eoghan of Kendrum
    - Ch. Quakertown Quality

Dam
Birkfell Sea Fury

Eriegael Storm Warning
- Ch. Eriegael Mercedes
  - Ch. Kirnbrae Symmetra Sailaway
    - Int. Ch. Cruben Moray
    - Denmohr Gay Girl
  - Eriegael Andrasda
    - Int. Ch. Tulyar of Trenean
    - Birkfell Solo
- Ch. Eriegael Stormchild
  - Ch. Kirnbrae Symmetra Sailaway
    - Int. Ch. Cruben Moray
    - Denmohr Gay Girl
  - Eriegael Marinette
    - Ch. Eriegael Mercedes
    - Eriegael Silhouette

Ch. Birkfell Sea Shanty
- Ch. Famecheck Jolly Roger
  - Ch. Famecheck Happy Knight
    - Ch. Calluna the Poacher
    - Famecheck Fluster
  - Ch. Famecheck Lucky Charm
    - Ch. Shiningcliff Sultan
    - Famecheck Paddy Scalare
- Birkfell Schottishe
  - Ch. Barrister of Branston
    - Ch. Hookwood Mentor
    - Bloom of Branston
  - Birkfell Snowfinch
    - Ch. Barrister of Branston
    - Birkfell Skylark

187

CHAMPION GLENGORDON FINEARTE PRINCE OF PEACE

Sire
Ch. Sarmac Heathstream Drummer Boy

- Ch. Lindenhall Drambui
  - Ch. Sollershott Soloist
    - Ch. Bandsman of Branston
      - Ch. Banker of Branston
      - Ch. Banessa of Branston
    - Citrus Silhouette
      - Ch. Sollershott Sun-Up
      - Famecheck Cygnet
  - Rainsborowe Bridie
    - Rainsborowe Ruskin
      - Ch. Bandsman of Branston
      - Rainsborowe Michala
    - Rainsborowe Trimma Donna
      - Ch. Famecheck Gay Crusader
      - Rainsborowe Trudy
- Heathstream Cedarfell Misty Dell
  - Whitebriar Jackson
    - Whitebriar Jacket
      - Whitebriar Jude
      - Whitebriar Jesse
    - Whitebriar Joybelle
      - Ch. Whitebriar Jimola
      - Gay St Trudy
  - Ch. Whitebriar Jillan
    - Can Ch. Whitebriar Jamie
      - Ch. Famecheck Happy Knight
      - Piegi of Kendrum
    - Whitebriar Jatoma
      - Ch. Famecheck Gay Buccaneer
      - Whitebriar Juna

Dam
Ch. Cedarfell Messenger Dove

- Whitebriar Jackson
  - Whitebriar Jacket
    - Whitebriar Jude
      - Ch. Famecheck Viking
      - Whitebriar Judith
    - Whitebriar Jesse
      - Ch. Furzefield Pilgrim
      - Judy of Marstonholme
  - Whitebriar Joybelle
    - Ch. Whitebriar Jimola
      - Ch. Famecheck Jolly Roger
      - Whitebriar Juna
    - Gay St. Trudy
      - Eriegael Hebrides
      - Blackhouse Delight
- Ch. Whitebriar Jillan
  - Can Ch. Whitebriar Jamie
    - Ch. Famecheck Happy Knight
      - Ch. Calluna the Poacher
      - Famecheck Fluster
    - Piegi of Kendrum
      - Ch. Furzefield Pilgrim
      - Maree of Kendrum
  - Whitebriar Jatoma
    - Ch. Famecheck Gay Buccaneer
      - Ch. Famecheck Gay Crusader
      - Ch. Famecheck Lucky Mascot
    - Whitebriar Juna
      - Famecheck Friendly Rival
      - Whitebriar Jacana

CHAMPION WHITEBRIAR JONFAIR

Whitebriar Johncock

- **Warberry Satellite**
  - **Ch. Symmetra Skirmish**
    - Tulyar's Boy
      - Int. Ch. Tulyar of Trenean
      - Penelope Chorta
    - Famecheck Lucky Star
      - Ch. Famecheck Happy Knight
      - Famecheck Paddy Scalare
  - **Eriegael Saidhe**
    - Ch. Kirnbrae Symmetra Sailaway
      - Int. Ch. Cruben Moray
      - Denmohr Gay Girl
    - Eriegael Andrasda
      - Int. Ch. Tulyar of Trenean
      - Birktell Solo

- **Whitebriar Jatoma**
  - **Ch. Famecheck Gay Buccaneer**
    - Ch. Famecheck Gay Crusader
      - Ch. Famecheck Happy Knight
      - Int. Ch. Famecheck Lucky Charm
    - Ch. Famecheck Lucky Mascot
      - Ch. Shiningcliff Sultan
      - Famecheck Paddy Scalare
  - **Whitebriar Juna**
    - Famecheck Friendly Rival
      - Ch. Famecheck Happy Knight
      - Ch. Famecheck Lucky Charm
    - Whitebriar Jacana
      - Ch. Hookwood Sensation
      - Piegi of Kendrum

Whitebriar Jeenay

- **Whitebriar Jaudari**
  - **Phlurry O'Petriburg**
    - Slitrig Simon of Lynwood
      - Ch. Famecheck Gay Buccaneer
      - Slitrig Sweet Suzette
    - Ch. Phluster O'Petriburg
      - Ch. Petriburg Mark of Polteana
      - Ch. Phancy O'Petriburg
  - **Whitebriar Juna**
    - Famecheck Friendly Rival
      - Ch. Famecheck Happy Knight
      - Ch. Famecheck Lucky Charm
    - Whitebriar Jacana
      - Ch. Hookwood Sensation
      - Piegi of Kendrum

- **Whitebriar Jinka**
  - **Whitebriar Jackson**
    - Whitebriar Jacket
      - Whitebriar Jude
      - Whitebriar Jesse
    - Whitebriar Joybelle
      - Ch. Whitebriar Jimola
      - Gay St. Trudy
  - **Whitebriar Jatoma**
    - Ch. Famecheck Gay Buccaneer
      - Ch. Famecheck Gay Crusader
      - Ch. Famecheck Lucky Mascot
    - Whitebriar Juna
      - Famecheck Friendly Rival
      - Whitebriar Jacana

CHAMPION CHECKBAR FINLAY MACDOUGAL

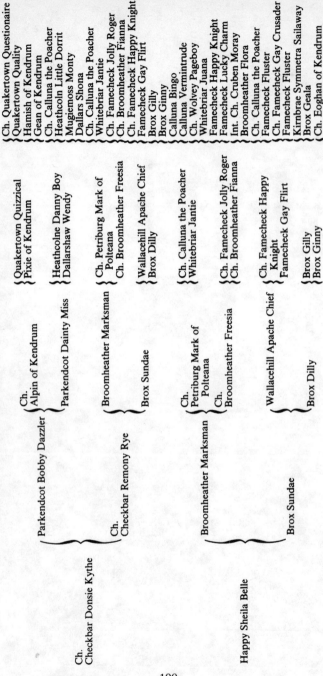

Ch. Checkbar Donsie Kythe

- Parkendcot Bobby Dazzler
  - Ch. Alpin of Kendrum
    - Quakertown Quizzical
      - Ch. Quakertown Questionaire
      - Quakertown Quality
    - Pixie of Kendrum
      - Hamish of Kendrum
      - Gean of Kendrum
  - Parkendcot Dainty Miss
    - Heathcolne Danny Boy
      - Ch. Calluna the Poacher
      - Heathcoln Little Dorrit
    - Dallarshaw Wendy
      - Mugiemoss Monty
      - Dallars Shona
- Ch. Checkbar Remony Rye
  - Broomheather Marksman
    - Ch. Petriburg Mark of Polteana
      - Ch. Calluna the Poacher
      - Whitebriar Jantie
    - Ch. Broomheather Freesia
      - Ch. Famecheck Jolly Roger
      - Ch. Broomheather Fianna
  - Brox Sundae
    - Wallacehill Apache Chief
      - Ch. Famecheck Happy Knight
      - Famecheck Gay Flirt
    - Brox Dilly
      - Brox Gilly
      - Brox Ginny

Happy Sheila Belle

- Broomheather Marksman
  - Ch. Petriburg Mark of Polteana
    - Ch. Calluna the Poacher
      - Calluna Bingo
      - Calluna Vermintrude
    - Whitebriar Jantie
      - Ch. Wolvey Pageboy
      - Whitebriar Juana
  - Ch. Broomheather Freesia
    - Ch. Famecheck Jolly Roger
      - Famecheck Happy Knight
      - Famecheck Lucky Charm
    - Ch. Broomheather Fianna
      - Int. Ch. Cruben Moray
      - Broomheather Flora
- Brox Sundae
  - Wallacehill Apache Chief
    - Ch. Famecheck Happy Knight
      - Ch. Calluna the Poacher
      - Famecheck Fluster
    - Famecheck Gay Flirt
      - Ch. Famecheck Gay Crusader
      - Famecheck Fluster
  - Brox Dilly
    - Brox Gilly
      - Kirnbrae Symmetra Sailaway
      - Ch. Eoghan of Kendrum
    - Brox Ginny
      - Brox Geala
      - Brox Geala

190

Eng. Sw. Nor. Fin: CHAMPION FAMECHECK EXTRA SPECIAL

Sire
Famecheck Royal Binge

Int. Ch.
Famecheck Royal Prerogative

- Am. Ch. Famecheck Consort
  - Int. Ch. Famecheck Trojan
    - Tri Int. Ch. Famecheck Hallmark
    - Ch. Famecheck Verona
  - Ch. Famecheck Maid to Order
    - Tri Int. Ch. Famecheck Hallmark
    - Famecheck Helen
- Ch. Famecheck Heirloom
  - Tri Int. Ch. Famecheck Hallmark
    - Int. Ch. Famecheck Marksman
    - Famecheck Caprice
  - Ch. Famecheck Air Hostess
    - Int. Ch. Famecheck Trojan
    - Famecheck Rowena

Famecheck Bingo

- Famecheck Cardtrick
  - Int. Ch. Famecheck Cardsharper
    - Tri Int. Ch. Famecheck Hallmark
    - Famecheck Royal Flush
  - Ch. Famecheck Dainty Maid
    - Tri Int. Ch. Famecheck Hallmark
    - Famecheck Juliet
- Ch. Famecheck Silver Charm
  - Tri Int. Ch. Famecheck Hallmark
    - Int. Ch. Famecheck Marksman
    - Famecheck Caprice
  - Ch. Famecheck Air Hostess
    - Int. Ch. Famecheck Trojan
    - Famecheck Rowena

Dam
Famecheck Special Order

Int. Ch.
Famecheck Firm Favourite

- Int. Ch. Famecheck Cardsharper
  - Tr Int Ch. Famecheck Hallmark
    - Int. Ch. Famecheck Marksman
    - Famecheck Caprice
  - Famecheck Royal Flush
    - Int. Ch. Famecheck Trojan
    - Ch. Famecheck Dainty Maid
- Ch. Famecheck Dainty Maid
  - Tri Int. Ch. Famecheck Hallmark
    - Int. Ch. Famecheck Marksman
    - Famecheck Turvey
  - Famecheck Juliet
    - Famecheck Jubilant
    - Ch. Sollershot Soloist

Ch.
Famecheck Maid to Order

- Tri Int Ch. Famecheck Hallmark
  - Int. Ch. Famecheck Marksman
    - Famecheck Jill
    - Ch. Famecheck Jolly Warrior
  - Famecheck Caprice
    - Int. Ch. Famecheck Madcap
    - Ch. Famecheck Gay Bucaneer
- Famecheck Helen
  - Am. Ch. Famecheck Romeo
    - Ch. Famecheck Lucky Choice
    - Ch. Famecheck Gay Crusader
  - Ch. Famecheck Gaiety Girl
    - Ch. Famecheck Lucky Mascot

191

CHAMPION ARNHOLME APRIL JESTER

- **Ch. Olac Moondrift**
  - Ch. Backmuir Noble James
    - Famecheck Major Domo
      - Int. Ch. Famecheck Domino
        - Int. Ch. Famecheck Hallmark
        - Famecheck Royal Flush
      - Ch. Famecheck Glamis
        - Int. Ch. Famecheck Hallmark
        - Shandwin Shantabella
    - Backmuir Mary Stuart
      - Ch. Heath of Backmuir
        - Ch. Sollershott Freshney Foy
        - Highstile Pick Me Up
      - Whitebriar Jylland
        - Ch. Whitebriar Jimolo
        - Whitebriar Jescot
  - Miranda Moon of Olac
    - Ch. Tasman March of Time
      - Ch. Highstile Prank
        - Ch. Sollershott Soloist
        - Wolvey Puffin
      - Pillerton Pollyann
        - Ch. Pillerton Peterman
        - Pillerton Polka
    - Subo Alpine Snow
      - Oldfold Birthday of Marank
        - Ch. Snow Goblin
        - Sheena Gay Girl
      - Subo Deborah Ann of Attwood
        - Strathairlie Scamp
        - Floss of Pantglas
- **Arnholme Tancharny Alicia**
  - Arnholme Apollo of Tancharny
    - S.A. Ch. Arnholme Abracadabra
      - Ch. Tasman March of Time
        - Ch. Highstile Prank
        - Pillerton Pollyann
      - Ch. Purston Petite
        - Ch. Pillerton Peterman
        - Birktell Screech Owl
    - Famecheck Fay
      - Int. Ch. Famecheck Domino
        - Int. Ch. Famecheck Hallmark
        - Famecheck Royal Flush
      - Ch. Famecheck Glamis
        - Int. Ch. Famecheck Hallmark
        - Shandwin Shantabella
  - Arnholme Athene
    - Clantartan Carnog Crest
      - Famecheck Knight Errant
        - Ch. Famecheck Jolly Warrior
        - Famecheck Rowena
      - Famecheck Fantasia
        - Famecheck Soloman
        - Famecheck Paprika
    - Arnholme Annabel Lee
      - Pillerton Perry
        - Ch. Sollershott Soloist
        - Ch. Pillerton Peta
      - Snowbelle of Bobbingay
        - Ch. Pillerton Peterman
        - Redhill Suzie

CHAMPION PILLERTON PETERMAN

Slitrig Simon of Lynwood

- Ch. Famecheck Gay Buccaneer
  - Ch. Famecheck Gay Crusader
    - Ch. Famecheck Happy Knight
      - Ch. Calluna the Poacher
      - Famecheck Fluster
    - Ch. Famecheck Lucky Charn
      - Ch. Shiningcliff Sultan
      - Famecheck Paddy Scalare
  - Ch. Famecheck Lucky Mascot
    - Ch. Shiningcliff Sultan
      - Ch. Melbourne Mathias
      - Walney Thistle
    - Famecheck Paddy Scalare
      - Freshney Fatamah
      - Freshney Futurist
- Slitrig Sweet Suzette
  - Slitrig Skipper
    - Ch. Furzefield Pilgrim
      - Furzefield Piper
      - Furzefield Purpose
    - Slitrig Sequin
      - Ch. Hookwood Mentor
      - Freshney Frill
  - Slitrig Sapphire
    - Ch. Wolvey Pirate
      - Ch. Wolvey Pageboy
      - Wolvey Playmate
    - Slitrig Sequin
      - Ch. Hookwood Mentor
      - Freshney Frill

Pillerton Pickle

- Ch. Calluna the Poacher
  - Calluna Bingo
    - Ch. Shiningcliff Simon
      - Ch. Leal Flurry
      - Walney Thistle
    - Cruben Miss Rustle
      - Am. Ch. Cruben Cranny
      - Cruben Oddity
  - Calluna Vermintrude
    - Furzefield Piper
      - Furzefield Provider
      - Furzefield Penelope
    - Calluna Nike
      - Ch. Melbourne Mathias
      - Calluna Victory Wings
- Blainy of Branston
  - Ch. Nice Fella of Wynsolot
    - Fanmail of Wynsolot
      - Party Manners of Wynsolot
      - Freedoms Fortune
    - Shiningcliff Starturn
      - Ch. Shiningcliff Sultan
      - Ch. Shiningcliff Dunthorne Damsel
  - Ch. Banda of Branston
    - Ch. Barrister of Branston
      - Ch. Hookwood Mentor
      - Bloom of Branston
    - Binty of Branston
      - Brigadier of Branston
      - Beau of Branston

CHAMPION BILLYBONG OF BRANSTON

Ch. Bandsman of Branston
- Ch. Banker of Branston
  - Ch. Barrister of Branston
    - Ch. Hookwood Mentor
      - Furzefield Piper
      - Bonchurch Bunty
    - Bloom of Branston
      - Brigadier of Branston
      - Baroness of Branston
  - Binty of Branston
    - Brigadier of Branston
      - Ch. Melbourne Mathias
      - Buzz of Branston
    - Beau of Branston
      - Bobby of Branston
      - Belinda of Branston
- Ch. Banessa of Branston
  - Ch. Nice Fella of Wynsolot
    - Fan Mail of Wynsolot
      - Party Manners of Wynsolot
      - Freedoms Fortune
    - Shiningcliff Starturn
      - Ch. Shiningcliff Sultan
      - Ch. Shiningcliff Dunthorne Damsel
  - Baffin of Branston
    - Int. Ch. Bannock of Branston
      - Ch. Barrister of Branston
      - Binty of Branston
    - Cheeky Cherubim
      - Baron of Branston
      - Stort Bedelia

June of Braddocks
- Ch. Citrus Warbler
  - Ch. Famecheck Jolly Warrior
    - Ch. Famecheck Happy Knight
      - Ch. Calluna the Poacher
      - Famecheck Fluster
    - Ch. Famecheck Lucky Charm
      - Ch. Shiningcliff Sultan
      - Famecheck Paddy Scalare
  - Famecheck Cygnet
    - Famecheck Saturn
      - Ch. Wolvey Poster
      - Freshney Futurist
    - Famecheck Gypsy
      - Ch. Shiningcliff Sultan
      - Famecheck Paddy Scalare
- Famecheck Wendy
  - Ch. Famecheck Gay Crusader
    - Ch. Famecheck Happy Knight
      - Ch. Calluna the Poacher
      - Famecheck Fluster
    - Ch. Famecheck Lucky Charm
      - Ch. Shiningcliff Sultan
      - Famecheck Paddy Scalare
  - Ch. Famecheck Lucky Charm
    - Ch. Shiningcliff Sultan
      - Ch. Melbourne Mathias
      - Walney Thistle
    - Famecheck Paddy Scalare
      - Freshney Fatamah
      - Freshney Futurist

194

CHAMPION HAWESWALTON HOUDINI

Ch. Cedarfell Merry 'N' Bright

- Cedarfell Man-O-Minx
  - Whitebriar Jackson
    - Whitebriar Jacket
      - Whitebriar Jude
      - Whitebriar Jesse
    - Whitebriar Joybelle
      - Ch. Whitebriar Jimola
      - Gay St Trudy
  - Ch. Whitebriar Jillan
    - Can. Ch. Whitebriar Jamie
      - Ch. Famecheck Happy Knight
      - Piegi of Kendrum
    - Whitebriar Jatoma
      - Ch. Famecheck Gay Buccaneer
      - Whitebriar Juna
- Cedarfell Minuet
  - Ch. Sollershott Soloist
    - Ch. Bandsman of Branston
      - Ch. Banker of Branston
      - Ch. Banessa of Branston
    - Citrus Silhouette
      - Ch. Sollershott Sun-Up
      - Famecheck Cygnet
  - Ch. Whitebriar Jillan
    - Can. Ch. Whitebriar Jamie
      - Ch. Famecheck Happy Knight
      - Piegi of Kendrum
    - Whitebriar Jatoma
      - Ch. Famecheck Gay Buccaneer
      - Whitebriar Juna

Haweswalton Veiled Venus

- Int. Ch. Famecheck Cardsharper
  - Int. Ch. Famecheck Hallmark
    - Famecheck Marksman
      - Ch. Sollershott Soloist
      - Famecheck Jill
    - Famecheck Caprice
      - Ch. Famecheck Jolly Warrior
      - Int. Ch. Famecheck Madcap
  - Famecheck Royal Flush
    - Ch. Famecheck Trojan
      - Int. Ch. Famecheck Hallmark
      - Ch. Famecheck Verona
    - Ch. Famecheck Dainty Maid
      - Int. Ch. Famecheck Hallmark
      - Famecheck Hallmark
- Kingsmere Katie
  - Glengordon Bally Toff
    - Am. Ch. Pillerton Prosper
      - Ch. Pillerton Peterman
      - Pillerton Polka
    - Glengordon Machylan Mirabelle
      - Ch. Sollershott Freshney Foy
      - Machylan Crystone Mandy
  - Kingsmere Caprice
    - Glengordon Morar
      - Ch. Citrus Warbler
      - Famecheck Trustful
    - Dizzy Lizzie
      - Int. Ch. Stoneygap Freddie
      - Dizzy Daz

CHAMPION ASHGATE CLAYMORE

Ch. Ashgate Lairg

- Nordic Ch. Ashgate Striling
  - Finearte Dove's Pride
    - Ch. Wadeshouse Waterboy
      - Int. Ch. Waideshouse Willoughbly
      - Ch. Waideshouse Woodlark
    - Ch. Cedarfell Messenger Dove
      - Whitebriar Jackson
      - Ch. Whitebriar Jillan
  - Shira of Ashgate
    - Famecheck Sylvan
      - Int. Ch. Famecheck Hallmark
      - Famecheck Jenny Wren
    - Am. Ch. Famecheck Pert
      - Int. Ch. Famecheck Domino
      - Ch. Famecheck Glamis
- Ashgate Linga
  - Tervin Pacey of Ashgate
    - Ch. Morenish Geordie
      - Ch. Sollershott Freshney Foy
      - Morenish Jane
    - Tervin Patsy
      - Can. Ch. Lymehills Proklee Pikador
      - Chalk White
  - Melinda of Millburn
    - Irish Ch. Millburn Monitor
      - Irish Ch. Eriegael Summer Rain
      - Snowee of Loughore
    - Misty of Longvale
      - Ch. Famecheck Bernard
      - Famecheck Honey

Nordic Ch. Ashgate Ciola

- Ch. Olac Moonraker
  - Pillerton Perry
    - Ch. Sollershott Soloist
      - Ch. Bandsman of Branston
      - Citrus Silhouette
    - Ch. Pillerton Peta
      - Slitrig Simon of Lynwood
      - Pillerton Pickle
  - Miranda Moon of Olac
    - Ch. Tasman March of Time
      - Ch. Highstile Prank
      - Pillerton Pollyann
    - Subo Alpin Snow
      - Oldfold Birthday Boy of Marank
      - Subo Deborah Ann of Attwood
- Cove of Ashgate
  - Ch. Checkbar Donsie Kythe
    - Parkendcot Bobby Dazzler
      - Ch. Alpin of Kendrum
      - Parkendot Dainty Miss
    - Ch. Checkbar Remony Rye
      - Broomheather Marksman
      - Brox Sundae
  - Keithall Tessa
    - Ch. Quakertown Quistador
      - Ch. Alpin of Kendrum
      - Ch. Quakertown Querida
    - Keithall Glamour Girl
      - Keithall Chieftain
      - Citrus Theme Song

CHAMPION QUAKERTOWN QUISTADOR

Ch.
Alpin of Kendrum
- Quakertown Quizzical
  - Ch. Quakertown Questionaire
    - Ch. Eogham of Kendrum
      - Ch. Barrister of Branston
      - Ch. Isla of Kendrum
    - Quakertown Questionmark
      - Ch. Mark of Old Trooper
      - Quakertown Quizette
  - Ch. Quakertown Quality
    - Ch. Calluna the Poacher
      - Calluna Bingo
      - Calluna Vermintrude
    - Calluna Miss Phoebe
      - Calluna Big Wig
      - Calluna Cutie Pie
- Pixie of Kendrum
  - Hamish of Kendrum
    - Fruin of Kendrum
      - Rory of Kendrum
      - Fenella of Kendrum
    - Gowan of Kendrum
      - Ch. Barrister of Branston
      - Ch. Isla of Kendrum
  - Gean of Kendrum
    - Fergus of Kendrum
      - Ch. Banker of Branston
      - Ch. Cotsmor Creambun
    - Ch. Maree of Kendrum
      - Furzefield Piper
      - Ch. Deirdre of Kendrum

Ch.
Quakertown Querida
- Quakertown Quarrelsome
  - Ch. Quakertown Questionaire
    - Ch. Eogham of Kendrum
      - Ch. Barrister of Branston
      - Ch. Isla of Kendrum
    - Quakertown Questionmark
      - Ch. Mark of Old Trooper
      - Quakertown Quizette
  - Ch. Quakertown Quality
    - Ch. Calluna the Poacher
      - Calluna Bingo
      - Calluna Vermintrude
    - Calluna Miss Phoeba
      - Calluna Big Wig
      - Calluna Cutie Pie
- Cara of Kendrum
  - Rory of Kendrum
    - Ch. Furzefield Pax
      - Furzefield Piper
      - Cassette of Eastfield
    - Ch. Deirdre of Kendrum
      - Roddy of Whitehills
      - Gyl of Kendrum
  - Rona of Kendrum
    - Ch. Calluna the Poacher
      - Calluna Bingo
      - Calluna Vermintrude
    - Pipit of Kendrum
      - Ch. Timoshenko of the Roe
      - Shira of Kendrum

CHAMPION CLAN CRINAN

Morenish Just William

Eng. Swed. & Nordic Ch. Tweed Tartan Caledonier
- Int. & Nordic Ch. Tweed Tory
  - Int. & Nordic Ch. Quakertown Quickmarch Tweed This Is It
    - Ch. Alpin of Kendrum
    - Quakertown Queen
    - Tweed Tavern
    - Sollershott So Sweet
- Int. & Nordic Ch. Tweed Tartan Maid
  - Int. & Nordic Ch. Whinkirk Woodsman Int & Nordic Ch. Tweed Thistle
    - Ch. Sollershott Soloist
    - Whinkirk Wanda
    - Int. Ch. Macmahons Motto
    - Sollershott So Sweet

Ch. Morenish Fanny MacDougal
- Ch. Checkbar Finlay MacDougal
  - Ch. Checkbar Donsie Kythe Happy Sheila Belle
    - Parkendot Bobby Dazzler
    - Ch. Checkbar Remony Rye
    - Broomheather Marksman
    - Brox Sundae
- Morenish Janie Alison
  - Ch. Alpingegay Sonata Morenish Jane
    - Warberry Satellite
    - Warberry Wideawake
    - Ch. Alpin of Kendrum
    - Eriskay Sweet Alison

Crinan Celtic Ayre

Famecheck Speciality
- Eng. Swed. Nordic & Fin. Ch. Famecheck Extra Special
  - Famecheck Royal Binge Famecheck Special Order
    - Int. Ch. Famecheck Royal Prerogative
    - Famecheck Bingo
    - Int. Ch. Famecheck Favourite
    - Ch. Famecheck Maid to Order
- Famecheck Gay Manner
  - Famecheck Gay Gordon of Stergo Famecheck Royal Manner of Greenveld
    - Famecheck Domino
    - Ch. Famecheck Busybody
    - Int. Ch. Famecheck Royal Prerogative
    - Ch. Famecheck Maid to Order

Crinan Christiana
- Ch. Heath of Backmuir
  - Ch. Sollershott Freshney Foy Highstile Pick Me Up
    - Ch. Sollershott Sunth Up
    - Freshney Faggot
    - Ch. Wolvey Permit
    - Wolvey Phantasy
- Eng. & Irish Ch. Candida of Crinan
  - Selig Rustin of Crinan Highstile Pixie
    - Pillerton Pip
    - Suriva Tina
    - Quakertown Quireboy
    - Ch. Highstile Poppet

APPENDIX V
REGISTRATIONS 1907 to 1988

1907 – 141	1935 – 718	1963 – 2744
1908 – 249	1936 – 757	1964 – 2884
1909 – 351	1937 – 682	1965 – 3113
1910 – 442	1938 – 633	1966 – 3094
1911 – 583	1939 – 424	1967 – 3611
1912 – 596	1940 – 138	1968 – 4160
1913 – 631	1941 – 135	1969 – 4837
1914 – 552	1942 – 175	1970 – 4933
1915 – 239	1943 – 277	1971 – 4097
1916 – 193	1944 – 494	1972 – 4510
1917 – 97	1945 – 675	1973 – 4472
1918 – 55	1946 – 1017	1974 – 4630
1919 – 126	1947 – 1056	1975 – 3913
1920 – 244	1948 – 1114	1976 – 1960
1921 – 371	1949 – 1193	1977 – 1447
1922 – 499	1950 – 1018	1978 – 3253
1923 – 587	1951 – 992	1979 – 4725
1924 – 688	1952 – 968	1980 – 4595
1925 – 758	1953 – 895	1981 – 3525
1926 – 721	1954 – 948	1982 – 3485
1927 – 715	1955 – 1080	1983 – 3950
1928 – 726	1956 – 1327	1984 – 4153
1929 – 663	1957 – 1263	1985 – 4864
1930 – 639	1958 – 1448	1986 – 5155
1931 – 540	1959 – 1785	1987 – 5339
1932 – 590	1960 – 2070	1988 – 5385
1933 – 598	1961 – 2344	
1934 – 628	1962 – 2614	

Because of the change to the registration system it is not possible to make a direct comparison of the number of registrations in 1976 and 1977 (in which only 'active' registrations are recorded above)) with that of the previous years.

Index